THE STREETS OF SAN FRANCISCO

**"Arrival in San Francisco is an experience in living,"
observed writer William Saroyan in the 1930s.
Most modern visitors would agree**

San Francisco is an enchantingly beautiful city, one of the most distinctive in the world, with panoramas from 43 different hills, watery vistas and a verdant park that seems to go on forever. The man-made landscape is mostly lowrise, wooden houses that delight the eye as they have since they were built a century or more ago.

The "city by the bay" is what many call it, and although there must be scores of cities beside scores of bays, almost everybody knows this reference to mean San Francisco. It's a big bay, too, 50 miles (80 km) around and crossed by no fewer than five bridges. One, the Golden Gate Bridge, perhaps the most famous bridge in the world, is as evocative of the city as the little cable cars, Fisherman's Wharf and, yes, Tony Bennett's timeless song. Even before he left his heart here, San Francisco was one of the favorite cities for tourists – and that includes all the people who haven't even been here yet.

San Francisco is also a city with a strong sense of neighborhood, each with its own distinct identity, overlapping and interrelating so that people mix and mingle and go through them instead of bypassing them on the highway when they want to visit some other part of town – which is more the familiar pattern in the United States.

Small as it is (pop. 750,000), San Francisco has many times featured on the world's front pages: the discovery of gold, the 1906 earthquake and fire, the founding and first home of the United Nations, the Bay Area tech revolution, the fierce battles of the gay community to be awarded equal rights. Most famously, perhaps, was the Haight-Ashbury "commune" that became an international magnet for 1960s hippies and the renowned attitude of tolerance that has served as a sort of metaphorical welcome mat for unorthodox lifestyles.

It will welcome you, too, whatever your tastes and inclinations, and will doubtless be everything you want it to be. You'll absorb the ambiance, be entranced by the sights, delight in the food and sleep well at night. You might even learn to appreciate the fog; some think it's kind of… romantic.

But, of course, those tend to be the people who live here. ❑

PRECEDING PAGES: taking a break overlooking the bridge and the bay; car crazy in California. **LEFT:** Coit Tower, standing sentinel on Telegraph Hill.

THE MAKING OF SAN FRANCISCO

In the early days California was a peaceful place.
Then came the Europeans, followed by the discovery
of a precious metal at Sutter's Mill that would
change the landscape forever

The Miwok, the Ohlone and the Wituk were some of the tribes that occupied much of northern California, living for years in harmony with the land that the most ecologically conscious can only dream of. Then the Spaniards arrived. Once the Europeans settled the land, the natives' decline was inevitable. Regarding the tribes as little more than animals, within a century the "the people of reason" had virtually obliterated the culture and ravaged the environment. The city of San Francisco was built from the aggressive companionship of greed and gold.

Early explorers

Precisely what Sir Francis Drake discovered in 1579 during his voyage around the world in the *Golden Hind* has never been established with certainty. Drake had a mission from Elizabeth I to "annoy" the Spanish provinces and had been obediently causing havoc up and down the west coast of Mexico. In his gentlemanly manner of operation, though, he had not had one person killed.

Apparently Drake passed by the bay's entrance without venturing inside or even noticing an opening, but his log shows that he did anchor just north of the bay and sent several landing parties ashore. It was believed that one of these groups left behind the small brass plate discovered in 1936 near Drake's Bay, though debate over its origin continues.

LEFT: opera has been part of San Francisco cultural life since the 1850s.
RIGHT: Sir Francis Drake sailed near the bay in 1579.

Rumors of riches enticed the Spaniards from the beginning. The early explorers were seeking a Northwest Passage that would lead them to the Orient and its valuable spice trade. Hernando Cortés, the conqueror of Mexico, had ordered a series of expeditions up the coast of Baja California – at the time thought to be an island – but it was not until 1542 that Juan Rodriguez Cabrillo discovered the land to the north. Cabrillo, too, passed by without noticing the immense natural harbor now called San Francisco Bay, but perhaps it was concealed in fog, as is still so often the case.

Later, Gaspar de Portolá, on his northern expedition to find a suitable harbor, also missed its significance, thinking it to be an open gulf. A later explorer, José Francisco Ortega, reported the bay to be "a great arm of the sea extending to the southeast farther than the eye could see." But discovery was slow, and it wasn't until the visit of Captain Juan Bautista de Anza six years later that a decision was made to build a mission at Yerba Buena.

San Francisco de Assisi

Captain José Moraga and Fray Francisco Palóu founded the mission with a handful of settlers in 1776, just days before the signing of the Declaration of Independence on the opposite side of the country. The church was dedicated to San

ily fallen to attacks from the sea had there been any. Northern California was still a remote outpost then, and held little appeal for foreign adventurers. Ironically, the Gold Rush that eventually ended the region's isolation might have come a century earlier if the tribes' discovery of the precious metal had been acted upon. Instead, the Spanish padres to whom it was shown advised silence, reasoning that knowledge of its existence would bring an influx of invaders.

By the end of the 18th century, however, foreign officials were beginning to show interest in the region. In 1792, the English sailor George Vancouver scouted the coast, bringing

Francisco de Assisi, but became known as Mission Dolores, probably because of the small lagoon on which it was built, Nuestra Senora de los Dolores.

Palóu acted for the renowned "Apostle of California," Fray Junipéro Serra, who was directly responsible for founding nine of the eventual 21 Californian missions, and personally baptized thousands of natives. Presidios (garrisons), like the one nearby – today's Presidio – were built at strategic points to protect a mission against attack from hostile tribes or foreign colonists.

The garrison was strong enough to sustain forays by hostile natives but would have eas-

with him the first American visitor, John Green, to the shores of California. The Russians had also arrived – their trading post and garrison only 50 miles (80 km) north at Bodega Bay was engendering nervousness on the part of the Californians, but they eventually departed in 1841. By this time Mexico had declared its independence from Spain and the secularization of the missions had begun – a process that had been intended to turn over the land and livestock to Native American families but which mostly resulted in their further exploitation by new owners.

When a certain Captain Beecher visited this part of northern California in 1826, five years after Mexico had declared its independence from Spain, he noted among the residents only ennui. "Some of them," he wrote, "were ingenious and clever men but they had been so long excluded from the civilized world that their ideas and their politics, like the maps pinned against the wall, bore the date 1772 as near as I could read forth fly specks." It wasn't until 20 years after his visit that the US flag was raised, the year (1846) that Samuel Brannan arrived with 230 Mormons to colonize what was then renamed San Francisco. There was also apprehension about the growing signs of interest by France and Britain in the West, and especially the value to a foreign power of San Francisco Bay, which an American diplomat described as, "capacious enough to receive the navies of all the world."

Stars and stripes

Immediate problems lay nearer to home. In May 1846, President James Polk engaged the United States in war with Mexico. Even before news of this declaration reached California, an independent group of nationalists at Sonoma, led by Ezekiel Merritt and William B. Idle, awoke the Mexican authority, General Vallejo, from his bed and obliged him to sign articles of surrender.

The action had been encouraged by the presence of a US expedition led by a cartographer and explorer, John Charles Fremont. As he declined to allow the rebels to raise the Stars and Stripes, they created a new flag depicting a grizzly bear racing a red star – the Bear Flag, as it became known. Accepting his acclamation as President of the Californian Republic, Fremont led a mission to capture the state capital at Monterey, but found Commodore John Sloat had sailed from Mazatlan and arrived there first. Whatever Mexican resistance there had been crumbled quickly. All across California, groups raised the Stars and Stripes and claimed the territory.

The war ended and California was ceded to the United States with the signing of the Treaty of Guadalupe in January, 1848. One

week before, James Marshall, who had just built a mill for John Sutter, discovered gold in the Sierra Nevada foothills. Sutter was an immigrant from Switzerland, whose 49,000-acre (19,800-hectare) Sacramento Valley ranch had been granted to him by the Mexican governor of California. He tried to keep the find a secret, but the news, of course, changed the landscape of this peaceable pastoral region forever.

Early arrivals made instant fortunes merely from washing nuggets out of a stream, or scraping the gold dust from easily accessible veins in the rock. It was estimated that the area was yielding as much as $50,000 (in value) of

the precious metal each day. As the risks increased, the supply dried up and prices of everything skyrocketed. The real necessities of life were buckets, shovels, rockers, dippers, and pans. Miners – called '49ers because of the year of their arrival – mainly lived in tents, sleeping on blankets atop pine needles, but for anyone who needed a roof overhead, the rental of a hut in town cost $3,000.

It wasn't long before those who serviced the prospectors grew considerably richer than most of the prospectors themselves. Levi Strauss arrived from Germany to sell tents but ended up turning his supply of canvas into durable, riveted work trousers. In 1850, a gold

LEFT: Miwok, Ohlone and Wituk Native Americans settled northern California long before the Europeans.
RIGHT: the Presidio was established in 1776.

digger wrote home: "You can scarcely form a conception of what a dirty business this gold digging is… A little fat pork, a cup of tea or coffee and a slice or two of miserable bread form the repast of the miners."

Hookers, prospectors, merchants, miners and adventurers – all seemed to regard San Francisco as their personal mecca. It had become a city in which unprecedented numbers of people thought they saw their future. In later years, Edwin Markham, comparing the city to Venice and Athens "in having strange memories," also said it was unlike the other places, "in being lit from within by a large and luminous hope."

GOLD! GOLD! GOLD!

By the end of May, 1848 word of the discovery at Sutter's Mill had spread all over California: the editor of *The Californian* newspaper announced the suspension of publication because his entire staff had quit.

"The whole country from San Francisco to Los Angeles and from the sea shore to the base of the Sierra Nevada," he wrote, "resounds with the sordid cry of GOLD! GOLD! GOLD! – while the field is left half-planted, the house half-built and everything neglected but the manufacture of shovels and pick-axes." Before the year was out more prospectors arrived, from Mexico, Peru and Chile. Gold fever had ignited the world.

Already in debt and lacking funds to keep law and order, much less provide shelter or health care for the newcomers, officials of San Francisco cast around for ways to raise funds. The city hit upon the idea of a steep tax on gamblers, of whom there seemed to be an unlimited and growing supply. "Gambling saloons glittering like fairy palaces … suddenly sprang into existence, studding nearly all sides of the plaza and every street in its neighborhood," an historian recorded. "All was mad, feverish mirth where fortunes were lost and won on the green cloth in the twinkling of an eye." As much as $60,000 could ride on the turn of a card.

Floating jail

The new license fees paid for policemen and the upkeep of a brig – moored at Battery and Jackson streets – used as a city jail. Virtual anarchy reigned in the streets, through which roamed gangs of hoodlums, some operating with almost military precision. The depredations of one group known as the Hounds were so outrageous that a group of citizen volunteers armed themselves, rounded up the criminals and tried and sentenced them, though they were soon released for lack of enough facilities to confine them. Two years later in 1851, by which time almost a dozen daily papers were operating, the citizens once again took control by forming a 200-member Committee of Vigilance.

"Whereas… there is no security for life and property," they declared they were "determined that no thief, burglar, incendiary or assassin shall escape punishment either by the quibbles of the law, the insecurity of the prisons, the carelessness or corruption of the police or a laxity of those who pretend to administer justice." This group managed to catch, try and hang a trio of burglars before a regular law-and-order policy could be brought into effect.

By this time the gold was beginning to peter out, but in its place were arising endless disputes over water rights, which continue to this day. Miners whose claims were staked far from stream beds collaborated to build ditches funneling water from sources whose "riparian rights" (i.e. ownership of the adjoining land) were in conflict with "appropriation rights."

The introduction of hydraulic mining, bringing streams of water to bear on hillsides, intensified the problem. The extensive network of canals and flumes that brought water a long distance from its source, came to be worth more than the claims it served, but the conflicting arguments over who had a prior right to the water were never fully resolved. *California as It Is and as It May Be, Or, A Guide to the Goldfields* was the title of the first book to be published in San Francisco (in 1849). In it, author F.B. Wierzbicki wrote that the city looked like it had only been built to endure for a day, so fast had been its growth and so flimsy its construction.

Islands sold for $1 apiece. Real-estate speculation reached epidemic proportions. Each boatload of new miners represented another batch of customers. As the burgeoning city burst from the confines of Yerba Buena Cove, "water lots" sold for crazy prices on the expectation they could be made habitable with landfill. The practise continued for decades, and many of today's downtown San Francisco neighborhoods are also built on landfill.

Fire hazard

A major hazard was fire in hastily built San Francisco, where most buildings were constructed of wood and cloth and where ocean

"The town has led the van in growth… there is nothing like it on record. From eight to ten thousand may be afloat on the streets and hundreds arrive daily; many live in shanties, many in tents and many the best way they can … The freaks of fortune are equally as remarkable in this place as everything else connected with it; some men who two years ago had not a cent in their pockets, count by thousands now…"

For most of the '49ers, the town was rough, ready and expensive. Eggs from the Farallone

winds constantly fanned the flames of wood-burning stoves and oil lamps used for heating and light. Half a dozen major conflagrations broke out between 1848 and 1851, every one of them destroying several blocks at a time, but each was followed by sturdier rebuilding.

By 1854, with a library, churches, schools and theaters among the many substantial stone or brick buildings, and horse-drawn streetcars traversing the now-tidy streets, it was becoming clear that the Gold Rush was coming to an end. Immigrants were still arriving, along with boatloads of supplies that could no longer be paid for, but stores and businesses were going bankrupt and the

LEFT: Gold Rush panhandlers hoping to strike it rich.
ABOVE: San Francisco's Market Street, 1865.

streets were filling with penniless and now jobless ex-miners.

About the only people still enjoying prosperity were the gaming bosses, whose money had thoroughly corrupted the city government. The gunning down of James King, a prominent editor whose *Evening Bulletin* had targeted police and the courts, brought a revival of the vigilante groups. This was a controversial move that incensed its many critics, but it did serve its purpose in chasing many undesirable elements out of town. Within months, the vigilante groups were disbanded and a majority of rational electors decided to vote in a new government.

Whatever chance California had of becoming placid was swept away in 1859 by yet another torrent of riches flowing down the Sierra slope. This time it was silver, not gold, that led to the rush.

Boomtown to fancy town

One of the most uncomfortable outposts of the Gold Rush had been centered around Nevada's Sun Mountain on the dry eastern slope of the Sierra near modern-day Lake Tahoe. There was a little gold up in the Virginia Range, but eking a living out of the area's irritating bluish clay was unrewarding work. In June 1859 a sample of that "blasted blue stuff" found its way to Melville Atwood, an assayer in Grass Valley. Atwood found an amount of silver worth an astounding $3,876 in that sample of ore. This seam of silver, called the Comstock Lode, was probably the greatest single mineral strike ever made.

At first it appeared that the Silver Rush would mimic the Gold Rush of a decade earlier. "Our towns are near depleted," wrote one spectator. "They look as languid as a consumptive girl. What has become of our sinewy and athletic fellow citizens? They are coursing through ravines and over mountaintops," looking for silver.

One of the young men who rushed up to the Virginia Range was Mark Twain. In his book *Roughing It* he describes how he and his fellow almost-millionaires "expected to find masses of silver lying all about the ground." The problem for Twain and the thousands like him was that the silver was in, not on, the steep and rugged mountains. And getting it out was not a matter of poking and panning.

The Silver Rush, it turned out, was a game for capitalists, men with money to buy the claims, dig the tunnels and install the expensive machinery and mills that transformed the blue stuff into cash. They were men like William Ralston of the Bank of California in San Francisco, and the four legendary "Bonanza Kings" – James Flood and William O'Brien, former saloon-keepers; and James Fair and John W. Mackay, old miners – whose Consolidated Virginia company regularly disgorged $6 million in a month.

As usual, the treasures of the Comstock Lode flowed downslope from the boomtown of Virginia City to San Francisco. By 1863, $40 million of silver had been wrestled out of the tunnels in, around, and through Sun Mountain. Two thousand mining companies traded shares in San Francisco's Mining Exchange. Fortunes were made, lost and made again as rumors of bonanza or borasca (profitless rock) swept into town. At one time, more speculative money was wrapped up in Comstock mining shares than existed in real shares on the whole of the Pacific Coast.

The Comstock lasted until the 1880s, plumping up California's economy with the $400 million the Virginia Range yielded. In San Francisco, William C. Ralston, the Comstock's greatest mine owner, had taken over as the city's top booster. Ralston poured his Comstock money into a myriad of grand schemes: he built the Palace, America's largest city hotel; he bought sugar refineries, lumber, stage and water companies; and as the 1860s drew to a close, he happily prepared for what he and his fellow plutocrats thought would be the capstone to the state's greatness – the long-awaited completion of the transcontinental railroad that had been foreordained by the building of California's first railroad, the 22-mile (35-km) Sacramento Valley line in 1856.

Newspaper tycoons

George Hearst, another successful mineowner, poured some of his millions into a newspaper, the *San Francisco Examiner*, turning it over to his son, William Randolph, in 1887. This was the beginning of what became the largest publishing empire the world had known.

By the time of his death in 1951, William Randolph Hearst had extended his empire to more than a score of daily papers (including two New York papers and two Chicago papers), 14 magazines in the US, and two in England, 11 radio stations and five news services employing a total of 38,000 people. Hearst served two terms as congressman for California but was beaten in his campaigns to be governor, mayor and president.

Hearst's personal spending was said to run to $15 million a year, of which at least $1 million went on art and antiques, the bulk of this destined for his hilltop ranch at San Simeon, south of San Francisco *(see page 196)*. He also owned a rambling estate in Mexico, St Donat's Castle in England, the 67-acre (27-hectare) estate Wyntoon in northern California, and commercial and residential property in various US cities.

An efficient transport system was one of San Francisco's earliest achievements, with half a dozen different companies operating horse-drawn services by mid-century. But the hills were steep and often slippery and watching a horse fall down on one of them, pulling

the carriage after it, was the event that inspired British engineer Andrew Hallidie with the idea for a cable car. By 1873, Hallidie's cable cars were operating on a 2½-mile (4-km) route along Clay Street *(see page 129)*.

The rush for gold had added a new impetus for contact between the East and West coasts. In addition to those in search of the gold itself were hundreds who sought to become part of the boom by shipping supplies, and although regional railroads were running, there were no transcontinental lines. It was not until 1853 that the Federal government allocated funds for the study of feasible routes, with California's gold boom making the state a top con-

tender for the terminus over previously favored Oregon.

The main form of transportation was clipper ships, which took six or eight months to sail from Boston to San Francisco. In the year 1849, after President Polk had declared that "the abundance of gold in (California) would scarcely command belief," almost 800 ships set off on from the East Coast. Within a dozen years, 50 steamers out of San Francisco were carrying passengers and freight not only up and down the West Coast, but to destinations as far away as China and Australia.

Concurrent with this development of clippers – and by 1860 this era was over – was the

LEFT: inventor and engineer Andrew Hallidie at the controls of the first cable car, 1873.
RIGHT: William Randolph Hearst ran the largest publishing empire in the world from 1887 to 1951.

growth of the overland stage. They were initially financed by regional postmasters, spurred on by a need to deliver the mail.

Pony Express and the railroads

For a brief period, the glamour of the Pony Express (relays of boy jockeys, unarmed, dodging Indian ambushes) captured the public's imagination, but the intervening Civil War also brought the telegraph system – the first on the West Coast was erected on North Beach's Telegraph HIll – and sending letters for $5 lost its appeal.

Plans for a railroad linking the East and West coasts had been mooted for many years.

Central Pacific's ownership of vast parcels of land along its right-of-way would drive prices of much-needed agricultural land shamefully high. George even foresaw the racial tensions that would result from the railroad's importation of thousands of Chinese laborers, who flooded the state's job market in the 1870s and became the targets of bitter discontent.

George's pessimism rang true with the coming of the first train. In San Francisco, real-estate dealing of $3.5 million a month fell to less than half that amount within a year. "California's initial enthusiasm soon gave way to distrust and dislike… an echo of the national conviction that the railroads were responsible

When the Civil War broke out, Congress was intent upon securing California's place in the Union, and the process was accelerated.

In the winter of 1862, the Pacific Railroad Act granted vast tracts of western land, low-interest financing and outright subsidies to two companies – the Central Pacific, building from Sacramento, and the Union Pacific, building from Omaha, Nebraska.

Henry George, a journeyman printer and passionate theorist, had warned that the increasing dominance of the railroads would be a mixed blessing. He predicted that western factories would be undersold by the eastern manufacturing colossus, and that the

for most of the country's economic ills," was the assessment of historian John W. Caughey in his book *California*.

But others took a different view. The genius of the Central Pacific was a young engineer named Theodore Dehone Judah, builder of the Sacramento Valley line, whose partners unfortunately were uncommonly cunning and ruthless men. Charles Crocker, Mark Hopkins, Collis Huntington and Leland Stanford, who became known as "The Big Four," had been lured West by the Gold Rush.

They were Sacramento shopkeepers when they invested in Judah's scheme. Shortly after Congress issued them with vast tracts of land, they forced Judah out. He died, aged 37, in 1863, still trying to wrest control from his former partners. The Central Pacific made the Big Four almost insanely rich.

The government's haste to get the railroad built, together with Leland Stanford's smooth political maneuvering, made the Central Pacific the virtual dictator of California politics for years. Between them the railroad barons raised private investment, earned government subsidies, acquired bargain-priced land, imported cheap "coolie" labor from China, and by their monopolist practises became multi-millionaires.

San Francisco railroad barons

As the largest landowners and biggest employers, the immensely wealthy railroad barons were able to manipulate freight rates, control water supplies, keep hundreds of thousands of acres of productive land for themselves and subvert politicians and municipal leaders. It was to be many years before state regulation of the railroads became the norm rather than the other way around.

In the beginning, at least, carping at the Big Four's use of the railroad's treasury as a kind of private money preserve was a game only for malcontents and socialists. In the mahogany boardrooms of San Francisco's banks, on the editorial pages of its newspapers and on the floor of the overheated Stock Exchange the verdict was clear: the railroad would bring firm and fabulous prosperity to the state of California.

In April 1868, five years after construction had begun on Sacramento's Front Street, the first Central Pacific train breached the Sierra at Donner Pass. On May 12, 1869, the Golden Spike was driven at Promontory Point, Utah, and the East and West coasts were linked. "San Francisco Annexes the Union," read one San Francisco headline.

But the rush of prosperity failed to materialize. In the winter of 1869–70 a severe drought crippled the state's agriculture.

Between 1873 and 1875 more than 250,000 immigrants came to California. Many were factory workers and few could find work: the "Terrible '70s" had arrived. For William Chapman Ralston, these years were a great calamity. As the head of the Bank of California in San Francisco, the former Comstock mining tycoon had presided over the endless boom mentality that was a legacy of the Gold Rush. But, by the mid-1870s, the booms had given way to the full bloom of depression.

On "Black Friday," April 26, 1875, a run on the Bank of California forced it to slam shut the huge oak doors at Sansome and California streets. Driven into debt by Comstock mining

losses and by the failure of the railroad to bring prosperity, William C. Ralston drowned the next day while taking his customary swim in San Francisco Bay. Ralston's death signaled the end of California's boom.

Hurt most by the shrinkage of capital in the 1870s were the working people. During the gold and silver rushes, California's laborers had enjoyed a rare freedom to move easily from job to job and to dictate working conditions. Now, with massive unemployment, unionization began to take hold. For the next 60 years, California suffered labor strife.

As if that weren't enough, early in the new century, disaster struck the Bay City.   ❏

LEFT: the Central Pacific Railroad made fortunes for the city's landowners and elite.

RIGHT: this cartoon from the *San Francisco Illustrated Wasp* shows the discrimination faced by Chinese immigrants brought in to work on the railroad.

THE 1906 EARTHQUAKE

A few terrifying seconds at 5:15am on April 18, 1906, marked the worst natural disaster the United States had ever suffered

In San Francisco, which in 1906 accounted for 40 percent of California's population, the effect of an earthquake on this scale (measured at 8.25 on the Richter Scale) was cataclysmic. The greatest destruction came from the subsequent fires, which raged for three days, and with its hydrant and alarm systems fatally damaged, the fire department was unable to cope. Experts were lacking, and the inexperienced commandant of the Presidio, Brigadier General Frederick Funston, exceeded his authority in a panic to take charge. His improvisations destroyed scores of beautiful mansions along Van Ness Avenue, and spread the fires still further. At least 300 people were dead or still trapped in smoking ruins as city blocks (like the Mission, above) were leveled. A handful of people were shot or bayoneted by Funston's ill-prepared militia, who poured onto the streets trying to bring order and prevent looting. Fortunately, aid poured in from all over the world, $8 million worth within the first weeks. Even the much-reviled Southern Pacific Railroad pitched in, offering goods and free passage out of the city.

BELOW: Soup kitchens were set up to feed those left homeless. Golden Gate Park was covered in tents and blankets, as 300,000 people camped out after the quake.

BELOW: Spectators gathered to watch as flames from the three-day fire – much deadlier than the quake itself – overtook the city. Estimates put the total damage at $350 million.

ABOVE: One of the first structures to collapse was City Hall, recently completed after three decades of construction. In total, 28,000 buildings were destroyed.

ABOVE: Although the earthquake lasted only 48 seconds, the rubble spread out over the whole city. At least 315 people were killed, six were shot, and another 352 were missing, many never to be found.

AN EYEWITNESS ACCOUNT

Author Jack London, whose San Francisco family homes were destroyed in the fires following the earthquake, filed this first-hand report:

Within an hour after the earthquake shock, the smoke of San Francisco's burning was a lurid tower visible a hundred miles away. And for three days and nights this lurid tower swayed in the sky, reddening the sun, darkening the day and filling the land with smoke.

I watched the vast conflagration from out on the bay. It was dead calm. Not a flicker of wind stirred. Yet from every side, wind was pouring in upon the city. East, west, north and south, strong winds were blowing upon the doomed city. The heated air rising made an enormous suck. Thus did the fire itself build its own colossal chimney through the atmosphere …

Just 24 hours after the earthquake, I sat on the steps of a small residence on Nob Hill… To the east and south at right angles were advancing two mighty walls of flame. I went inside with the owner… He was cool and cheerful and hospitable. "Yesterday morning," he said, "I was worth six hundred thousand dollars. This morning, this house is all I have left. It will go in 15 minutes."

ABOVE: San Franciscans have never allowed anything to stand between them and a good meal. In this picture, a couple sit down at a linen-covered makeshift table with a friend, to dine and to watch their city burn.

MODERN TIMES

Out of the ashes of the 1906 earthquake rose a city
that gave a home in the 1950s and 1960s to beatniks,
hippies and, later, yuppies. In the 1990s, their children
were at the forefront of the tech revolution

Before the 20th century, San Francisco was already California's most prosperous center, a city of 27,000 buildings, a place with 1,700 architects perfecting the "tall, narrow rowhouse with vertical lines and a false front to make the house look more imposing," as described by the city archivist. These characteristically Victorian and Queen Anne-style homes, or those of them that survived the 1906 fire, still feature in at least half a dozen neighborhoods today.

San Andreas Fault

A geologist named Andrew Lawson had discovered and named the San Andreas Fault more than 10 years previously, yet, despite two earthquakes in the 1890s, little attention was given to planning for geological emergencies. When the Big One arrived, there had been the warning of strange behavior by domestic animals like dogs and horses on the previous evening, but no alarm was raised.

A prediction in *Zadikiel's Almanac* for 1906 also went unheeded. It read: "In San Francisco Mars and Saturn are on the fourth angle, or lower meridian. In the vicinity of that great city underground troubles – probably a serious earthquake – will be destructive about Christmas day or the latter half of February. The winter will be stormy and cold."

When the quake did hit (*see page 26*) there was widespread devastation, though most of it

came from the resulting fires, but a spirit of determination rose to meet the challenges. The Committee of Forty on the Reconstruction of San Francisco was formed to define the tasks to be done and A.P. Giannini's tiny Bank of Italy, making loans to small businesses intent on rebuilding, was at the forefront of those determined to revive the city's fortunes. The bank was later to become the Bank of America, the country's largest.

Two happier events in successive years held great significance for San Francisco: the first was the opening of the Panama Canal in 1914, which cut days off the ocean route from the East while making the long journey around

LEFT: San Francisco in the Summer of Love, 1967.
RIGHT: the Panama Pacific International Exposition was held in San Francisco in 1915.

Cape Horn obsolete. Then, on January 25, 1915, only a month after San Francisco's Thomas Watson received the very first transcontinental phone call, from inventor Alexander Graham Bell, the Panama Pacific International Exposition opened in San Francisco. During the year of the exposition, 19 million visitors traveled to the city to marvel at the new fashions and inventions.

The distant war in Europe had few repercussions in the Bay Area beyond boosting industry, manufacturing and mining, with a consequent steep drop in employment when World War I came to an end. The city languished in the fog for the next few years.

purple pelargoniums, its tranquil setting was a contrast to the harsh realities of a sentence on "the Rock." One of the prisoners described his time on Alcatraz as "like living in a tomb."

The prison's administrative code was "Complete Control." At no time did the main building's 450 cells hold more than 250 captives, and the staff ran as high as 100 people.

This did not prevent three inmates – Frank Lee Morris and John and Clarence Anglin – from tunneling out with sharpened spoons in 1962. The feat took years, and the prisoners were never found, although speculation as to how they could survive in the frigid waters surrounding the island lead most to conclude they

Major labor troubles typified the Depression and the following years, culminating in the General Strike of 1934 when the International Longshoremen's Union immobilized traffic in the port. During one demonstration, two strikers were killed and 100 people – police and strikers – were injured.

Alcatraz

In 1934, Alcatraz island – lying just over a mile away from the city in tide-ripped San Francisco Bay – became the site of what was for 30 years to be America's most famous prison. A beautiful site blanketed with flowers like lavender lippia, orange nasturtiums, red fuchsias and

BUILDING BRIDGES

Although it is the Golden Gate that is San Francisco's enduring image, the Bay Area's other bridges are also spectacles in their own right. The gorgeous and sometimes overlooked San Francisco-Oakland Bay Bridge, completed in 1936, brought about new engineering challenges due to the depth of the water and a bay floor of mud. So successful was it, the Bay Bridge was declared the seventh wonder of the world in 1955 by the American Society of Civil Engineers. The San Mateo-Hayward Bridge earned the same organization's "outstanding civil engineering achievement" honor when it opened in 1967. (See also page 161.)

drowned or froze to death. Nevertheless, the escape of the "Alcatraz three" was a factor in the Prison Board's decision to phase out the institution not long after.

Around the same time that Alcatraz became a prison, ground was broken nearby for the Golden Gate Bridge, although it wasn't dedicated until 1937, six months after the even longer Bay Bridge joined San Francisco to Oakland. Only a few weeks before the Golden Gate ceremony, 11 workmen died when their scaffold collapsed.

The Golden Gate, more than any other image, has been responsible for the romantic vision the city retains in the national psyche. In tion, the Army Corps of Engineers and the city's Public Utilities Commission and Public Works Authority. Attached to the new Bay Bridge, it was completed within 18 months, just in time to house the Golden Gate International Exposition which was visited by 17 million people from all over the world. The Expo lasted two years, and 27 countries took part.

World War II

Marshall Dill, the Expo's 1940 president, said it would become an enduring memory – "another chapter in San Francisco's prismatic history in which we can all take pride... The fest is over and the lamps expire." World War II had begun

1987, traffic on the bridge came to a standstill for hours as more than half a million people walked across to celebrate its 50th birthday. "To pass through the portals of the Golden Gate," wrote Allan Dunn, "is to cross the threshold of adventure." And Gene Fowler asserted: "Every man should be allowed to love two cities; his own and San Francisco."

In 1937, work was begun on the creation in the bay of Treasure Island, a joint project of the federally funded Works Progress Administra-

by the time the fair closed, and with such a group of architectural marvels, it is not surprising that the founders of the United Nations came here in 1945 after the war was over, for their first conference.

Even with the thousands of new workers to staff the wartime factories and the bustling port, in addition to the numbers of servicemen who had remained behind when the war was over, the city's population was still only 700,000 – less than half that of Los Angeles, its rival 450 miles (725 km) to the south. Nevertheless, World War II had a tremendous impact on the local economy –"as great as any event since the Gold Rush," wrote historian Oscar Lewis.

LEFT: steelworkers constructing the Golden Gate bridge, which opened in 1937.
ABOVE: the exercise yard of Alcatraz.

Beatniks, Hippies, Riots and a Rebellious Heiress

In the 1950s, San Francisco was the birthplace of a new cultural renaissance beginning with what local columnist Herb Caen termed "beatniks." Led by writers Allen Ginsberg (*Howl*) and Jack Kerouac (*The Dharma Bums*) and supported by Lawrence Ferlinghetti of North Beach's City Lights Bookstore, the Beats led a life centered around poetry readings, marijuana and dropping out of the mainstream – a potently attractive example that came to have a wide appeal

and soon brought a stream of youthful admirers to the coffee houses of North Beach and, in the following decade, to the streets of the Haight-Ashbury district.

Over on the Berkeley campus of the University of California the axis of dissent was the Free Speech Movement, which kept up a steady assault against racism, materialism and what the students regarded as the stifling effects of the "multiversity" itself, and its aid and encouragement to the Vietnam war machine. Antiwar protests, which eventually spread around the world, swelled and took root here with the writers and protesters clustered around Max Scherr's *Berkeley*

Barb, one of America's five earliest "underground" newspapers. Max Scherr, a bearded radical who had previously operated a bar called Steppenwolf, took to the streets himself to sell his paper which, at its peak, reached a circulation of 100,000 – an astonishingly high figure for a newspaper that was still largely put together by a group of amateurs around a crowded kitchen.

Stimulated by the burgeoning rock music scene and steered by underground newspapers, thousands of gaudily dressed hippies – successors to the Beats – descended on Golden Gate Park in January 1967 to celebrate what was termed a Human Be-In. Among those who addressed the 100,000-strong gathering were Ginsberg, psychedelic drug guru Tim Leary ("Turn On, Tune In, Drop Out"), Mario Savo and other representatives of the Free Speech Movement from Berkeley, plus a daredevil parachutist who dropped from the clouds straight into the center of the (largely stoned) gathering.

The resultant worldwide publicity made the Haight-Ashbury district irresistible to disaffected young people throughout the world, substantial numbers of whom began to clog San Francisco's streets, with predictable results. The euphoria was short-lived and within a year or two it was all over, with begging, drug dealing and exploitation by greedy landlords the most notable side effects. It was from Haight-Ashbury that the notorious murderer Charles Manson recruited some of his most earnest disciples. Nevertheless, the memory of enchantment lived on.

One offshoot of the rebellious era was the kidnapping in 1974 of Patty Hearst, daughter of the newspaper tycoon, by a group who called themselves the Symbionese Liberation Army whose members later died in a fiery shootout with the city police after Hearst had been rescued, but not before the heiress turned the tables and took up arms, describing herself as an "urban guerrilla."

The hippie movement, the struggles, the poetry and the New Left helped to shape and change the American psyche, nowhere more so than in San Francisco itself. ❏

LEFT: FBI-released photo of heiress Patty Hearst as a Symbionese Liberation Army member, 1974.

Since long before the war, San Francisco, with its obvious ties to Oriental ports, had begun to harbor a large component of Asian immigrants. At least 110,000 *Nisei* (second-generation Japanese) were rounded up and sent to detention camps in the xenophobic days after Pearl Harbor. Accused of no crime, they lived behind barbed wire under military guard. Americans of Japanese heritage were estimated to have lost $365 million in property from having to sell their homes at under-market prices at this time.

The 1950s, 60s and early 70s were a time of unparalled turmoil and creativity, as San Francisco repeatedly hit the headlines of the world's newspapers *(see feature opposite.)*

and Harvey Milk, an openly homosexual city official, were murdered in City Hall by an outraged homophobe.

Taking to the streets

On May 21 of the following year, when Dan White was convicted of manslaughter with a lenient sentence rather than first-degree murder, 5,000 gays took to the streets and rioted, causing more than $1 million in damages to public property, including City Hall and a number of police cars. A plaza in the Castro District was named in honor of Harvey Milk and in 1986, a few blocks away, another significant memorial to gay victims was established, with

ABOVE: the National Guard trains guns on Berkeley students who are giving peace signs, 1969.

By the late 1970s, gay men and women were commonplace and most variances from the currents of mainstream America were accepted benignly. This part of the state is a major player in the country's ecology movement, providing a home to such groups as the Sierra Club, Friends of the Earth and Greenpeace. Towns like Petaluma passed no-growth ordinances, and San Franciscans have fought long and hard to avoid big-city urbanization.

The battles have not always been peaceful: in 1978, San Francisco mayor George Moscone

a gallery specially built to house the Names Project Memorial Quilt – each patch commemorating a victim of Aids. Today there are tens of thousands of these patches across the US and an active community in San Francisco to promote the quilt *(see page 51).*

The political tide turned irrevocably in 1978 when local politician Dianne Feinstein, with massive support from the gay population, was elected mayor. For 10 years, from 1978 to 1988, San Francisco's reputation for tolerance and liberalization flourished, as gays moved into all areas of the political arena, from the police department to the fire department to the Board of Supervisors.

Natural disasters have never been long out of the city by the bay. In October 1989, a major earthquake estimated at 7.1 on the Richter Scale collapsed a freeway, killed nine people and caused approximately $10 billion worth of damage. The fact that more people were not killed during the mid-afternoon quake is put down to the fact that the Bay Area's two "home teams" were competing in the World Series championship at the time, and that most people were either at the baseball stadium or at home glued to their television screens, the streets uncharacteristically deserted.

Within a year of the 1989 tremblor, a US Geological Survey report said that it had re-corded more than 7,000 aftershocks, some ranging as high as 5.4 on the Richter Scale. In 1992, the Oakland hills were ravaged by exten-sive fires that burned 3,000 homes.

San Francisco's political climate changed dramatically in the mid-1990s when State Assembly speaker Willie Brown – forced out by term limits after a 15-year tenure – ran a divisive campaign that resulted in his being elected mayor.

Willie Brown quickly endeared himself to San Franciscans with a gigantic celebratory party at Fisherman's Wharf and by 1997 was basking in the acclaim awarded to him for pre-siding over a booming economy displayed in an $80 million budget surplus. "A dapper and jaunty cricket of a man (who) has long had about him a sportive, Cyrano-esque panache not unlike the raffish flair of the Bay City itself," is how one reporter described him in a 14-page *New Yorker* profile.

Dot-com boom and bust

The first two years of the 21st century were fer-tile times for the city and the technology indus-tries in nearby Silicon Valley. Small and large companies made millions from innovative, or sometimes just shiny ideas that dominated the internet and became the basis of the "new econ-omy." With stock prices inflating to unbeliev-able heights, often accompanied by equally innovative business practices, the dot-com bub-ble crashed on October 9, 2002, leading to cat-astrophic losses for the NASDAQ Composite and resulting in one of the greater crashes of the stock market.

FASCINATING FIGURES ABOUT SAN FRANCISCO			
Here are a few figures about one of the world's most fabulous cities:		43	number of hills in the city
		118	nightclubs and dancehalls
		215	landmark buildings
8.25	magnitude of the 1906 earthquake	225	parks, playgrounds and squares
5	number of bridges	29½	miles of shoreline
10	historic districts	961	licensed taxis
14	number of islands in the bay	1,017	number of acres in Golden Gate Park
26	number of fog signals around the bay	14,000	Victorian houses
4½	feet in the narrowest city street	260,0000	commuters per day
65	museums	751,682	population of San Francisco County
7½	miles of waterfront	1,200,000	number of visitors to Alcatraz annually
90	theaters	9,600,000	yearly cable-car riders

Gone were the flashy cars, but other beginnings started to emerge as the atmosphere became charged with recovery and new ideas. An above average number of unemployed 20-somethings contributed to a heated mayoral election in 2003 between the Green Party candidate Matt Gonzales and Democratic Party front-runner Gavin Newsom. Newsom won and started to shake up City Hall. On February 12, 2004, 15 same-sex couples were married, and dozens of marriage licenses to same-sex couples were issued, sparking a national debate.

Three days later, more than 1,600 same-sex marriages were performed and hundreds of people who were lined up around City Hall were

Life and lifestyles

Elsewhere, new building and new projects, some started before the bust, continued apace. Baseball's Pacific Bell Park (now SBC Park), opened up the South Beach area to new life and a new clientele. The Asian Art Museum moved to the Civic Center; the 1898 Ferry Building was turned into a rapturously received farmers' market; City Hall got a facelift and the most significant buildings in Golden Gate Park – the de Young Museum, the Steinhart Aquarium and the Morrison Planetarium, are being spruced up for the future.

Appetites for consciousness expansion, Eastern philosophies and the exploring of new

turned away. A few months later, President George Bush called for a ban on same-sex marriages across the country.

Later, in August of the same year, the California Supreme Court voided the marriages, citing Mayor Newsom as having exceeded his authority. Clearly, a fight had begun and today the debate rages on, with an uncertain outcome, avidly watched by many San Franciscans.

LEFT: in 1989, an earthquake collapsed a freeway and killed nine people; hundreds were injured.
ABOVE the opening of baseball's PacBell (now SBC) Park spearheaded a revival of the South Beach and China Basin area near the Bay Bridge.

lifestyles are characteristic of many San Francisco residents, as are ecological movements and personal, gender and other single-issue political movements. San Francisco's local legislation, innovative or "whacko," depending on your view, is propelled by the regular plebicites – lists of propositions put to the electoral vote that help make a San Francisco voting form resemble a smaller city's telephone book.

New Yorkers often claim scornfully to be too busy living their lives to have time to think about ways to improve them, but the lifestyles pioneered in those Californian adventures are often the lifestyles adopted by East-Coasters and others later on. Watch this space. ❏

Decisive Dates

Pre-1500s Miwok, Ohlone and Wituk native tribes occupy much of the land now known as northern California.

1535 Spain's Hernando Cortés sets foot on California's shore, followed later by Portugal's Juan Rodriguez Cabrillo.

1579 Sir Francis Drake lands at Port Reyes, reporting to Europe that California is an island.

1769–1823 the Spanish establish a chain of 21 missions along between San Diego and Sonoma.

1776 Both the Presidio of San Francisco and Mission Dolores, located nearby, are founded.

1792 British explorer Captain George Vancouver sails into San Francisco Bay.

1834 Governor Figueroa assigns boundaries to the pueblo of San Francisco.

1846 John Fremont christens the entrance to the Bay the "Golden Gate."

1848 Gold is discovered in the nearby Sierra Nevada foothills, precipitating an unparalled boom in the city's economy.

1850 San Francisco is almost completely destroyed by fire.

1852 Wells Fargo begins transporting freight by stagecoach.

1854 First US Mint opens on Commercial Street.

1859 More discoveries in the Sierra Nevadas – this time a boom following silver discoveries.

1862 San Francisco Stock Exchange opens.

1869 The transcontinental railroad line is completed, and the first train arrives at Alameda.

1870 A contract is awarded for a topographical survey of what will eventually become Golden Gate Park.

1873 The world's first street cable railroad runs along Clay Streeet.

1880 George Hearst pours huge sums of money into the *San Francisco Examiner*, turning it over to his son William seven years later.

1901 First publication of *The Octopus* by Frank Norris, a devastating criticism of the Southern Pacific Railroad.

1906 An earthquake estimated at 8.25 on the Richter Scale levels much of the city, followed by a disastrous fire.

1907 Destroyed by the 1906 earthquake, the Fairmont, Nob Hill's first hotel, is rebuilt.

1911 Formation of the San Francisco Symphony Orchestra.

1914 The first transcontinental telephone conversation takes place: Alexander Graham Bell in New York talks to Thomas Watson in San Francisco.

1915 The Panama Pacific International Exposition, celebrating the birth of the Panama Canal, opens; centerpiece is SF's Palace of Fine Arts.

1920 The first transcontinental airmail flight is completed, and mail arrives from New York.

1923 First season of the San Francisco Opera.

1924 Palace of Legion of Honor is dedicated.

1933 Golden Gate Bridge construction begins.

1934 US Government converts Alcatraz island into a federal prison.

1936 The Bay Bridge opens, linking San Francisco and the East Bay.

1937 Pan American begins flights between San Francisco and New Zealand.

1938 Herb Caen's column begins in the *San Francisco Chronicle* and runs for nearly half a century, earning him the nickname "Mr San Francisco."

1939 The Golden Gate International Exposition opens on Treasure Island.

1942 San Franciscans of Japanese ancestry are rounded up and sent to "internment camps" for the duration of World War II.

1945 The United Nations' first headquarters is established in San Francisco.

1949 Treasonous wartime broadcaster "Tokyo

Rose" (Iva Toguri D'Aquino) is tried in San Francisco and sentenced to 10 years in jail.

1950s Birth of the "Beats," a loose literary group centered in North Beach.

1951 The Japanese premier signs a peace treaty, at the SF Opera House, that officially ends World War II.

1960 The House Unamerican Activities Commission meets at City Hall. Mass arrests and abuse of protesters foreshadow the protest movement of later years.

1965 Entrepreneur Bill Graham opens The Fillmore for staging weekly rock concerts.

1967 The "Human Be-In" gathering of hippies takes place in Golden Gate Park.

1970 Native Americans take over Alcatraz island and celebrate "Liberation Day."

1971 The last link on the BART subway system is completed.

1972 The first Gay Pride parade takes place in the Castro.

1973 The National Park Service begins guided tours of the decommissioned Alcatraz.

1974 Patricia Hearst, granddaughter of William Randolph, is kidnapped by the Symbionese Liberation Army.

1977 Harvey Milk makes headlines by becoming the first gay to be elected to the city's Board of Supervisors. The Gay and Lesbian Film Festival is established.

1978 Milk and Mayor George Moscone are assassinated by conservative political opponent Dan White. Dianne Feinstein, with massive support from the gay movement, begins a 10-year stint as mayor.

1980s Local computer industry booms: Silicon Valley and Apple become household words.

1982 San Francisco 49ers win the Superbowl.

1985 Dan White, killer of Harvey Milk and Mayor George Moscone, commits suicide.

1986 The Names Project Memorial Quilt commemorating Aids victims is started, and then travels around the world.

1989 An earthquake measuring 7.1 on the Richter Scale hits the Bay Bridge, collapses a freeway, kills nine people, injures hundreds and causes billions of dollars of damage.

1991 The legendary rock promoter and music guru Bill Graham dies in a helicopter crash.

1992 Pro-gay politican and former mayor Dianne Feinstein enters the US Senate.

1993 The city's Board of Supervisors votes to ban smoking in the workplace.

1995 The new Museum of Modern Art opens in the resurgent South of Market (SoMa) area.

1998 A city-wide smoking ban in restaurants and bars is introduced.

1999 City Hall reopens after a refurbishment. The Hearst Corporation buys the *San Francisco Chronicle* newspaper for $660 million and sells its sagging historic flagship, the *Examiner*.

2000 The Asian Art Museum moves from Golden Gate Park to the Civic Center. Base-

ball's Pacific Bell Park (now SBC Park), opens in South Beach, spearheading refurbishment and gentrification of the area.

2003 Protests over America's invasion of Iraq lead to the arrest of hundreds. Democrat Gavin Newson defeats Green Party candidate Matt Gonzalez in a tight race.

2004 Mayor Gavin Newsom authorizes the city clerk to issue marriage licenses to same-sex couples, sparking a national debate.

2005 The new de Young Museum opens in Golden Gate Park, replacing the original.

2008 The California Academy of Sciences due to have completed a massive renovation and move back to Golden Gate Park. ❑

LEFT: the St Francis window in Mission Dolores.
RIGHT: the Asian Art Museum completed a successful move from Golden Gate Park to the Civic Center.

SAN FRANCISCANS

Since long before the the Gold Rush,
San Francisco has held promise for
people of all kinds from all over the world

Cars pause at crossroads, unprompted, to allow pedestrians to pass in the street. San Francisco is the only town in the United States, probably the world, to have proposed allowing beggars to take credit-card swipes, because of the lack of change in the pockets of generally wealthy locals. This is the place that legalized gay matrimonial unions.

San Francisco is a town that is keen to accommodate, to include. It has grown and evolved through waves of migration. But there's another explanation for its enduring popularity: for most, the City by the Bay is not a way-station – it's where people want to be. It's beautiful, the climate is agreeable, the food is good and almost every kind of outdoor activity is available. Most tastes for indoor recreation are also catered for. People like it here. And once they're here, they want to stay.

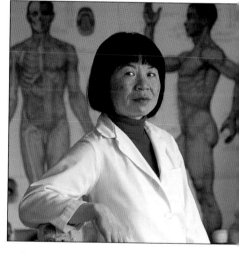

Go West

Besides being west, as in "Go West, young man, and grow up with the country" (a quote originally from an 1851 editorial by John Soule in the Indiana *Terre Haute Express*, but usually attributed to Horace Greely), the very landscape has offered hope and the promise of opportunity to countless generations. Native Americans found the hunting plains and fertile lands of California hospitable, and deemed Yosemite Valley "a holy place." Mexicans came north to work the rich fields, and Spanish

PRECEDING PAGES: Hispanic haircuts in the Mission District. **LEFT:** twins step out in style on Market Street. **RIGHT:** Asian acupuncturist.

settlers saw what Sir Francis Drake missed – a world-class natural harbor.

In the late 1840s, California land grants beckoned to many, who saw the risks of pioneering a better prospect than their present lives. Then the glitter of gold drew just about everyone. Even the US government took notice, and plans for a trans-continental railroad, long discussed, suddenly stretched into steel rails across the country. The railroad's construction brought an influx of workers, many of them Chinese, and led in part to the development of the world's largest Chinatown outside China. The "Beat" counter-culture thrived here in the 1950s, then flower children came to "be" in the 1960s. Just down the peninsula, the next generation was gearing up – bright computer pioneers who would reinvent the tools of work and communication, just in time for the internet to ignite in the 1990s.

Statistics

San Francisco is the United States' 13th largest city, with 750,000 people dwelling snugly in an area only 7 by 7 miles (11 by 11 km). According to the most recent census, the population is 46 percent white, 29 percent Asian (most of whom are Chinese), 14 percent Hispanic and 11 percent African-Americans. In recent years, the city has also drawn increasing numbers of

Filipinos and Southeast Asians, and a certain proportion of eastern Europeans.

The city's demographic mix includes a high percentage of young unmarrieds, with the number of single people between 25 and 34 years of age having increased dramatically in the past few decades. Only 20 percent of San Francisco households include children, fewer than one-fifth of adults under 45 own their own home, and nearly 100,000 people – almost one in seven residents of the city – live with a friend, a lover or with roommates.

San Francisco is a decentralized metropolis, where many of its inhabitants root themselves in cozy neighborhood enclaves; where their distinct cultures and identities grow and thrive; and where each is characteristically tolerant of the other. The gay and lesbian population crosses all ethnic divisions, and wields cohesive political power in the city. According to most estimates, between one in five and one in seven city residents is gay.

All that glitters

People of almost every state, nation and race came in the rush for gold; by 1850, Mexican, Irish, German and French immigrants made up four-fifths of the foreign-born population. Once the miners arrived, as historian James Adams noted, "…every type of citizen of every social grade or profession came, not to hew forests, farm and make homes, but to get as rich as possible as quickly as possible."

San Francisco became a boomtown almost overnight. Between 1848 and 1851, the population jumped from 1,000 to 40,000 – a staggering spurt of growth. Among the people who made their way here in search of instant riches were thousands of free blacks from the old South. In the city, black settlers organized and took action to secure their civil rights.

A Franchise League was formed to campaign for the repeal of a law forbidding blacks the right to testify in trials involving whites. Five hundred white San Franciscans signed the petition in 1860, and by 1863, the campaign had succeeded and a course of integration had, at least, been set. One black pioneer, J.B. Sanderson, became famous for founding city schools for poor Indian, Asian and black children, many of whom had been barred from local institutes. Sanderson himself taught lessons until he was able to recruit other people to replace him.

Genovese sailors had been trading along the western shore for years, but the remote towns and harbors offered little to interest the worldly seafarers. When the shout rang out that there was gold in the Sierra foothills, the Genovese were the first Italians to settle the "promised land" by the Golden Gate. Within months, tales of streets paved with gold spread to the old country, and people of the northern Italian provinces soon followed their pioneering cousins. Rural Ligurians, Luccans, Florentines and Venetians all made the grueling five-month journey from the old world to the new.

Not all their dreams came true, but California was a land rich in possibilities. The soil was fertile, the bay was filled with fish, and the town was starved of commerce. For a diligent people accustomed to hard work and saving, San Francisco was close enough to *paradiso*.

North Beach and the New World

By the 1860s, Italians were a strong presence in North Beach *(see pages 85 and 92)*. The new San Franciscans called their relatives over, and whole families – sometimes entire villages – arrived in the New World. Being Italians, provincial differences crossed the ocean with the pioneers. People of different regions spoke

unskilled, Sicilians took up the hard manual labor to which they were accustomed. As an island people, though, they were able fishermen. Soon they had displaced the Genovese from Fisherman's Wharf, and filled the bay with their colorful *felucce*. To this day, in North Beach's Saints Peter and Paul Church, a priest conducts the Blessing of the Fleet.

By 1851, there were 25,000 Chinese working in the mines, the majority of them eventually settling in San Francisco. These Chinese fortune-seekers shared a common dream that Gum San, the Gold Mountain, would provide them healthy fortunes with which they could return home and rejoin their anxious families.

distinct dialects and followed their own customs. The battles that rocked the newly unifying Italy were fought with equal vigor in the New World. The sea-faring Genovese mostly stuck to trade and fishing; Ligurians grew and sold produce; and the others opened stores or established businesses. In the 1880s a second wave of immigrants arrived, this time from southern Italy. As in the old country, the northerners considered Sicilians second-rate citizens, calling them *terrone* (dirt-eaters). Largely

The first Chinese men who came to San Francisco and northern California were called "coolies" – workers willing to do hard labor in the mines and, later, on the railroads for significantly lower wages than whites. Coolie comes from the Chinese phrase *ku li*, meaning "bitter strength." This new life was unimaginably harsh: a newspaper of the time reported that 20,000 lbs (9,000 kg) of bones were collected from shallow graves along the railroad tracks where Chinese workers had died. The bones were sent home to China for burial.

Wherever they worked, Chinese laborers formed communities. In San Francisco they lived in crude, segregated barracks in a section

LEFT: portrait of a diner.
ABOVE: San Francisco Giants fans float on inflatable baseball gloves in McCovey Cove, outside SBC Park.

soon known as Chinatown *(see page 99),* where goods and services were often cheaper than those of their white competitors.

The gold and railroads brought riches to a small number of people, but prosperity to entire communities of business folk who catered to the needs of the workforce. An enduring Gold Rush success is Levi's jeans, first rivetted for the miners who were excavating the hills.

Excellence in products and services was widespread; Hinton R Helper, a commentator of the time, wrote, "I have seen purer liquor, better segars, finer tobacco, truer guns and pistols, larger dirks and bowie-knives, and pret-

pines had been under the American flag since the end of the Spanish-American war, so they arrived without restriction, and although expected to return home after their studies, many remained. A second wave came in the 1920s, when farmers hired contractors to recruit Filipino laborers, who were often treated with the same anti-Asian sentiment that affected the Chinese community.

From Mexico, an astonishing 10 percent of the population migrated to the southwestern US in the first 30 years of the 20th century, the majority to Texas and California. In California, their numbers swelled from 8,000 to 370,000. Most came to harvest cotton, can-

tier courtesans here in San Francisco than in any other place. California does furnish the best bad things obtainable in America."

Influx of immigrants

In the first decade of the 20th century, the number of Japanese in the US increased from 6,000 to 25,000. Most of these immigrants settled in California, with a large number choosing San Francisco. Local trade unions protested against the hiring of Japanese workers and, after the great earthquake of 1906, many fled south to Los Angeles.

The first Filipinos came to the US between 1903 and 1910, usually as students. The Philip-

taloupe and lettuce crops. Working the fields until harvest was over and returning to their families across the border as soon as possible, the migrants were transient to the point of being virtually homeless.

Settling in temporaray colonies or *barrios,* with cheap rentals but no zoning requirements – no sewers, no paved roadways or street lighting – these immigrants were often prey to illnesses. The Hispanic activist Cesar Chavez, leader of the United Farm Workers Union and commemorated in Cesar Chavez Boulevard in the Mission District, lived in such a *barrio* in Santa Clara county, 50 miles (80 km) south of San Francisco.

Angel Island

From 1890 to 1940, the Chinese faced harsh discrimination, both locally and across the United States. New laws prohibited them from marrying non-Asians, becoming citizens, holding skilled jobs or owning property. When San Francisco's immigration station on Angel Island was opened in 1910, it established separate facilities for Asians.

Conditions were similar to prisons of the day, with new arrivals subjected to humiliating physical examinations and long months of waiting without any idea of whether they would be allowed to enter the city. Many Asians were turned back and had to board

headed for the urban centers of the West Coast, and the thriving war industries. During World War II, a huge influx of blacks also came from the South, to work in shipyards and the increasingly popular defense businesses.

The navy contributed a migration of gay men during the war, discharging them from the ships when they berthed at the San Francisco docks. They, too, formed a community, establishing the haven that now draws soulmates from around the globe. These wartime migrations all fueled a housing shortage in San Francisco. While many Japanese had fought against their mother country during World War II, on the side of the United States, thousands more

ships for the long journey home. Some of the inscriptions and poetry etched into the concrete walls of the barracks on Angel Island can still be seen. Fortunately, much of this discriminatory legislation was eradicated in the 1940s. And in subsequent years, as immigration quotas were relaxed, entire families arrived in San Francisco to make new lives for themselves.

In the 1930s "Dust Bowl" years, many poor white farmers fled from Louisiana, Oklahoma and Texas, memorably chronicled by John Steinbeck in *The Grapes of Wrath*. They

LEFT: internet entrepreneurs.
ABOVE: surveying the sailboats around Fort Mason.

(DON'T) CALL IT FRISCO

Newspaperman Herb Caen, chronicler of things San Franciscan, felt strongly enough to name his book *Don't Call It Frisco*; in Hayes Valley a coin-operated laundry is called the "Don't Call It Frisco Laundromat." Unpopular with locals since the 1930s, the name is not a corruption of "Francisco," but is thought to be from an old English word, "frithsoken," meaning refuge, and used by sailors to refer to a port with repair yards. Recently, there has been a backlash to the backlash: the term is appearing on the hooded tops and T-shirts of young residents, and the folks who run "Frisco Tattoo" in the Mission District say that "Frisco" is one of their most popular indelible etchings.

had their possessions confiscated and/or were detained in concentration camps. Japanese people, returning from this long, harsh internment, came back to find they could no longer afford homes. Reparations from the Federal government 40 years later did little to erase the bitter memories.

Power to the people

After 1946, when the Republic of the Philippines was established, strong economic and military ties to the US continued and the immigration quota was raised. Revised immigration laws in 1952 brought another wave of Filipino immigration and recent census figures

show the Filipino community to be among the city's fastest-growing "Asian-Pacific" immigrant groups. Lacking the regional and family organization of the Chinese and the Japanese to establish settlements, Filipino immigrants, many from remote islands, finally found unity through the American labor movement. They ultimately merged with Mexican-American union members to form the United Farm Workers Union.

More recent arrivals from the Philippines have been professional people, who tend to specialize in fields like engineering and medicine. Today, a huge Filipino community occupies the area just south of San Francisco in

Daly City. Black migrants, in the meantime, had congregated in housing projects, in areas like Hunters Point and the Fillmore District, where they were charged high rents for dilapidated Victorian dwellings. Shortly after the Watts riots in southern California in 1965, a smaller uprising took place in Hunters Point. When the plight of the tenants of the black ghettos could no longer be ignored, municipal job training programs were instituted and new businesses were established. The Office of Economic Opportunity and other agencies came in to help provide skills and advice, and Hunters Point received $3 million a year from the federal Model Cities Program.

Enter the dragon

Until 1970, Korean immigration to the Bay Area had been slight, and when the Koreans did arrive, they often had the capital to start small businesses, unlike the Chinese, who worked for other people and lived among themselves in Chinatown. As a result, modern Chinatown is not just for sightseeing; it is the focal point of a community that has become one of the most important segments of the population, wielding political power and making cultural contributions to the city.

Like the Chinese, the local Japanese-American community draws its cultural strength, customs, celebrations and power from its long history. Today, roughly 12,000 Japanese live in San Francisco, most in the area called Nihonmachi, or Japantown.

Refugees from Kampuchea, Vietnam and Laos have recently settled in record numbers and, predictably, have faced some discrimination. There have been clashes between Vietnamese fishermen and local white fishermen, who feel threatened by the newcomers. Although laws regarding the use of certain types of nets have been established (laws aimed specifically at inhibiting Vietnamese fishing), a number of strong-advocate legal groups have emerged to serve the interests of the Vietnamese people.

Conversely, the black population of San Francisco is shrinking, having dropped to 60,000. Most of those who leave are moving to the suburbs that have begun to push the Bay Area's outer limits into the San Joaquin Valley and others parts of central California.

Star tech

The most recent Gold Rush, the massive internet land-grab of the 1990s, has been a major factor in shaping the modern San Francisco landscape. Boutiques, wine bars, cool restaurants and computer stores began to spring up, seemingly on every street corner. Everything, and everyone, became wired. New media companies moved into old warehouses, and districts like South Beach became trendy overnight. SBC Park breathed new life into McCovey Cove, as techies spent their few leisure hours and abundant dollars frequenting the new ball park and the watering holes that opened around it. Sleek sailboats cruised into

anti-pollution laws. Tolerance of cultural, religious, racial and gender divergences are hard-wired into the city's civic codes and legislation.

While there is certainly no shortage of personal wealth in San Francisco, unlike in other places this is not displayed so much in clothes and accessories, but in discreet displays of what can best be described as "tech toys." Status is quietly conveyed with personal organizers, cell-phones and, of course, vehicles, although parking is such a trial all over the city that most people's cars spend much of their time standing in garages.

The tech that drives the toys is clearly from the hottest tip of the cutting edge. The first

the Marina and Fort Mason districts. Property prices soared to breathtaking heights, and landlords with rentals were able to write long checklists of requirements for potential tenants. Applicants would line up, and apartments would be let within hours, sometimes minutes.

The Californian body-culture is accompanied here by spiritual and personal development, and this has lead in turn to social and ecological pioneering; in the nation that pollutes the planet's atmosphere the most, San Francisco has some of the world's toughest

internet café was established across the bay in Berkeley, and a sizeable portion of the world's foremost technology and communications companies are headquartered in the Bay Area. Groovy gadgets show up here first.

Immigration still surfaces as an issue in political campaigns, as politicians will often inflame the emotive issues as an easy ride to further their own agendas, and discrimination does occur here, as it does everywhere. The difference is that the city usually meets these challenges head-on, positively and pro-actively. All in all, San Francisco's cultural atmosphere is bright, confident, accommodating and optimistic. Much like its people and its landscape.   ❏

LEFT: shades of cultural diversity.
ABOVE: Elvis (and Elvis and Elvis) lives!

THE GAY COMMUNITY

Since World War II, this creative and sociable
community has introduced a vital pulse
into the San Franciscan cultural mix

After rioting in the streets, refurbishing entire neighborhoods of decaying Victorian homes, wielding a powerful voting bloc in local politics, taking government posts in national politics and building substantial businesses, the San Francisco gay community has earned the city its reputation as an international gay mecca.

The emergence of the city's out-front, unabashed and sometimes highly volatile gay community represents the most significant sociological development in San Francisco's history since the early days of the beatniks and the hippies. There is no definitive record to give the exact number of gays and lesbians living in San Francisco – although city officials speculate endlessly – but this city of 750,000 is home to at least 80,000 same-sex snugglers.

Like nearly every aspect of San Francisco's history, the transformation of the Gold Rush town into a homophile Oz grew from the most improbable beginnings.

Boot camp

It started in the waning days of World War II. The US military began systematically purging its ranks of gays, booting out suspected homosexuals at their point of debarkation. For the massive Pacific theater of the war, this meant San Francisco.

The purges created an entire class of men who had been officially stigmatized as homosexuals. Unable to return home and face inevitable shame, they stayed in the Bay Area, socializing in discreet bars or, more often, at intimate soirées. Another migration of professional gays came during the early 1950s in the gray days of the anti-communist McCarthy era, when the federal government drummed thousands of homosexuals out of apparently secure government jobs.

Local authorities, meanwhile, did not take a liking to the idea of gays grouping in the bohemian bars of North Beach. They treated any gathering of more than a few dozen as an armed insurrection. Bar raids, mass arrests and harsh prosecutions of men and women accused of frequenting "disorderly houses" became distressingly commonplace.

Activist origins

By 1960, gays had begun moving toward an open campaign for civil rights, a course unthinkable a few years earlier. Ultimately, institutions like the US military establishment and the San Francisco Police Department provoked this politicization, since the activism was a response to anti-gay excesses.

It started humbly enough in 1955 with the formation of the US's first lesbian group, the

Daughters of Bilitis. The notion of homosexuals banding together in pressure groups was considered novel, but quickly caught on. Cadres of politically active gays were soon forming, such as the Society for Individual Rights and the Mattachine Society, whose then-radical publication tentatively asked whether homosexuality was a "disease or way of life," and whether gays should be rehabilitated or punished.

In 1961, José Sarria, a prominent female impersonator who was sure he was neither diseased nor in need of rehabilitation, got so irate over police raids on his Black Cat bar that he took off his dress and high heels and donned a three-piece suit to run for the Board of Super-

visors, San Francisco's style of city council. Sarria polled a then-astounding 7,000 votes, and clued the fledgling gay groups to the fact that their future power could lie in the ballot box. By 1964, liberal candidates for the Board of Supervisors were seeking gay endorsements, their careers safe from pious moralists, a minority breed in San Francisco. When the 1969 board election came along, so did a 35-year-old political newcomer named Dianne Feinstein. Later to become mayor from 1978 to 1988, and a US Senator in 1992, Feinstein campaigned energeticaly among gays, later crediting the margin of her landslide victory to gay ballots.

Having seen the effectiveness of the political voice, studies suggest that, proportionately, gays vote in larger numbers and give more money to political candidates than heterosexuals.

Hippie influence

As Feinstein campaigned at the Society for Individual Rights, hippie counter-culture was in full bloom in Haight-Ashbury. This was fertile territory for the Gay Liberation Movement sweeping west from New York City on the heels of the antiwar movement.

It didn't take long for the flower children to question whether the do-your-own-thing hippie ethos might mean more than simply wearing love beads, growing long hair, puffing on "weed" and swallowing LSD. Slowly, a few dozen, then a few hundred, gay hippies moved over the hill from Haight Street into Castro Street, a nearby Irish-American enclave.

Many working-class Catholics were terrified by the "gay invaders," as they called them, and moved out in panic. They left behind a huge, if somewhat dilapidated, stock of quaint 1880s Victorian homes, perfect for gay gentrification. The area quickly evolved into the nation's first neighborhood owned and run by and for gay people. The city's first Gay Pride Parade (now San Fransisco Pride) was held in 1972, an event now attended by hundreds of thousands.

Castro Street rapidly became the embodiment of the gay drive for acceptance, and in late 1975, gay votes elected George Moscone, the first mayor wholly sympathetic to gay voters. Two years later, neighborhood voters elected Harvey Milk to the Board of Supervisors. A Castro Street camera shop owner and gay activist, Milk organized the area's merchants' group, and became the first openly gay city official to be elected in American politics.

In 1978, former supervisor Dan White, the city's most anti-gay politician, gunned down Supervisor Milk and Mayor Moscone in cold blood right in their City Hall offices. The city reeled in shock, and a somber, mixed crowd of 40,000 marched the familiar path from Castro Street to City Hall, silently bearing candles.

White Night riots

Six months later, a jury sentenced double-murderer White to only five years, sparking the massive "White Night" riots. White, paroled in 1985, killed himself in the same year that

Cathedral, 1100 California Street (*for more information, go to www.aidsquilt.org*).

In 1981, the first openly lesbian judge, Mary Morgan, was appointed to the San Francisco Municipal Court and three years later Berkeley became the first city in the world to award the same spousal benefits to lesbian and gay city employees as to other employees. For years now, the city has had openly gay and lesbian elected officials, supervisors, police officers, congressional aides and bureaucrats, as well as judges on the Municipal Court.

On February 12, 2004, at San Francisco City Hall, 15 same-sex couples married, and dozens of marriage licenses were issued to same-sex

The Life and Times of Harvey Milk won the Oscar for best documentary.

The menace of Aids was cited when, in April 1984, San Francisco's Department of Public Health used emergency powers to close all the city's bathhouses. Two years later, Cleve Jones began the Names Project Memorial Quilt; tens of thousands of patches commemorating victims of the virus. Originally in a gallery/workshop on Market Street, portions of the quilt are now on view all over the country, the San Francisco patches in the Interfaith Chapel at Grace

couples. A national debate ensued with personal interventions from the President demanding that the practice be ended, and the story still has some way to go.

The advent and ravages of Aids have been a dark catalyst, transforming gay culture in recent years. The illness and deaths of friends and lovers have become part of the way of life, and the once-lusty nightlife has toned down. More conservative dating and courtship practices have become the norm.

Nevertheless, revelers remain on the scene in sufficient numbers, and with wild enough abandon, to give the city some of the liveliest and most colorful gay bars anywhere on earth. ❏

LEFT: Harvey Milk in front of his Castro camera shop.
ABOVE: lovely ladies in the Bay to Breakers race.

THE GOURMET'S CITY

California cuisine, cultural diversity, celebrity chefs
and bounty from the sea and the trees –
the City by the Bay has a hungry
appetite rich in history

When it comes to food, the Bay Area has always been slightly ahead of the competition. Consider this: the city once claimed to have the only restaurant in America serving pizza; opened the first Chinese and Japanese restaurants in the West; insists it invented the fortune cookie; and gave rise to that nebulous culinary catch-all, "California cuisine."

With over 3,000 eating and drinking establishments in San Francisco – said to be more per capita than anywhere else in the world – and a compact array of ethnic neighborhoods spilling over into one another, it's no surprise that an appetite for fresh and innovative cuisine, combined with a spirit of experimentation, helped to confirm San Francisco's reputation for fine food.

It has always been this way, or so it seems. At the time of the Gold Rush in 1849, which forever changed the face of the West, San Francisco was nothing but a transient, shanty town, filled with houses made of paper and men with dreams of gold. Populated by hotel-dwellers and apartment renters, none of which were provided with kitchens, eating out became a tradition by necessity.

A free lunch

Perhaps the noblest practice in the city's memory is the "free lunch" saloon. In even the simplest corner grocery or "bit" saloon, hard-working clerks and brokers could, for the

LEFT: the Garden Court at the Palace Hotel.
RIGHT: Ferry Building Marketplace.

meager price of a mug of beer, feed on an impressive array of cheeses, bologna and pickles. Author Jack London wrote of one, south of Market Street: "Especially I liked the San Francisco saloons. They had the most delicious dainties for the taking – strange breads and crackers, cheeses, sausages, sardines – wonderful foods that I never saw on our meagre home-table."

In the more elegant saloons, adorned with crystal chandeliers and mahogany tables, brandy-sipping bankers and merchants were offered an even more elaborate spread. On the ground floor of the Palace of Fine Arts, a free lunch at the Lick House included pig's head, crab salad, terrapin stew, Holland herring and smoked salmon. There were, of course, plenty of places for those who struck it rich on gold to spend their new fortunes. The Poulet d'Or, the city's first French restaurant, opened in 1849, and was soon renamed "The Poodle Dog" by miners who couldn't cope with the French vowels.

By the turn of the 20th century, the city had become known as the "American Paris." When the 1906 earthquake leveled San Francisco, some muttered that the city was perhaps getting its just desserts and prophesied that this would teach it to appreciate a more modest appetite.

They were wrong, of course. Amidst the rubble, restaurateurs set up trestle tables and served meals (*see photo on page 27*). Dinner over, they set about the business of rebuilding. The rest of the country soon learned that it took more than an earthquake to dull the appetites of San Franciscans.

If the 1906 earthquake failed to turn the city sober and serious, Prohibition made another attempt. With one bar for every 100 inhabitants, San Francisco may have been the most bibulous city in the States. When alcohol was outlawed by the government, the locals merely shrugged their shoulders and said, "We might as well eat."

The early ethnic diversity of the city always offered plenty of fare for San Franciscans to choose from. Mexican missionaries were joined by scores of Chinese, French and Germans who arrived in the city in 1849 – enticed by the Gold Rush, but who remained to cook. Vietnamese, Thai, and Cambodian immigrants have since added Asian options to the city's international and endless variety of dishes.

Historical appetite

Word of the culinary riches soon whet the appetites of food connoisseurs the world over, who were drawn to the intrigue of the American Paris. Once in San Francisco, visitors could sample and purchase – as they still can today – Crab Louis salad and fresh petrale sole from the dockside stands of Fisherman's Wharf; Italian gnocci and oven-fresh *foccacia* bread from the tiny storefronts of North Beach; armsful of French bread; warm tortillas and chili-laden *salsas* from the Mexican-influenced Mission; and Thai fish cakes and Chinese pot stickers from Clement Street, deep in the heart of the Richmond area.

In 1935, after a trip to San Francisco with her companion Gertrude Stein, Alice B. Toklas recalled her adventures in her cookbook: "In San Francisco we indulged in gastronomic orgies. Sand dabs *meuniere*, rainbow trout in aspic, grilled soft-shell crabs, *paupiettes* of roast fillets of pork, eggs Rossini and tarte Chambourde. The tarte Chambourde had been a specialty of one of the three great French bakeries before the San Francisco fire. To my surprise, no one in Paris had ever heard of it."

While the unique French tart may have been news to Parisians, it could not have surprised long-time San Franciscans, raised on such a cross-cultural stew. They began to feel that they ate so much sushi, pasta, dim sum and pâté that they began to reinvent these favorites as part of a new, native cuisine.

Fueled by the culinary riches of the world, local chefs rebelled against the convention that French food belonged in French restaurants, Chinese in Chinese restaurants, and so on. Experimentation became the *notion du jour*, and over the years, the mixing and melding of international ingredients – along with a decidedly Western touch – gave rise to a culinary revolution. Chefs aren't fond of the term, but for better or worse, the food media and grateful gourmands christened the result "California cuisine."

California cuisine

The gourmet "revolution" was happening all over San Francisco, but nowhere with more passion than across the Bay Bridge in nearby Berkeley, where eclectic cuisine was introduced most dramatically. In 1971, Alice Waters opened Chez Panisse (see page 169). Waters set out with no formal training, just a year spent abroad experiencing European food. To Waters, freshness was the cardinal virtue and foods were cooked simply so as to

Armed with local ingredients, the Chez Panisse kitchen went to work. The result? The strictly French food became less "French," and the menu suddenly offered dishes like ravioli made like gnocci from potato starch and garlic, and the very English jugged hare.

Waters-trained chefs began to branch out on their own, and the Chez Panisse philosophy spread to other restaurants, as the public ate with interest. The fervor for fresh ingredients chimed with the Californian ethos, and in a few short years, chefs had been elevated to celebrity status. Fashion-hungry customers now follow chefs' careers from one restaurant to the next.

foster their natural flavor. Chez Panisse opened as a typical French bistro. Frustrated by an inability to get quality goods as they did in France, Waters began encouraging local purveyors to bring produce to her kitchen door. Farmers grew special vegetables to complement a specific dish and raised handfed livestock and poultry according to careful specifications. Small-time fishermen sold her their catch and, for the first time in years, local oysters were farmed.

A recent addition to the cuisine scene is the revamped 8,000 sq. ft (743 sq. meters) Ferry Building at the foot of San Francisco's Market Street. The old warehouse interior has been transformed into a hugely popular farmers' market and high-end eating destination, where everything is locally grown and produced. You can choose from homemade beef jerky, oysters from Hog Island (in Tomales Bay), a caviar bar, cheeses from the Cowgirl Creamery and the now-famous Slanted Door restaurant with its redwood bar and views of the bay. An afternoon in the Ferry Building is a gourmet's dream, and gives hungry visitors a chance to sample real California living. ❑

LEFT: Alice Waters of Chez Panisse, the "godmother" of California cuisine.

ABOVE: shaken, not stirred, at Zam Zam in the Haight.

BAY CITY ARTS

The light, the hills, the evocative fog
and the exuberant diversity of San Francisco
are the lifeblood of a dynamic arts community

It's nearly impossible to go a day in San Francisco without rubbing elbows with an artist, poet, actor or writer – or at the very least, a well-informed critic. While traditional artistic expressions such as opera, symphony and ballet are well-respected and hold a firm place in the city's cultural story, the Bay Area has really built its reputation as a breeding ground for experimental – and often outrageous – work.

Conventionally, artists of all media and inclinations flock here, then travel to Los Angeles and New York to be marketed; this holds true in theater, visual arts and the music industry. Some historians may trace this appetite for new creative ventures back to the city's Barbary Coast era, but it's more likely due to the national upheaval of the 1960s, when San Francisco became the quintessential counterculture city.

These days, San Francisco's tolerance seems inexhaustible: African-American, Asian-American and Latin American artists have made bi-culturalism an integral part of their work and the Bay Area culture. The influence of the Pacific Rim has contributed too, though as a port city, San Francisco has always felt the presence of other influences.

Visual arts

The first group effort to bring visual art to the forefront of the city's culture was in 1871, when 23 visual artists formed the San Francisco Art Association, exhibiting in a loft above a market.

By the 1890s, art had become a social concern, and a rich patron donated a Nob Hill palace to the Art Association to display its work.

A flamboyant neo-Egyptian Exhibition Hall, built for 1894's Midwinter International Exposition in Golden Gate Park, evolved into the de Young Museum. The permanent collection includes important works in the California School of Painting, characterized by Thomas Hill, Alfred Bierstadt and William Keith. These landscapists specialized in huge mountain gorges, vast Yosemite landscapes and natural light. A 2005 renovation of the de Young highlights the harmony between modern architecture and the natural landscape of the park.

LEFT: the soaring interior of the San Francisco Museum of Modern Art.
RIGHT: San Francisco Ballet dancers in *Continuum*.

In 1915, the huge Panama Pacific International Exposition brought a $40 million collection of paintings and sculpture to San Francisco and local artists discovered and adopted elements of French aestheticism. Bernard Maybeck's Palace of the Legion of Honor, devoted primarily to French art, opened in the 1920s.

Money, the climate and the University of California at Berkeley brought Diego Rivera and Mark Rothko to San Francisco. With them, public murals and abstract expressionism came into the regional culture, traditions followed not only by the muralists of Coit Tower, but also by the contemporary Hispanic artists with their Mission District murals, notably in Balmy Alley.

Visual Arts appreciation gained serious momentum in the 1990s with the opening of two major art centers in the once run-down area of SoMa. The spectacular San Francisco Museum of Modern Art, designed by Swiss architect Mario Botta, opened in 1995 to display a permanent collection that include works by Henri Matisse, Georges Braque, Vasily Kandinsky, Joan Miró, Georgia O'Keefe, Frida Kahlo, Jackson Pollock, Clyfford Still, Jasper Johns, Robert Rauschenberg, and Bay Area artists Richard Diebenkorn, Elmer Bischoff, David Park and Sam Francis.

The vast Yerba Buena Center for the Arts holds four rounds of visual arts exhibits each year. The contemporary space features national and international artists with strong ties to popular culture. The center also has year-round theater, dance and cross-disciplinary performances. Other recent additions to the SoMa area will be the Mexican Museum, the Jewish Museum, the Museum of Craft and Folk Art and the Museum of African Diaspora.

Known for his magnificent and extensive portfolio of American landscape photography, Ansel Adams was raised in his family's home near Golden Gate Bridge and spent most of his life here. His exquisite photos of Yellowstone and the Sierra Nevada are his best known works. Many Ansel Adams pictures are on permanent display at SFMoMA.

Bad-boy rock 'n' roll photographer Jim Marshall, a San Franciscan legend with a salty wit and a fondness for guns and whisky, is famous for his archetypical '60s photography. His images of musicians such as Jimi Hendrix, Janis Joplin, Jim Morrison and Johnny Cash earned him worldwide recognition. Portraitist Annie Leibovitz burst into the limelight from *Rolling Stone* magazine (created in San Francisco by publisher Jann Wenner). Her work regularly graces the pages of *Vanity Fair*, and she studied at the San Francisco Art Institute.

Music

When San Francisco was a young city, a passion for opera sprouted alongside the music halls and cabarets. Along with the newcomers to the city in the 1850s, opera houses appeared. Fire brigades escorted favorite divas through the crowds to performances, and San Francisco became a regular stop for European troupes. In the Bay Area there are no fewer than seven opera companies. Every fall, Free Opera in the Park is hosted in the bandshell in Golden Gate Park. There are more classical concerts per capita here than in any other city in the country, a phenomenon described by one critic as an "unreasonable profusion." Chamber music, too, is well-served.

The concerts and light shows held at the Fillmore and Avalon ballrooms became the standard for rock gigs all around the world. Locally based artists like the Grateful Dead, Jefferson Airplane and Janis Joplin regularly appeared at these venues, and performed in high-profile concerts in Golden Gate Park.

For the biggest names in rock, pop and alternative music, the venerable Warfield Theater and The Fillmore (both still run by Bill Graham Presents, years after the promoter's death in a helicopter accident in 1991), are joined by the Great American Music Hall and Slim's as the city's larger venues.

Regardless of the dance moves, there are plenty of places to pick up your feet in San Francisco. Although nightclubs are all over the city, there are two main neighborhoods for music. The most vibrant and varied is along Mission and Valencia streets between 16th and 26th Street. One single block of 11th Street between Folsom and Harrison has several rock clubs.

More "serious" theater dates from the turn of the 20th century, when San Francisco regularly hosted stock companies from England and from other parts of the United States. Fifty years later and across the country, Herbert Blau and Jules Irving founded New York's Actors Workshop in 1959 on the premise that theater belonged to actors and directors – *not* to producers and promoters. Local theaters began to develop new works and talent rather than simply staging Broadway shows.

Most notable was the American Conservatory Theater (ACT) led by Bill Ball, a visionary who helped create the model for regional theaters throughout the country. From the start,

The best bet to see what's up is the listings of *SF Weekly* or the *Bay Guardian*, the two largest free weekly papers.

Theater

San Francisco has a long, although varied, theater tradition. In the second half of the 19th century, melodeons (theater-bar-music halls) proliferated. The bawdiness and musicals are still here. Big productions from New York arrive each season, and burlesque surprisingly popular. Most theaters are located near Union Square.

ACT had a penchant for Molière and other classical European works. Other regional theaters were dedicated to developing young writers.

At the Magic Theatre, a brilliant young playwright named Sam Shepard began a career that has made him one of the best-known contemporary dramatists, in addition to starring in movies. The Eureka Theatre, Asian-American Theatre Company and Berkeley Repertory Theatre also provide a forum for new playwrights; David Henry Hwang (author of *M. Butterfly*) first produced his plays at AATC.

Just about every theatrical form thrives in San Francisco, from poetry performances to agitprop, to Shakespeare. ❏

LEFT: Bay Area theater troupe.
ABOVE: opera at Caffé Trieste in North Beach.

THE CITY ON SCREEN

San Francisco's iconic views have played supporting roles in movies from *Vertigo* to *Star Trek*. Francis Ford Coppola has headquarters here, and George Lucas has just moved into the Presidio

San Francisco has always offered high-value locations for moviemakers, with a range of romantically iconic views and backdrops. Barbra Streisand deftly maneuvered her Volkswagen between two cable cars in *What's Up Doc?*; Kim Novak hurled herself from a (non-existent) tower in *Vertigo* with a backdrop of the Golden Gate Bridge; and Steve McQueen bounced a Mustang over the city's hills in *Bullitt*. More recently, with more than a nod to *Bullitt*, the car chase in *The Rock* was like a pyromaniac's travelogue for the City by the Bay.

San Francisco's movie identity dates back to the 1930s with Howard Hawks' *Barbary Coast* and W.S. Van Dyke's *San Francisco*, which depicted the city collapsing in the 1906 earthquake. In 1941, John Huston's *The Maltese Falcon* had Humphrey Bogart, Peter Lorre and Sydney Greenstreet skulking in the alleys and backways of Nob Hill.

Bedroom to film set

The Fairmont Hotel, atop the same hill, has featured in movies from *Vertigo* in 1958 to *Petulia* (with Julie Christie and George C. Scott) exactly a decade later, to the Sean Connery drama *The Rock* in 1996.

The North Beach area is regularly jammed with lights, camera cranes and trailers. The renowned Saints Peter and Paul Church on Washington Square was the site of a shoot-out in 1971's *Dirty Harry,* and the Bank of America at 555 California Street became "America's tallest skyscraper" in 1974 as 86 fictional stories were added and then torched in Irwin Allen's disaster movie *The Towering Inferno.* The Transamerica Pyramid, one of the city's emblematic buildings, has featured in dozens of films including the 1991 *Shattered,* starring Tom Berenger.

Four blocks north, City Lights Bookstore was the setting for *Flashback,* a 1960s film starring a radical played by Dennis Hopper. The bookstore also featured in the 1980 Beat-inspired movie *Heart Beat* with Nick Nolte, Sissy Spacek and John Hurt.

The Tosca Café, across the street at 242 Columbus Avenue, featured in *Basic Instinct,* starring Michael Douglas and Sharon Stone, as did the Country & Western bar Rawhide on

7th Street. "Hollywood studios like to film in San Francisco," says former actor turned location scout Ellen Winchell, "the city has so many unique looks. It has its own magnetism." Winchell rents parking lots, pacifies neighbors, photographs potential sites, secures permits and hires security. She needed extra guards for the daily protests by gay activists on the sets of *Basic Instinct* – they thought the script was homophobic and should be banned or censored.

In other cities, sites featured in movies become tourist attractions. Here, the places most often chosen are already famous. Alcatraz, of course, has made regular appearances

Skywalker and Zoetrope

Two years after Francis Ford Coppola left Hollywood with George Lucas in 1969, he announced; "Just say Francis Coppola is up in San Francisco in an old warehouse making films." Since then he has built an empire with the movie studio American Zoetrope; a library and a winery in Napa; Chrome Dragon Productions; a TV production company; and a restaurant. Coppola's 1974 *The Conversation* starring Gene Hackman was shot around Union Square. Coppola's son, Roman, is a big fan of Hong Kong cinema, and helped launch Chrome Dragon Productions with Wayne Wang, who directed *The Joy Luck Club* here.

(The Birdman of Alcatraz 1962*; Escape from Alcatraz* 1979*; The Rock* 1996*)*, as has City Hall (*The Right Stuff*, 1983; *Class Action*, 1990) and the Golden Gate Bridge (*Superman*, 1978; *A View to a Kill*, 1985; *Interview with the Vampire*, 1994, and many more). The bridge, and Mission Dolores provided backdrops for *Vertigo*, whose Carlotta Valdez (Kim Novak) lived in an apartment at 940 Sutter Street, now the York Hotel.

LEFT: Steve McQueen and *Bullitt* sparked a vogue for SF car chases *and* inspired a new Mustang by Ford.
ABOVE: James Stewart and a mysterious Kim Novak in Alfred Hitchcock's 1958 classic, *Vertigo*.

Meanwhile, Lucas has assembled 1,300 employees at his Skywalker Ranch near the Bay Area town of Nicasio and other Marin County locations. His $2 billion business includes the *Star Wars* movies, *Indiana Jones*, the THX sound system and Industrial Light & Magic. Lucas's company has recently constructed another filmmaking unit in San Francisco's coveted Presidio.

Another movie success story has been across the bay in Emeryville near Berkeley, headquarters of Pixar Studios, part-founded by Apple Computer's Steve Jobs, and creators of the computer-animated adventures *Toy Story*, *Monsters Inc.*, *Finding Nemo* and *The Incredibles*. ❑

LITERARY SAN FRANCISCO

**From the Beats and Dashiell Hammett
to Amy Tan and Armistead Maupin,
the City by the Bay inspires its own writers
and lures others from all over the world**

A bronze plaque in Union Square's Burritt Alley, just off Bush Street, reads: "ON APPROXIMATELY THIS SPOT, MILES ARCHER, PARTNER OF SAM SPADE, WAS DONE IN BY BRIGIT O'SHAUGHNESSY." The memorial doesn't mention the classic detective story *The Maltese Falcon* or its author, but leaving the alley and walking toward Powell Street, the mystery is solved as you pass "Dashiell Hammett Street" on the right. Don't be surprised if you cross paths with other literati as you stroll around the city. A plan proposed by the celebrated City Lights Bookstore has been a great success: to rename 12 streets for prominent writers and artists who lived and worked in San Francisco.

What is the special appeal of this place for would-be wordsmiths? In part, its vital literary scene is self-propagating; a rich past, as well as books by and about San Francisco's writers, inspires others who would follow in their heroes' footsteps. What's more, with its jumble of ethnic neighborhoods spilling over into one another, San Francisco is alive with languages and cultures. It's a welcoming and romantic literary breeding ground, offering the golden promise of the West.

Mark Twain's jumping frogs

"San Francisco is a truly fascinating city to live in… The climate is pleasanter when read about than personally experienced," wrote

---

LEFT: the influential City Lights Bookstore.
RIGHT: Ken Kesey, Merry Prankster and author of *One Flew Over the Cuckoo's Nest*.

Mark Twain in his 1871 memoir, *Roughing It*. Twain, born Samuel Clemens, came from Missouri in 1861 following his brother Orion, who was a newly appointed secretary to the governor of the Nevada territory. When Twain's dreams of riches in the gold mines didn't pan out, he took to writing humor and travel for Virginia City's *Territorial Enterprise* newspaper, and quickly became a local celebrity. His travels continued westward, and in 1864 and 1865, Twain worked in San Francisco, covering the police, fire and theater beats for the *Morning Call* newspaper, before writing lampoons and commentaries for the *Golden Era* and the *San Francisco Chronicle*.

You won't find many traces of Twain's brief stint here, but it was a crucial time in his development as a writer. While in San Francisco he wrote the *Notorious Jumping Frog of Calaveras County*, based on a tall tale heard in a saloon in the town of Angels Camp. An annual jumping-frog contest held there every spring pays homage to the story.

Other Gold Rush literary figures included Bret Harte (who befriended Twain during his stay) and Ambrose Bierce. Like Twain, Harte contributed to the *Golden Era*. He was also the most popular western writer of his day, earning $10,000 in 1870 from the *Atlantic Monthly*, and contributing to every issue.

Bierce, author of the flawlessly cynical *Devil's Dictionary* – "Birth; the first and direst of all disasters," "a bride; a woman with a fine prospect of happiness behind her" – in addition to acclaimed short stories about the Civil War, was one of the first recognized columnists in American journalism. His unmissable Sunday column, "Prattles," appeared in William Randolph Hearst's *The Examiner*, and skewered pomposity with a fierceness that earned him the nickname "Bitter Bierce."

Robert Louis Stevenson is honored by several monuments in San Francisco, despite spending less than a year in northern California. In 1879, he traveled from his native Scotland in pursuit of Fanny Osbourne, a married woman with whom he had fallen madly in love in France. Trying unsuccessfully to support himself by writing, he spent several impoverished months living in a room at 608 Bush Street, waiting for Mrs Osbourne's divorce to be finalized. Afterward, Osbourne and Stevenson were married and sojourned in Napa Valley, where Stevenson recuperated from tuberculosis.

Although Stevenson didn't write his major works until after his return to Scotland in July 1880, a monument dedicated to him in the northwest corner of Chinatown's Portsmouth Square depicts the *Hispaniola*, the galleon featured in the classic pirate novel, *Treasure Island*. The inscription below the ship is taken from his "Christmas Sermon." Stevenson often came to Portsmouth Square to write and to watch the ships.

An oyster pirate named Jack

Born in San Francisco in 1876, Jack London kept close ties with the Bay Area through the course of his short, celebrated life. In *Martin Eden* (1909) and *John Barleycorn* (1913), London recalls the Oakland waterfront where he grew up. At the age of 14, he bought a sloop, the *Razzle Dazzle*, and became an oyster pirate along the shoals of the San Francisco Bay. Though he was known as the "Prince of the Oyster Pirates," the following year London had a change of heart and went to work as a deputy for the Fish Patrol.

London traveled across the US and Canada, on a sealing schooner off the Japanese coast and, in 1897, to the Klondike with the Gold Rush. After each adventure, he came back to Oakland. Returning from the Klondike with scurvy, London began to write about his experiences on the rugged Alaskan frontier. *The Son of the Wolf* (1901), his first collection of short stories, brought him immediate success and he continued writing in this vein, producing acclaimed, best-selling novels.

Apart from the plaque at 605 3rd Street marking his birthplace, there are few Jack London landmarks in San Francisco itself; most of his family's homes were destroyed in the fires following the 1906 earthquake (*see page 26*). But the city of Oakland has not forgotten him: Oakland renamed its waterfront shopping plaza Jack London Square in 1951, where you'll find Heinhold's First and Last Chance Saloon, an actual haunt from London's waterfront days. Supposedly, London sealed the purchase of his first sloop here. A house was brought from Alaska where he lived, and there are others in East Oakland, among them 575 Blair, where in 1903 he wrote his popular novel, *The Call of the Wild*.

Two years after, London and his wife Charmain moved north to a ranch (dubbed "Beauty Ranch") in Glen Ellen, in Sonoma's wine country. At the then-incredible cost of $70,000, London built his dream home, Wolf House, only to see it burn down in 1913 – the

grew up. She traveled east in 1891 to study at Radcliffe and Harvard, and eventually, in 1901, journeyed on to Europe where she remained an expatriate for years.

In 1934, Stein and her companion Alice B. Toklas revisited the area during a US lecture tour. She is still remembered in Oakland, not always fondly, for having written "There is no *there* there," about the city, in her 1937 memoir, *Everybody's Autobiography*.

New-style detective

Dashiell Hammett lived in San Francisco from 1921 to 1929, when he produced such books as *Red Harvest* and *The Dain*

night before he and his wife were to move in. Since 1959 the ranch has been open to the public as the Jack London State Historic Park. A short path from the house leads to the ruins of Wolf House and the grave where London's ashes were buried after his death in 1916.

Although writer Gertrude Stein was born in Allegheny, New York in 1874, the Steins moved west to Oakland in 1880 where she

LEFT: stop by the First and Last Chance Saloon in Oakland, made famous by Jack London.
ABOVE: the Beats in Mexico; photo by Allen Ginsberg. Clockwise from top left: Jack Kerouac, Ginsberg, Peter Orlovsky, Lafcadio Orlovsky, Gregory Corso.

DASHIELL HAMMETT

In 1921, Dashiell Hammett moved to San Francisco to marry Josephine Dolan. Though they had planned to return East, they stayed on, living in rented apartments. Based on his experience as a private detective, Hammett created an indelible character in Sam Spade, the cynical gumshoe inhabiting foggy San Francisco nights, memorably portrayed by Humphrey Bogart in John Huston's 1941 movie of *The Maltese Falcon*. Like many others in the 1950s, Hammett fell on the harsh mercies of the House Un-American Activities Committee for reported associations with Communists. He was jailed, and his career destroyed.

Curse, a hard-boiled style of novel writing that redefined the American mystery story.

Born in Maryland in 1894, Hammett was raised in Baltimore and Philadelphia. At 14, he dropped out of high school to help support his family, and shortly afterward joined the Pinkerton Detective Agency. Many of the shady characters in his fiction were based on types he had encountered in his five years as a Pinkerton man. Aficionados of *The Maltese Falcon* can still stop by John's Grill, at 63 Ellis (between Powell and Stockton streets).

Established in 1908, John's Grill is one of the few restaurants mentioned in the novel that is still open for business. Its second-floor Mal-

tese Falcon room is filled with Hammett memorabilia, and more photos are displayed on the restaurant's third floor.

The Beats and beyond

In the mid-1950s, the writing emerging from the cafés and bars of North Beach commanded national and international attention as the arbiter of a cultural revolution. The "Beat Generation" had been first defined on the East Coast a decade earlier by Jack Kerouac, Allen Ginsberg and John Clellon Holmes experimenting with spontaneous writing based on the rhythms of jazz and be-bop. But it wasn't until Kerouac and Ginsberg came out West in 1954

and 1955, encountering writers Lawrence Ferlinghetti, Gary Snyder, Michael McClure and others, that the Beats galvanized a literary movement *(see also page 88)*. All of this came together in San Francisco on October 7, 1955, at a poetry reading at the Six Gallery, an artists' cooperative. Organized by Kenneth Rexroth, the "Six Poets at the Six Gallery" reading featured Rexroth, Snyder, McClure, Ginsberg, Philip Whalen and Philip Lamantia and introduced the first public reading of Ginsberg's incendiary poem, *Howl*. Kerouac recounts the event in his novel *The Dharma Bums*.

The poem created a sensation when it was published in 1956 and was immediately confiscated by officials who deemed it "obscene" literature. Ferlinghetti's City Lights Bookstore, the first paperback bookstore in America, and he the publisher of *Howl & Other Poems*, was brought up on criminal charges. The ensuing trial brought against the bookstore, which City Lights won, established a legal precedent and brought the Beats to national prominence, as did Kerouac's book *On The Road*, published in 1957.

As the beatniks gave way to the hippies, so were the Beats followed by the Merry Pranksters. Led by Ken Kesey, author of *One Flew Over the Cuckoo's Nest*, the Pranksters were early experimenters with hallucinogens and organized massive LSD-tinged gatherings, or "Acid Tests," among them the legendary Trips Festival in January 1966. Held at Longshoreman's Hall in Fisherman's Wharf, the event reportedly drew 20,000 adventurers: Tom Wolfe's *The Electric Kool-Aid Acid Test* recounts these exploits in full detail.

At the same time, San Francisco was home to *Rolling Stone* magazine and its infamous correspondent, Hunter S. Thompson. Thompson lived in the Haight-Ashbury district during the mid-1960s when he was researching *Hell's Angels*, his off-kilter look at the motorcycle gang of the same name.

Armistead Maupin is a North Carolina native who relocated to San Francisco in 1971. His serial, "Tales of the City" began chronicling the lives of young gay and straight San Franciscans in the *San Francisco Chronicle* in 1976. The series was warmly received by the public, and reproduced in several best-selling volumes of books. It was later made into a successful series for British television.

While San Francisco lacks the publishing clout of New York, authors have always found the Bay Area a place of inspiration. Not only was there the late, great columnist Herb Caen (immortalized with a section of the Embarcadero now renamed "Herb Caen Way"), but the community nurtured poet Adrienne Rich, Chicana playwright and poet Cherríe Moraga, and many feminist erotica writers.

Internationally known writers Amy Tan (*The Joy Luck Club*), Alice Walker (*The Color Purple*) and Anne Rice (*Interview with the Vampire*) have all lived and worked in San

Local writers vie for a desk at the exclusive SF Writer's Grotto, which hosts see-and-be-seen events, and has been a workspace for Mary Roach, Po Bronson, Ethan Canin and others. At 826 Valencia is San Francisco's official Pirate Supply Store and home to a literary re-birth in the Mission District. Run by writer Dave Eggers, author of *A Heartbreaking Work of Staggering Genius*, the store provides premises for McSweeny's and The Believer, also a youth literary center where local writers teach classes and inspire the next generation of San Francisco wordsmiths.

The filmmaker Francis Ford Coppola rejuvenated the North Beach literary scene with

Francisco, and most have used the city as a backdrop in one or another of their highly charged novels.

The Modern Lit scene

The literary tradition still thrives in San Francisco, through underground readings, a lively café culture, innumerable writers' groups, and independent publishers like Manic D Press, City Lights, Last Gasp and McSweeny's.

LEFT: Amy Tan, whose *The Joy Luck Club* chronicles the lives of mothers and daughters in Chinatown.
ABOVE: John's Grill, 63 Ellis Street, opened in 1908; it was frequented by Sam Spade in *The Maltese Falcon*.

his magazine *Zoetrope: All Story*, headquartered in the copper-clad North Beach Sentinel Building. In addition to online workshops (*www.zoetrope.com*), Zoetrope hosts literary events, many at his Café Zoetrope at Kearny Street and Columbus Avenue.

Poetry, spoken word, fiction, non-fiction and other related arts intersect every September at LitQuake, a four-day festival that celebrates the city's literary present. Local celebs like Michael Chabon (author of *The Amazing Adventures of Kavalier and Clay*), Marin County resident Isabelle Allende and others join in making sure the city's literary tradition is on the map for decades to come. ❑

PLACES

A detailed guide to the city with the principal sites
clearly cross-referenced by number to the maps

For a city just a few miles wide and long, San Francisco covers a huge
variety of terrain, natural and social. At least a dozen distinct neighborhoods are tucked inside the narrow city limits, with an array of
fascinatingly different styles, all set in a sea-fringed frame of stunning natural beauty. Social, cultural and ethnic diversity is an easy backdrop, with
class boundaries softly blurred. The most visible extremes are the wealthy
elite on top of Nob Hill, and the homeless of the Tenderloin District, but
San Francisco is a collage of cultures – ad hoc, yet somehow hanging
together with a comfortable sense of permanence.

The many and varied hills offer visitors to the city a variety of panoramas and vistas. On foot these can be a challenge, but by bus, auto or cable
car, every trip is an adventure. Whether walking or riding, the views make
it all worthwhile, unfolding glimpses of the bay, the bridges and the streets
that so often retain a Victorian or Georgian character, but with an individual, urban West Coast style.

A visit is happily unpredictable, although a healthy attitude to surprise
(and a good pair of walking shoes) are useful equipment. There are also
wonderful treats, especially if you venture away from the beaten path. Just
don't underestimate those hills: a guide published a few decades ago
advised that when you finally get tired of walking San Francisco, you can
always just stop and lean on it.

The following sections are mapped out as a series of city neighborhoods
full of attractions, experiences and activities. After these essential sites,
we travel farther afield, around the bay from the Bay Bridge to the Golden
Gate, and to Oakland, Berkeley and the Bay Area. Finally, for those with
more time for spectacular northern California, there are a series of excursions: wild coastlines, pleasing wineries and hot-tub heavenly spas just
waiting for you to savor before heading back to San Francisco.

Oh, and if you do leave your heart, as so many often do, you can always
come back for it next time.   ❑

PRECEDING PAGES: the dizzying view of the city and the bay from Twin Peaks; Nob Hill:
do not adjust your book. **LEFT:** *Beach Blanket Babylon*, at North Beach's Club Fugazi, is
the longest running musical review in San Francisco's history.

San Francisco

0 ___ 500 yds
0 ___ 500 m

N

Golden Gate Bridge

PRESIDIO

Geary Blvd

Fulton Street

GOLDEN GATE PARK

Lincoln Way

19th Ave

Sunset Blvd

Great Hwy

Sloat Blvd

Skyline Blvd

HARDING PARK

Pacific Ocean

San Francisco Bay

Bay Bridge

3rd St

Evans Ave

3rd St

Bayshore Blvd

Army St

Mission St

McLAREN PARK

Guerrero St

17th St

Van Ness Ave

Divisadero St

California

Hill St

Broadway

Lombard St

Bay St

Market St

Mission St

Ocean Ave

Alcatraz

San Francisco Bay

San Francisco Bay

Oakland

Pier 1
Pier 3
Pier 7
Pier 9
Pier 15
Pier 17
Pier 19
Pier 23
Pier 27
Pier 29
Pier 31
Pier 33
Pier 35
Pier 39
Pier 41
Pier 43
Pier 45
Pier 47

SIDNEY

Davis
Front St
Battery
Sansome
Montgomery
Kearny
Grant
Stockton

Way

Caen

Herb

NORTH BEACH

Broadway
Vallejo
Green
Union
Filbert
Greenwich
Lombard
Chestnut
Francisco
Bay

TELEGRAPH HILL

Colt Tower

Saints Peter and Paul Roman Catholic Church

WASHINGTON SQUARE

North Beach Museum

Columbus

COOLBRITH PARK

Powell-Mason

Mason St

Taylor

Jones

Leavenworth

Hyde

Larkin

Polk

Van Ness

Franklin

RUSSIAN HILL

RUSSIAN HILL PARK

Powell-Hyde

FISHERMAN'S WHARF

The Anchorage

The Cannery

Musée Mécanique

USS Pampanito

Jefferson
Beach
North Point
Bay
Francisco
Chestnut
Lombard
Greenwich
Filbert
Union
Green
Vallejo

Ghirardelli Square

Hyde Street Pier

Municipal Pier

San Francisco Maritime National Historic Park

The Embarcadero

FISHERMAN'S WHARF

San Francisco's busy waterside, famed
for seafood and boisterous sea lions,
is also a place to explore the
city's maritime history

The city's 45-acre (18-hectare) **Fisherman's Wharf** ❶ is one of the most visited places in San Francisco. A bright, family-oriented carnival of attractions, despite the crowds and occasional tackiness, the Wharf also has great seafood restaurants, good little stores tucked in between the souvenir stands, two garden parks with open space for picnicking, and mouthwatering places to buy the food to picnic with.

During the summer months, when the narrow boardwalks are jammed with people, it's easy to forget that this is one of the city's more important historic spots. Alongside hundreds of sailboats and yachts and the ferries packed with visitors and commuters, much of San Francisco's maritime past is moored here.

Landmark ships

The waterfront retrospective starts at **Hyde Street Pier** ❷ (tel: 415-447-5000; pier free, charge to board vessels), where the Maritime Museum *(see page 78)* opens a fleet of vintage vessels to public inspection. Built in 1890, the steam-driven *Eureka* is the last of 50 paddle-wheel ferries that transported people and cars over the bay between San Francisco and Tiburon, until the eye-catching Golden Gate and Bay bridges stretched across to become so much a part of

the scenery. The *Alma*, a scow-schooner, hauled hay, produce and lumber around the bay, while the *Eppleton Hall*, built in England in 1914, traveled as far as Panama. The wooden-hulled *C.A. Thayer* was a hard-working lumber ship that sailed the California coast. Her last captain captured the final voyage on film, which can be seen during a tour. Built in 1886, the *Balclutha* made 17 trips around the Cape, was shipwrecked and served a brief stint in movies before her final voyage in 1930.

Map on pages 78–9

LEFT: roll up, roll up to Pier 39.
BELOW: a perfect spot for a picnic.

Musée Méchanique at Pier 45 is an exercise in nostalgia: see coin-operated pianos, antique slot machines and a 1910 steam-driven motorcycle.

Headquartered in the handsome premises of the former Del Monte cannery is the helpful **San Francisco Maritime National Historic Park Visitor Center ❸** (495 Jefferson Street at Hyde, tel: 415-563-2800; open 9.30–7pm, until 5pm in winter; free). Inside the headquarters of the park's **Maritime Museum ❹** (900 Beach Street, tel: 415-561-7000; open daily 10am–5pm free) are intricate models, muralist Hilaire Hiler's surrealist vision of Atlantis and all manner of ocean-going memorabilia. The whimsical, ship-shaped building was commissioned by the federal government as a Works Progress Administration project in the 1930s, a relief measure established to give jobs to the unemployed.

Much of this watery area west of the Hyde Street Pier has been designated by the National Historic Register as an historic district, under the banner of **Aquatic Park ❺**.

South of the Maritime Museum and occupying the entire block bounded by North Point, Polk, Beach and Larkin streets is **Ghirardelli Square ❻** (tel: 415-775-5500; open daily until 9pm in summer; until 6pm Sun, until 9pm Fri, Sat in winter), a shopping center geared toward visitors, with its own interesting past.

First chocolate, then gold

Before gold in California, there was chocolate: Domingo Ghirardelli's factory opened just 13 days prior to the discovery of that precious metal at Sutter's Mill in the Sierra foothills. So much chocolate was made here that, it is said, when it rains, chocolate still oozes from the old walls. Although the original chocolate vats – and working factory – have moved to the East Bay, there is still a retail outlet and candy store. (Be sure to try an ice-cream sundae).

If you don't have a sweet tooth, Ghirardelli Square also has over 50 restaurants and stores, many with

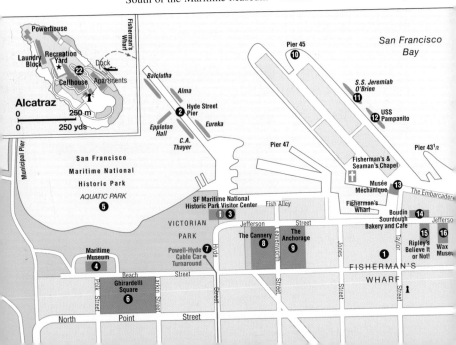

wonderful views of the bay. The courtyard shelters 120-year-old olive trees that provide perfect spots for resting and people-watching.

The corner of Hyde and Beach is a good place to stop for a hot drink if San Francisco's "summer days" have given you a chill. At the **Buena Vista Café** *(see page 81)* you can enjoy an Irish coffee served to perfection, as it has been for more than 50 years. At the same time, watch the busy cable car activity at the **Powell-Hyde Cable Car Turnaround 7**.

A short walk east leads to the **Cannery 8** (2801 Leavenworth Street, tel: 415-771-3112), a three-story shopping complex housing more than 40 stores, restaurants and bars. Relax in the beer garden and listen to live music on the brick patio, or explore the individual shops located in the underground passageways. Among the Cannery's nightspots is the **Green Room Comedy Club** (tel: 415-674-3540), a stand-up showcase

in the courtyard near the Beach Street entrance. Comic careers have been launched at Fisherman's Wharf, including that of actor Robin Williams. Next door to The Cannery is the **Anchorage 9**, another shopping and dining complex.

Fisherman's Wharf is one of the best places in the US for seafood. The corrugated metal sheds lining the docks are known as **Fish Alley**, where the catch of the day is packed, ready to be sold.

Pier 45

An appetite for fruits of the sea can be satisfied in a more relaxed fashion by strolling down **Jefferson Street**, the wharf's main drag, where sidewalk vendors boil and steam shellfish all day long. Arrive there by walking east and back along the waterfront to **Pier 45 10**, which remains as much of a working site as Fisherman's Wharf can offer. Here, fishermen depart each day before dawn and return with sand

Alioto's is just one of many seafood places on the Wharf. Try the Dungeness crab; the season runs from mid-November through June.

BELOW: the place Domingo Ghirardelli built from chocolate.

Fisherman's Wharf

0   200 yds
0   200 m

N

atraz,
el Island

er 41

★ Sea Lions

19 Riptide Arcade

20 Turbo Ride

21

San Francisco Carousel

Pier 39
17

Ferry Building, Oakland

Alcatraz
★ Jumping off point

Red and White
Fleet Ferry

Blue and Gold
Fleet Ferry

Theatre
39 **18**
The
Aquarium
of the Bay

The Embarcadero

Powell

Stockton

Street

Street

Point

Street

Grant St

Ann T

Ghirardelli

Map
on pages
78–9

*Boudin's Sourdough
bread got its start in
1849. The premises at
136 Jefferson are
where you can watch
bakers at work or buy
picnic supplies.*

BELOW: travel to
Fisherman's Wharf by
boat, trolley or cable car.

dabs, scallops, Dungeness crabs and
sea bass. The **SS *Jeremiah O'Brien***
⑪ (tel: 415-544-0100; open daily
10am–4pm; charge) is moored here.
It was one of a great fleet that operated during World War II, and is
America's last unaltered Liberty ship
still in operating condition.

The **USS *Pampanito*** ⑫ (tel: 415-
775-1943; open usually until 8pm in
summer, shorter hours in winter;
charge) a 300-ft (90-meter) subma-
rine that played an active role in
World War II, is berthed here, too.
Audio tours are available on board.

On Pier 45 at the end of Taylor
Street is the **Musée Méchanique** ⑬
(*see page 78*), while nearby is the
**Boudin Sourdough Bakery and
Café** ⑭. Things can get pretty
bizarre at **Ripley's Believe It or Not!**
⑮ (175 Jefferson, tel: 415-771-
6188; charge), a museum based on
the collection of eccentric illustrator
Robert Ripley. Almost as creepy (and
as silly) is the **Wax Museum** ⑯ (tel:
800-439-4305; charge).

If the Wharf triggers an impulse for
angling, you can charter a fishing trip
(tel: 415-346-2399) or sign up for a

boat that offer day trips for salmon
fishing, halibut or other catch,
depending on the season. **Pier 41** is
the place for trips around the bay,
including **Alcatraz** (*see pages 82 and
231*) and Angel Island (*see pages 174
and 231*). Be sure to double-check
where boats will depart from, as this
information can vary.

For a change of pace from the
cheap trinkets and souvenir stores,
head to **Frank's Fisherman Supply**
(366 Jefferson Street, tel: 415-775-
1165), where nautical antiques are
mixed in among marine supplies,
cool nautically-themed gifts and sea-
worthy hats and clothing. You might
catch a glimpse of local San Franciscan rivals on the wharf at one of the
city's clubs, the **South End Rowing
Club** or the **Dolphin Club** that stand
next door to each other.

Pier 39

Pier 39 ⑰ is Fisherman's Wharf's
major tourist area, and home to some
of its most photographed inhabitants;
the boisterous **sea lions** (*see photo on
page 82*). It also has more than 110
stores, restaurants and attractions. The
Aquarium of the Bay ⑱ (tel: 415-
888-SEA DIVE for tickets), is an
attraction that allows visitors to travel
through the ocean environment as if
they were diving themselves.

Thumb twitching and flashing-
light fun is to be found in the **Riptide
Arcade** ⑲, the largest games arcade
in the city, and the **Turbo Ride** ⑳,
where high-resolution film and digi-
tal-control hydraulics take passengers
on an thrill ride where the seats move
in sync with the on-screen action. For
a more nostalgic ride, try the **San
Francisco Carousel** ㉑. Handcrafted
in Italy, the two-tier structure depicts
famous local landmarks.

So, despite its initial, good-natured
tackiness, the picture is a pretty one
down at the water's edge, where San
Francisco and the bay meet with
crowd-pleasing exuberance. ❏

RESTAURANTS & BARS

Restaurants

A Sabella
2766 Taylor St. Tel: 415-771-6775. Open: D. **$$$**.
Fisherman's Wharf is famous for Dungeness crab and *cioppino* (a type of fish stew), and this is the place to sample both. A bay view, old world hospitality and a renowned wine list combine with 110 years of experience.

Albona
545 Francisco St. Tel: 415-441-1040. Open: D. **$$**.
This Istrian restaurant serves Northern Italian dishes influenced by flavors of Central and Eastern Europe. Think pan-fried gnocchi in a cumin-spiced sirloin sauce. Owner Bruno makes you feel like you're in his own private living room.

Alioto's #8 Restaurant
8 Fisherman's Wharf (Taylor at Jefferson). Tel: 415-673-0183. Open: L, D. **$$**.
The Alioto name stands for politics, feuds, family and fine food in San Francisco. For generations, this family-owned establishment has ruled the Wharf with fresh, local seafood dishes and Sicilian preparations.

Ana Mandara
891 Beach St, Ghirardelli Square. Tel: 415-771-8600.

Open: L, D. **$$$**.
French-Vietnamese inspired fare at this place, maybe a little upscale for Fisherman's Wharf. Starters include crispy rolls with crab, striped bass ceviche, and seared lobster with ginger rice.

Buena Vista Café
2765 Hyde St. Tel: 415-474-5044. Open: B, L, D. **$$**
A San Francisco institution and home of legendary Irish Coffee, a delicious elixir made with Irish whiskey, frothed cream and coffee.

Eagle Café
Pier 39 Fisherman's Wharf. Tel: 415-433-3689. Open: B, L, D. **$**
A great alternative to overpriced Wharf restaurants, the Eagle is a lively institution known for large portions, hearty breakfasts, stiff cocktails and stellar views.

McCormick & Kuleto's Seafood Restaurant
900 North Point St, Ghirardelli Square. Tel: 415-929-1730. Open: L, Br, D. **$$$**.
Ghirardelli Square seafood spot popular for fabulous views, a huge variety of fresh, imaginative seafood dishes and other American fare.

Scoma's
Pier 47 on Al Scoma Way. Tel: 415-771-4383. Open: L, Br, D. **$$$**.

For a glimpse of the workingman's Wharf, dine right on the pier at this old-school Italian that has been serving seafood, pasta and their acclaimed chowder for 40 years.

Bars and Clubs

Fiddler's Green
1333 Columbus Ave. Tel: 415-441-9758. Open: B, L, D. **$**
Tip back a pint of Guinness and tuck into shepard's pie among locals and Irish transplants at this tiny pub that stays open late and sometimes hosts live music.

Jack's Cannery Bar
2801 Leavenworth St. (in The Cannery). Tel: 415-931-6400. Open: B, L, D. **$$**

An impressive menu of brews are a feature of this comfortable pub with an enclosed beer-garden outside and a cozy fireplace inside.

Lou's Pier 47
300 Jefferson St. Tel: 415-771-LOUS. Open: L, D; music nightly
Upstairs has live music and dancing every night, with an emphasis on blues. Downstairs has casual Wharf dining with a Cajun twist.

RIGHT: seafood at the Wharf any way you want it.

ALCATRAZ

A windswept island and former fort just over a mile out into the bay became home to some of America's most notorious criminals

TIP

Take a sweater as the ferry crossing can be windy. The Alcatraz audio tour, narrated by inmates and prison guards, is well worth the extra charge.

BELOW: Alcatraz from Fisherman's Wharf.

For decades, any escape from **Alcatraz** ㉒ (tel: 415-705 5555, www.nps.gov/alcatraz/ open, 9.30am–6.30pm, 9.30am–4.30pm, in winter) would require a treacherous, 1½-mile (2.5-km) swim to San Francisco. Today, triathletes swim the same course in about 25 minutes, but they don't have to tunnel through solid rock, or slip past armed guards under cover of darkness to get started. Nor do any of the more than one million willing tourists who visit each year.

Frigid waters

Surrounded by the frigid waters and swift currents of San Francisco Bay, 22½-acre (9-hectare) Alcatraz island was once residence for the most notorious criminals of the 20th century, including Chicago mob boss Al Capone and "Machine Gun" Kelly. Set in the middle of one of the world's most beautiful harbors and accessible by ferry from Fishman's Wharf, this remote hump of rock is – surprisingly – a very beautiful spot, with rare plants and wildlife on

its outer fringes that many visitors miss. The island is so close to the city, it's said the inmates could hear chattering and laughing from mainland cocktail parties that caught the breeze and floated across the bay.

Alcatraz was christened *La Isla de los Alcatraces* (the island of the pelicans) by Spanish explorers in 1775. Its strategic position in the middle of the bay made it ideal for use as a defensive and disciplinary facility, and by the mid-1800s, US Army soldiers stood guard on the island's rocky bluffs.

Tales from "The Rock"

The island began serving its time as a prison in 1895, when Modoc and Hopi tribe leaders were held at Alcatraz. The first American military prisoners to serve time in the concrete cell block were among those who built it in 1912.

Two decades later, in the wake of the Prohibition-induced nationwide crime waves, the Federal Bureau of Prisons decided on Alcatraz as the ideal facility to house its most hardened criminals. That year, 1,953 men were rounded up and sent to "The Rock." On Alcatraz, just three privileges were available to the best-behaved inmates: the recreation yard, the library or a job in one of the on-site factories.

Prison cells were designed for maximum security. Just 5 ft by 9 ft (1.5 meters by 3 meters), inmates had to spend 16 to 23 hours a day in them. All privileges had to be earned by good behavior, and infractions of the rules were punished by confinement in the Segregation Unit, otherwise known as solitary confinement, where even light could be denied to an inmate deemed "unworthy."

The solitary life of a prison inmate was conveyed to a wide audience in *The Birdman of Alcatraz*, starring former circus acrobat Burt Lancaster.

The movie is based on the life of Bob Stroud, who spent his 53 years of incarceration studying the science of birds, and eventually became a world authority (although, contrary to Hollywood lore, Stroud never kept birds while at Alcatraz).

Perhaps the most surprising chapter of The Rock's history began on November 20, 1969, six years after the prison facility had been closed. A large band of Native Americans under the banner "Indians of All Tribes," led by Mohawk Richard Oakes, broke into the disused penitentiary. The occupation was mounted as a protest against the US government's broken promises to the tribes, and lasted 18 months, until June 11, 1971. The group finally dissolved into factions, and the protest was ended with none of their demands having been met. ❑

Daily tours are operated by the Blue & Gold Fleet (tel: 415-705-5555 for reservations; 415-773-1188 for general information), departing from Pier 41 at Fisherman's Wharf. For more on tours, see page 231.

Chicago mobster Al Capone (1898–1947) was one of Alcatraz island's better-known residents.

BELOW: the island is now run by the National Park Service.

NORTH BEACH TO TELEGRAPH HILL

Beatniks, Sicilian sailors, history-lovers, gourmets and club-goers are all drawn to this Italian neighborhood beneath Coit Tower

talian immigrants called **North Beach ❶** "Little City" when they settled here more than 100 years ago. Situated below Telegraph Hill's Coit Tower, North Beach is – loosely speaking – the bohemian, low-lying neighborhood that occupies the area bordered by Broadway and Washington Square.

Although subsequent trends and events have overlaid the perception of North Beach in the public's imagination, its Italians – and Italian roots – are still much in evidence. In the past, a number of *prominenti* distinguished themselves from the anonymous faces in the neighborhood and succeeded in winning the respect of the city as a whole. A.P. Giannini brought financial power to the common folk with his Banco d'Italia, an enterprise some people disparaged as "that little dago bank in North Beach." The name was later changed to the Bank of America, and Giannini's bank became one of the largest financial institutions in the world.

A fascinating history of literary figures, comedic celebrities and strip joints has added immeasurably to the neighborhood's great color. The Beat poets once gathered here for java and inspiration; a young Woody Allen and Bill Cosby had their taste of the limelight at the Hungry i; and Barbra Streisand, Johnny Mathis and Lenny

Bruce plied their trades in the area's nightclubs, like the Purple Onion *(see page 95)*. In recent years the Italians and other longstanding communities of Irish, Basque and Mexican families have been joined by Asian ethnic groups, all of whom add to the cosmopolitan mix.

On Broadway

The two blocks of **Broadway ❷**, north of Montgomery toward Columbus Avenue, were once San Francisco's "Great White Way," an

Map on page 86

LEFT: Molinari's Deli.
BELOW: Caffé Trieste was the first espresso coffee house on the West Coast.

Woody Allen and Bill Cosby performed comedy sketches at the Hungry i early in their careers. The name has been taken by a local strip joint, but will always be associated with North Beach.

assemblage of video parlors and strip joints offering the standard variety of commercial vice. Sleazy bars, watered-down liquor and live sex acts were the norm. Carol Doda made "silicone" history here. Sitting topless on a piano, she was lowered onto the stage, much to the delight of the audience who got a chance to see what implants were all about.

Late night spot

A 1990s swing-dance revival saw the Broadway area reinvigorated with swanky retro clubs. Some of these have closed now that the fad is over, but new nightspots have sprung up in their place. North Beach has always been a late night spot, and intends to stay that way.

A good place to start a tour is just south of Broadway in a part of town now known as **Jackson Square ❸**. The name is deceptive: you'll find no square here, just as you'll find no beach in North Beach, and no tele-

graph on Telegraph Hill. What can be found, however, are a few vestiges of the Barbary Coast (*see page 90*) and a handful of beautifully restored buildings from the Gold-Rush era. It's a pleasant place for a stroll – but only in the daytime.

Alternatively, an overview of North Beach's history can be gleaned by a quick visit to the **North Beach Museum ❹** (tel: 415-391-6210, ask for museum) inside the US Bank office at 1435 Stockton. Before the Gold Rush, North Beach was the home of Juana Briones and her family, who built their adobe house in 1836 near the intersection of Powell and Filbert streets. Señora Briones operated a small *rancho* on the outskirts of the village (which was then called Yerba Buena), supplying fresh meat and produce to passing ships, and occasionally giving shelter to a deserting sailor.

When gold was discovered in the Sierra foothills in 1848, thousands of

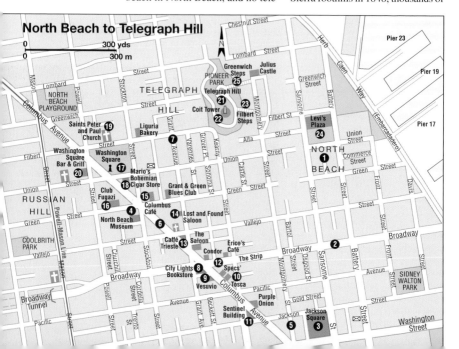

immigrants poured into Yerba Buena Cove in one of the wildest booms ever to hit the West. Settlers began squeezing into the valley between Russian and Telegraph hills toward the northern shore, from which North Beach takes its name.

Why the name?

In early days, the bay reached as far inland as Francisco Street to the north and Montgomery Street to the south, before landfill extended the area to accommodate boatloads of new San Franciscans, many of whom had just deserted ship. Now, entire city blocks stand on land that was once a harbor in which sailors left ships to rot while they abandoned uniforms and official orders in order to make their fortune from gold nuggets.

When fires swept through the area after the earthquake of 1906 devastated most of the city (*see page 26*), the Italians on Telegraph Hill who were trapped without water reportedly fought the blaze with buckets of "dago red," the neighborhood's local vintage. For many months, the homeless occupied Washington Square as

Map on page 86

survivors set about the arduous task of reconstruction, but within little more than a year North Beach was almost completely rebuilt, becoming one of the first districts to recover from the earthquake.

Most homes, built without the benefit of architects, took on variations of a simple Edwardian style. Many buildings have since been renovated, some being given an Art Deco stucco finish during the 1930s, but for the most part the homes in North Beach remain unadorned two- or three-story wooden frames with bay windows and back alleys.

Both the buildings and their layout give North Beach the feel of a European *quartier*, an intimate enclave of simple homes sheltered from the towering modern architecture located only a few blocks away. Fans of urban restoration might be interested in checking out the 700 block of **Montgomery Street ❺**. Notable among the renovations are the fine **California Steam and Navigation Building**, the **Ship Building** and the **Melodeon Theater Building**, all from the late 1850s or 1860s.

North Beach's Banco d'Italia later became the Bank of America. The Italian community allegedly once put out a fire using gallons of wine instead of water.

BELOW: North Beach Italian style.

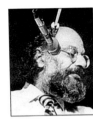

In 1956, the infamous poem Howl, *by Allen Ginsberg, was published by City Lights founder Lawrence Ferlinghetti.*

BELOW: a younger Lawrence Ferlinghetti outside the bookstore he founded in 1953.

Columbus Avenue ❻ cuts diagonally across Broadway, leading directly into the heart of North Beach. This is the district's main thoroughfare, and every year on Columbus Day hordes of revelers fill the street in a celebration of its namesake (although in recent years, indigenous populations who found Columbus' discovery gave little cause for rejoicing, have protested against these activities).

Restaurants, delis, pastry shops and cafés line the avenue. For the most part, the cuisine here is northern Italian with a few Chinese, Mexican, Creole and sushi places mixed in for good measure. The ambience ranges from no-frills slop houses to first-class dining rooms.

The intersection of Broadway, Columbus and Grant marks the meeting place of at least four distinct neighborhoods. **Grant Avenue** ❼ is the center of North Beach's social world, and every day here is a celebration of the incongruities that give North Beach its special character. There are still several family-run Italian businesses on Grant, while in

between them are galleries, boutiques, bars, antiques shops, restaurants, cafés and Chinese markets.

Beatnik haunts

Columbus's most famous location is **City Lights Bookstore** ❽ (261 Columbus, tel: 415-362-8193; open daily 10am–midnight), a National Literary Landmark. Owned by Lawrence Ferlinghetti, who founded it in 1953, this was the first bookstore in the country to sell only paperbacks. The cornerstone of "beatnikdom" in San Francisco, City Lights received notoriety for publishing Allen Ginsberg's incendiary poem *Howl*, subject of an obscenity trial (*see page 66*).

To this day, City Lights remains one of San Francisco's most important literary centers. The shop is known for its leftist leanings, and accordingly has a good selection of books on social change. Poetry, of course, is also well-served, with a whole room dedicated to the bards. City Lights also sponsors a schedule of readings by new and established writers; check the bulletin boards in

Map on page 86

the shop or ask a clerk for details of upcoming events.

Next door to City Lights is another beatnik haunt, **Vesuvio Café** ❾ (tel: 415-362-3370), a bar adorned with colorful stained-glass windows that got to be known for the words, "We are itching to get away from Portland, Oregon," painted over the entranceway. In its heyday, Vesuvio was owned by Henri Lenoir, whose collections of exotic bar-room paraphernalia still adorn the delightful but cramped bar. Near the front door is a list of names drawn in wet cement, which commemorates a handful of North Beach's "mad ones."

Before taking over Vesuvio Café, Lenoir managed **Specs'** (12 Saroyan, tel: 415-421-4112), across Columbus in a tiny alleyway. Specs' was a bohemian hotspot in the 1940s, a famed lesbian bar called 12 Adler Place, a nightclub featuring jazz, belly dancers and Middle Eastern music. Tucked away in the corner of this blind alley, Specs' has somehow managed to maintain a low profile throughout its long tenure as a watering hole for San Francisco's under-ground. The offbeat bar is decorated with an exotic hodge-podge of sailor and dock-worker memorabilia, fine Inuit carvings, posters, scrimshaw, wartime propaganda – even a dried whale penis. The large round tables encourage everyone to talk to the strangers sitting next to them.

Literary alleyways

A few years ago, North Beach alleys took on the names of famous writers. The tiny street that divides City Lights from Vesuvio became **Jack Kerouac Street**, and Specs' insisted that its end of the alley be called **Saroyan Place**, after the late Armenian-American novelist William Saroyan. Not far away is **Tosca** ❿, (242 Columbus Avenue, tel: 415-986-9651), a famous stomping ground with its original red Naugahyde booths, operatic selections on the jukebox and signature coffee drinks. Tosca maintains a regular clientele of locals, bohemians, socialites and politicos.

Stepping out of Tosca, turn left and walk south on Columbus to the intersection of Kearny Street.

Dashiell Hammett Street is just one of the thoroughfares named after writers who lived or worked in San Francisco.

BELOW: off the road, Jack Kerouac Street.

BELOW:
Mario's *focaccia* sandwiches might be the greatest food ever made by man.

The fabulous flatiron structure on the southwest corner is the **Sentinel Building** ⓫, which houses the headquarters of Francis Ford Coppola's production company, American Zoetrope. There's a small bistro inside serving Coppola's wines *(see page 95)*, and Francis himself can often be seen in the nearby cafés. Local etiquette prohibits anyone from approaching Mr Coppola and quoting lines from *The Godfather*.

Head north on Columbus, cross Broadway and turn right. This is the heart of the **Strip** ⓬, a hangover from North Beach's bawdier days, with adult bookstores, strip clubs and peep show booths.

But not that much has changed, because bars and clubs abound. At the intersection of Grant and Vallejo is **Caffé Trieste** ⓭ (tel: 415-982-2605), a favorite haunt of musicians where you can enjoy a real treat – live opera on Saturday afternoons. Farther up Grant next to the **Lost and Found Saloon** ⓮ (live music Wed through Sun) is the **Grant & Green Blues Club** (tel: 415-986-1801). Open noon to 2am, this is a down and dirty North

Beach institution with dark corners, Anchor Steam beer on tap and live music every night.

Half a block away around the corner on Green Street is **Gino & Carlo**, a neighborhood watering hole with all the qualifications of the quintessential North Beach bar: strong drinks, pool tables and lots of Sinatra on the jukebox. A few doors down are other atmospheric places, like the **Columbus Café** ⓯, with a mural on its wall depicting the mighty nautical journey of its namesake, Christopher Columbus, and **O'Reilly's Pub & Restaurant** *(see page 95)* .

Farther up Green is **Club Fugazi** ⓰ (tel: 415-421-4222), home to the fantastically campy and perpetually sold-out *Beach Blanket Babylon*, the longest-running musical review in San Francisco's theatrical history.

Since 1974, it has told the tongue-in-cheek story of Snow White and the quest for her prince, while meeting such updated characters along the way as Arnold Schwarzenegger, Hillary Clinton and Elvis. This is a fantastic way to cap an evening in North Beach, but don't wait until

The Barbary Coast

Modern-day Jackson Square is a pleasant place to stroll around, but it is ironic that one of the city's quieter neighborhoods was, during the Gold Rush, a place of unparalled vice. The Barbary Coast (as it was then named) was a vast marketplace of flesh and liquor where sailors and miners found fleeting pleasures, fast money and, just as likely, a violent end.

Second to gambling, shoot-outs were the favored participant sport, and fortunes often rode on the wink of an eye. Most businessmen in the Barbary Coast made their money trafficking in human bodies; either selling sex to '49ers or selling kidnapped sailors to the captains of hell ships.

Both enterprises produced high profits, and local politicians were more than happy to turn a blind eye in exchange for a piece of the action. A red light burned on almost every block, signaling both high-class "parlors" and squalid "cribs," where prostitutes worked in rooms barely big enough to fit a bed into. In the worst cases, Chinese girls were bought as slaves and made to work until they became sick or died.

you're here to buy a ticket, and be sure to get in line at least 45 minutes prior to show time. The Sunday matinee leaves out the racier elements for a kid-friendlier version.

Washington Square

Proceed west down Green Street, turn right on Stockton and head north one block to cross Union Street. Here is **Washington Square ⑰**, where, depending on the time of day, you might see Chinese tai chi practitioners or a flock of brilliantly colored wild parrots that frequently roost in the park's lush treetops. At the park's southwestern corner is **Mario's Bohemian Cigar Store ⑱** *(see page 95)*. On nearby Stockton Street, quaint little **Liguria Bakery** has occupied the same corner for over 50 years producing melt-in-the-mouth *focaccia* bread. They close when they sell out — usually by 3pm, so get here early to buy provisions for a picnic in Washington Square.

In characteristic North Beach fashion, the statue located in the center of Washington Square is not of anyone named Washington but, rather, of Benjamin Franklin. The statue was a gift to the city from an eccentric dentist named H.D. Cogswell, who amassed a fortune by putting gold into miners' teeth – a sign of some status in a town that all but worshipped the gleaming metal.

Cogswell, an avid teetotaler, swore to build one public fountain for every saloon in San Francisco. Famous for his offbeat humor, he labeled the three water spouts at the base of the statue Cal Seltzer, Vichy and Congress. On the west side of the square is a statue dedicated to the city's volunteer firemen, bequeathed to the city by Lillie Hitchcock Coit, the heiress who was also responsible for Coit Tower *(see page 97)*.

Here, too, you'll find **Saints Peter and Paul Church ⑲**, a picturesque, 80-year-old cathedral with a Romanesque facade that is still a favorite setting for traditional Italian weddings. The inscription above the entrance is from the first canto of Dante's *Paradiso:* "*La Gloria Di Colui Che Tutto Muove Per L'Universo Penetra E Risplende*" (The glory of Him who moves all things

Map on page 86

The Sentinel Building.

LEFT: Vesuvio.
BELOW: Café Zoetrope.

TIP

North Beach is an impossible place to park a car. A much better idea is to walk or take a taxi to its many bars, clubs and restaurants.

shines throughout the universe). On any given Saturday, you're likely to see yards of white silk billowing in a bridal breeze next to dapper, olive-skinned young men in razor-sharp Italian-cut tuxedos.

A sign in the vestibule promises all San Franciscans of Italian descent the right to receive special religious services here; another sign lists schedules for English, Italian and Chinese masses. Soon after it was built, the newly opened church was the target of anarchistic bombings, and a closer look shows the scars on its white facade left by the explosions.

Blessing of the fleet

On the first Sunday in October, Sicilian parishioners from the church conduct a procession honoring *Maria Santissima del Lume* (Mary, Most Holy Mother of Light) along Columbus Avenue to Fisherman's Wharf, where the traditional Blessing of the Fleet takes place *(see page 43)*.

The **Washington Square Bar & Grill** ⓴ *(see page 95)* across the square attracts well-known literati for dinner, drinks and late-night chatter. Established in 1886, Fior d'Italia claims to be the oldest Italian restaurant in America. Its food and location – directly across from the square with a view of Saints Peter and Paul's spires – has ensured continued success. But in 2005, Fior d'Italia burned to the ground; at press time the search was on for new premises.

Telegraph Hill

From Washington Square, the easiest way to get to **Telegraph Hill** ㉑ is to walk directly up Union Street, where the sidewalk gives way to flights of stairs that make the climbing easier (as long as you're fit.) From the top of Union, visitors can take one of the several footpaths that wind around the uppermost peak to eventually arrive at **Pioneer Park**.

Telegraph Hill has always been a part of, and apart from, North Beach. It was largely ignored by early settlers, who preferred to fill in the shallows of the bay below rather than build on the hill's steep shoulders. Irish stevedores were among the earliest inhabitants, although the Italians

BELOW: O'Reilly's Pub & Restaurant is the place for Guinness and good Irish food.

soon displaced them. San Francisco's bohemian crowd were often seen partying on the hill in clapboard shacks, until the well-to-do figured out what all the fuss was about and swiftly claimed the ground for their own. Today, real estate around Telegraph Hill is among the most desirable in San Francisco.

Signal Hill

Originally named *Loma Alta* ("high hill") by the Spaniards, the hill has gone under a number of names over the years, including Goat Hill, Windmill Hill, Tin Can Hill and Signal Hill. The last name refers to the efforts of two enterprising merchants who constructed a signaling station at the top of the hill to notify curious townspeople of ships approaching the harbor. Some years later in 1849, the semaphore was replaced by the first telegraph on the West Coast, later by an observatory, and most recently, by Coit Tower.

During the Gold Rush, Chilean prostitutes put up tents in "Little Chile," a shanty town of South American immigrants on the hill's western slope. On the eastern side of the hill was a similar cluster of ramshackle homes known as "Sydneytown," where Australian convicts called "Sydney Ducks" settled around the same time. In February 1849, the Ducks clashed with members of a gang that called itself the "Hounds," later renamed the "Regulators," men who made a career of extorting from local shopkeepers and harassing the Chilenos. When a Chilean shopkeeper in fear and frustation eventually shot one of their members, the gang stormed Little Chile, killed and wounded several people, and raped a number of the immigrant women.

The attack outraged many upstanding citizens, and a group of 250 vigilantes came together to capture the worst offenders. They arrested 19 people, but only two went to prison; the others got off with little more than a slap on the wrist. Although largely ineffective, this early display of public action set the stage for the Vigilance Committees of 1851 and 1856, which were both far more aggressive than the earlier 250-member committee.

Map on page 86

A salty dog on North Beach, a beach that's not a beach.

BELOW: listen to local opera singers on Saturday afternoons here.

Map on page 86

Learn about Levi Strauss (1829-1902) and the history of blue jeans by visiting the headquarters in Levi's Plaza.

BELOW: the courtyard of Levi's Plaza is guarded by Coit Tower.

At the top of Telegraph Hill is, of course, **Coit Tower** ㉒, styled as a giant fire hose. It's a simple, fluted monument with fantastic 1930s murals inside. The tower was constructed with funds left by the eccentric heiress Lillie Hitchcock Coit (*see page 96*).

Steep steps

When you're ready to head down the hill, the **Filbert Steps** ㉓ are somewhat precarious but well worth the effort to see some of San Francisco's oldest buildings. The rambling staircase begins at the top of the hill on the southeastern side of Coit Tower at Telegraph Hill Boulevard and winds past lovely gardens bursting with wild roses, poppies, bougainvillea, lilies and fruit trees. Through the foliage, there are breathtaking views along the way.

After reaching Montgomery Street, you can continue on down or head north to **Julius' Castle** (1541 Montgomery, tel: 415-392-2222), an elegant restaurant clinging to the hillside in perhaps the loveliest corner of the city. The restaurant specializes in

northern Italian and French cuisine. Continuing down Filbert Steps, narcissus and fuchsia grow among palm trees and ferns. Some gardens are manicured while others are unkempt and overrun with wild irises.

The steps end on Sansome Street, directly across from **Levi's Plaza** ㉔, the corporate headquarters of Levi Strauss & Co., which has a large, sunny brick-and-granite courtyard with an impressive water sculpture. A small but interesting museum in the main building's lobby chronicles the company's story, the evolution of blue jeans and Levi's ground-breaking advertising campaigns. Stores, restaurants and cafés line the plaza, but if you prefer, stop by **Il Fornaio** at 1265 Battery, for brunch or delicious pastry.

One block north of Sansome, you can climb the hillside parallel to the Filbert Steps. These lesser-traveled **Greenwich Steps** ㉕, made of steel and concrete, are nearly enveloped by the dense, lush landscape – so much so that you may forget that you're actually within the limits of a big, international city. ❑

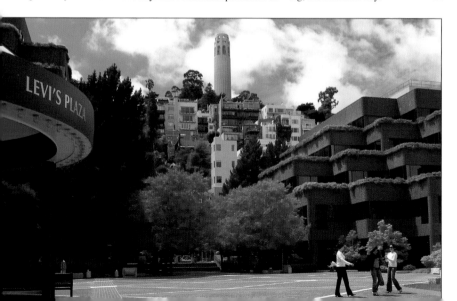

RESTAURANTS & BARS

Restaurants

Caffè Prague
584 Pacific St.
Tel: 415-433-3811. Open:
7am-3pm. **$**
Artsy, intellectual, friendly
and affordable, Caffè
Prague is a great place to
meet to discuss Kafka,
down some Pilsner, or
slurp tasty soups.

Café Zoetrope
916 Kearny St. Tel: 415-
291-1700. Open: L, D. **$$**
This small bistro in the
flatiron Sentinel Building
features tasty food, and
wines from Francis Ford
Coppola's Niebaum-
Coppola winery.

Franchino's
347 Columbus Ave. Tel: 415-
982-2157. Open: D. Closed
Mon. **$$**
Family owned and oper-
ated, friendly Franchino's
serves huge portions of
classic Italian dishes at
reasonable prices.

Golden Boy Pizza
542 Green St. Tel: 415-982-
9738. Open: L, D. **$**
Golden Boy's Sicilian-style
pan pizza is a favorite of
North Beach bar-goers,
and usually ordered by
the slice. Look in the window and choose what
whets the appetite.

Helmand
430 Broadway. Tel: 415-362-
0641. Open: D. **$$$**.
Afghani cuisine bursting
with flavor and spice. Try
the *bowlawni* – pastry
shells stuffed with pota-
toes and leeks.

Mama's
1701 Stockton St. Tel:415-
362-6421. Open: 8am-3pm.
Closed Mon. **$**
Featuring huge egg dishes
and pancakes, Mama's is
a local favorite, but be
sure to avoid weekends –
the line can be outra-
geous and reservations
are not accepted.

**Mario's Bohemian
Cigar Store**
556 Columbus Ave. Tel: 415-
362-0536. Open: L, D. **$**
Try the *focaccia* sand-
wiches, relax, and enjoy
Washington Square at
this tiny fixture.

Moose's
1652 Stockton St.
Tel: 415-989-7800. Open:
Br, L, D. **$$$**.
Overlooking Washington
Square and Sts. Peter &
Paul Cathedral, with an
open kitchen and jazz
piano nightly, Moose's is
popular with local
celebrities and politicos.

Myth
470 Pacific St. Tel:415-677-
8986. Open: D. **$$$**
There's amazing food,
modern décor, and an
open kitchen. Best to
order half-plates so you
can sample more of
Myth's fantastic flavors.

North Beach Restaurant
1512 Stockton St. Tel: 415-
392-1700. Open: L, D. **$$$**.
This venerable institution
serves hearty Tuscan cui-
sine featuring homemade
pastas, house-cured
proscuitto and a dizzyingly
comprehensive wine list.

**O'Reilly's Pub &
Restaurant**
622 Green St. Tel: 415-989-
6222. Open: Br, L, D. **$$**.
This re-creation of an Irish
pub is a cozy place for a
hearty brunch or any
other meal, either in the
cool, stoneworker interior,
or on the pleasant side-
walk tables. Be sure to try
the Guinness-battered
fish & chips.

Pena Pacha Mama
1630 Powell St. Tel: 415-646-
0018. Open: D. **$$**.
Experience the Bolivian
hospitality of the Navia
family and the robust
organic flavors from their
native country. Live traditional music most nights
makes for an unforget-
table experience.

Sushi on North Beach
745 Columbus Ave. Tel: 415-
788-8050. Open: L, D. **$$$**.
This family-run Asian
establishment is a real
find in the middle of Ital-
ian North Beach. Unique
rolls, good-sized pieces of
fresh fish, and fantastic
miso soup set it apart
from the rest.

**Washington Square Bar
& Grill**
1707 Powell St. Tel: 415-982-
8123. Open: L, Br, D. **$$$**.
On Washington Square,
and celebrated in count-
less *San Francisco Chronicle* columns, "The
Washbag," has had a culi-
nary revival lately to equal
its legendary atmos-
phere. Jazz and good
times nightly.

Bars and Clubs

Amante
570 Green St.
Tel: 415-362-4400.
Amante is surprisingly
unpretentious despite its
elegant interior. An inexpensive bar menu helps.

Blind Tiger
787 Broadway
Tel: 415-788-4020
Local young people dance
to DJ music featuring
house, hip-hop and pop.

The Lusty Lady
1033 Kearny St
Tel: 415-391-3126
Open Late - 25¢ a peep
This is SF's infamous
peep-show style all-nude
establishment, unique as
the country's first union-
ized strip joint. More of a
novelty than a turn-on.

Purple Onion
140 Columbus Ave
Tel: 415-217-8400
Open: intermittently – call
This club was a launching
pad for the Smothers
Brothers, Phyllis Diller,
and the Kingston Trio.
After a beautiful renova-
tion, it again features
comedy and music.The
Italian restaurant upstairs
is one of the best.

PRICE CATEGORIES

Prices for three-course
dinner per person with a
half-bottle of house wine:
$ = under $20
$$ = $20–45
$$$ = $45–85
$$$$ = more than $85

COIT TOWER AND TELEGRAPH HILL

Eccentric heiress Lillie Hitchcock Coit bequeathed this landmark, styled after a firehose, to reflect one of her grandest passions

Coit Memorial Tower rises 212 ft (55 meters) including its base, above 284-ft (87-meter) Telegraph Hill, the site of an early telegraph station. The architect was Arthur Brown Jr, a protégé of Bernard Maybeck, creator of SF's Palace of Fine Arts. Inspiration for the tower's then-controversial Art Deco modernism came from the current European vogue in power stations, notably Sir Giles Gilbert Scott's Battersea Power Station in London. The monument was built in 1933 with a bequest of $125,000 left by heiress Lillie Hitchcock Coit *(see story, right)*.

Coit Tower, 1 Telegraph Hill Blvd, tel: 415-362-0808. Open daily 10am–5pm. The murals are free; there's a charge for the elevator to the top. Take MUNI bus No. 9 from Washington Square.

Murals and marvelous views

Inside Coit Tower, spectacular murals depict images and themes from American labor in the 1930s. After seeing them, visitors can take advantage of the elevator to ride to the top of the tower. On a clear day, a splendid panoramic view awaits: the bridges and hills of the city, the bay islands, farther out to Marin County, and all the way north to the forested summit of Mount Tamalpais.

BELOW: Mural artists painted for 30 hours a week and were paid up to a dollar an hour. The Public Works of Art Project was part of President Franklin D. Roosevelt's New Deal initiative, and was much reviled at the time for producing "pinko art."

ABOVE: This mural is a pastiche of Downtown locations, including City Hall, the Main Library and the Stock Exchange.

BELOW: Mural detail of the San Francisco public library system; it features the names of classic and contemporary authors.

LILLIE HITCHCOCK COIT

Lillie Coit was born at West Point Military Academy on August 23 in 1843, the daughter of an army surgeon. She came with her family to San Francisco in 1851. As a teenager – before the family moved to France for many years – she was a firebuff, hitching rides on outgoing fire engines and spending long hours playing cards and parading around in the uniform of Knickerbocker Engine Company No. 5, who adopted her as their mascot. Returning to the Bay Area in 1925, she spent her last four years speechless after a stroke, and left one-third of her fortune to the city in her will. The Coit Advisory Committee had the area around Telegraph Hill rezoned after the tower was completed in 1933, so that future buildings would not exceed four stories. The tower is built on the site of the first West Coast telegraph, a semaphore completed in 1849, later replaced by an observatory that burned down in 1903.

ABOVE RIGHT: Artist Bernard Zakheim and his assistant.
BELOW: A team of 26 artists started work on the Coit Tower murals in 1934. Together they depicted the ideals of the national New Deal program to lift the economy out of the Great Depression.

CHINATOWN

This city within a city, one of the largest Chinatowns outside Asia, has fine temples, peaceful squares and a great line in dim sum

San Francisco's **Chinatown ❶** is the quintessential city within a city. Shop windows beckon with crowded displays of silk, porcelain, teakwood furniture and hand-wrought jewelry, in addition to the more usual and mainstream Chinese bric-a-brac. The entrance to this exoticism is at the corner of Bush Street and Grant Avenue, the **Chinatown Gate ❷** – a monument of jade-green tiles, crouching stone lions, dolphins and dragons. At the top of the gate, four gilded Chinese characters in raised relief translate as: "Everything in the World is in Just Proportion." Walk a little deeper into the area and you'll find aromatic open-air markets, glitzy emporiums, busy alleyways and herbalists' stores packed with jars of strange roots and spices.

At the time that gold was discovered in 1848, China was undergoing a period of upheaval. The Manchu Dynasty was corrupt and weakening; floods and droughts resulted in widespread famine; peasant rebellions were becoming commonplace, and the decade-long T'ai-p'ing Rebellion in the 1850s severely reduced the population of Southern China. Many Chinese took the opportunity to leave and come to California's new mining towns in order to seek their fortunes. Of the

estimated 30,000 Chinese immigrants in the state during the 1850s, half of these people made their homes in San Francisco.

Little Canton

Chinatown grew up around what was then the heart of San Francisco – Portsmouth Square – with merchants setting up shop near the major hotels and rooming houses. This area became known as "Little Canton" in 1850 and had 33 retail stores, 15 pharmacies (Chinese

Map on page 108

LEFT: Waverly Place is called the "Street of Painted Balconies."
BELOW: Chinese New Year parade.

There are currently 240,000 Asians in San Francisco, though not all of them live in Chinatown.

BELOW:
buy exotic herbs here.

herbal cures were much in demand in a city with few doctors), and at least six restaurants serving both Chinese and non-Chinese food. This was the beginning of San Francisco's "Chinatown," as it was heralded in 1853 in the local press.

Grant Avenue ❸, which extends seven blocks from Bush Street to Pacific Avenue, is considered Chinatown's main strip. One of San Francisco's oldest roads, it used to be named Dupont Street when it was the main thoroughfare of the Mexican pueblo of Yerba Buena, established in 1834. The street was renamed Grant, after the devastating earthquake of 1906, in honor of Ulysses S. Grant.

Grant also remains the major tourist shopping street of Chinatown, with most stores open daily until 10pm. A restaurant that has been an institution for years is the narrow, three-level **Sam Wo** (tel: 415-982-0596; open until 3am) on Washington Street, just off Grant, but better known for its charm, cheap fare and hustling staff than top-flight cuisine. What you save on

food you could spend elsewhere on drinks, at, for instance, the **Lipo Bar** at 916 Grant, named for the famous 1st century Chinese poet, Li Po, who was well known for his verse celebrating the joys of drunken revelry. There is a Buddhist shrine in the corner, Chinese men playing dice for shots of Remy and unbeatable drinks prices over the counter.

From the Chinatown Gate it's a two-block walk north along Grant Avenue to California Street and **St Mary's Church** ❹, which served as the main Catholic church in San Francisco from 1853 to 1891. Its sturdy granite foundation, imported from China, and walls brought from the East Coast, survived the devastation of 1906 and the more recent earthquake of 1989. The church's brick tower is engraved with the famous Biblical motto from Ecclesiastes: "Son, Observe the time and fly from evil."

In the past, this area of Chinatown was known for its somewhat seedy array of brothels and gambling and opium dens, and often became the setting for violent outbursts between

Early Chinatown

Early Chinatown was remarkable for its lack of women. According to the US census of 1890, the ratio of Chinese men to women in San Francisco was roughly 20 men to one woman. This was primarily because these early immigrants, or "sojourners," did not intend to settle in the United States; their goal was to make money and return home as soon as possible. In order to realize this quickly, the Chinese were driven by entrepreneurial zeal.

In 1850, there was a large watering hole at the base of Russian Hill known as Washerwoman's Lagoon. This was the largest "laundry" in the city, much of the work done by Native American and Spanish women. This lagoon, however, was not large enough to serve the city, and it was not unheard of for laundry to be sent by sea to Honolulu or Canton to be washed, then returned by steamer some months later. Obviously there was a need for laundries closer to hand. The opportunity was seized upon, as little capital was needed to start up such small neighborhood businesses. Once the Chinese entered the market, the price for laundering shirts plummeted from $8 a dozen to $2.

the Chinese and other residents of San Francisco. In the late 1800s, there were a number of attempts to clean up the area. All of them failed, until the fire that came in the wake of the 1906 earthquake destroyed most of the commercial establishments.

Squares and statues

After the great fire, the area surrounding St Mary's was decreed and renamed **St Mary's Square** ❺. Now quiet and peaceful, it rests on top of a large underground parking garage. In the morning, the square is often filled with Chinese and Americans practicing tai chi, moving in balletic slow motion.

An impressive 14-ft (4-meter) granite structure, the **Sun Yat-Sen statue**, named after the first president of modern China, stands at the northeast corner of the square. Dr Sun lived in Chinatown briefly in 1910 and published a newspaper. The sculpture in his honor was commissioned by the federally funded Works Progress Administration and was placed here in 1938. Its well-known sculptor, Beniamino Bufano,

also created the statue of St Francis at Taylor and Beach streets, and several other sculptures around the city, often whimsical animals.

Day-to-day life in Chinatown is mainly conducted on **Stockton Street** ❻. This is the place where most of the produce and fish markets, herbal pharmacies, butchers, shops and bakeries are found. Spices are also sold here, in large import-export shops.

Another important meeting place is **Portsmouth Square** ❼ just to the east, the center of San Francisco in the Gold Rush era and the site in the past of rallies, riots and hangings, as well as today's romantic trysts and countless family picnics. The square is somewhat run-down, but still popular with the older generation of Chinese men who gather daily to play mahjong at the small tables dotted around the square.

Many of these men grew up under the shadow of the Exclusion Act *(see page 102)*: unable to find wives, they grew accustomed to a life of bachelorhood.

East of the square, at 750 Kearny

Map on page 108

Restaurants began as early as 1849 because few rooming houses had kitchens, and the Chinese craved their native foods. These cafés became popular with local white miners bored by a diet of bread and potatoes.

BELOW: the Chinese Gate at the corner of Bush Street and Grant Avenue is the entrance to Chinatown.

The Bank of Canton building used to be the Chinese Telephone Exchange.

Street, is a hotel with a difference: on the third floor is the **Chinese Culture Center** ❽ (tel: 415-986-1822, guided tours available), a valuable research facility for the study of Chinese life in the Western world. Shows are held in its art galleries and entertainment is provided in its own theater.

North of Portsmouth Square is **Buddha's Universal Church** ❾ (720 Washington Street, tel: 415-892-6116), which was built entirely by volunteers. Once the site of a nightclub, the building was purchased by church members in 1951 for a mere $500, only to have the city condemn it as structurally unsound. Volunteers rebuilt it, and the temple was dedicated in 1963. Free tours of the Universal Church's altar, library and rooftop garden are available on specific days of the month; call for details.

Farther along, at 743 Washington Street, the Chinese Telephone Exchange is where the first San Francisco newspaper, the *California Star*, was printed in 1846. Currently, this attractive, pagoda-like building

is home to the **Bank of Canton** ❿; in earlier years it was the local office of the Pacific Telephone and Telegraph Company.

Recently relocated to 965 Clay Street is the **Chinese Historical Society** ⓫ (tel: 415-391-1188; donations welcome), which has a library and a small museum for people wanting general information about Chinese-American history. Dedicated to tracing the Chinese contribution to the growth of the United States and particularly California, its collection includes Gold Rush artifacts, a papier-mâché dragon's head, and an altar from a Napa Valley Taoist temple.

Immigration problems

In 1882, Congress passed the Chinese Exclusion Act, suspending Chinese immigration for 10 years. The act insured that foreign-born wives and children of Chinese-American citizens would be the only Chinese allowed to enter the country. The Exclusion Act was reinforced (and made even more stringent) by the Scott Act of 1888 and, later, by the Immigration Act of 1924. As a result of these measures, the Chinese population in the United States dropped from 132,000 in 1882 to 62,000 by 1920. (Today, the Chinese population in the US is approximately 2,300,000).

Still, from the 1880s to the 1920s, Chinatown expanded from its six-block length and two-block width until it covered eight city blocks, from Bush to Broadway, and three blocks from Kearny to Powell. The area was rebuilt after the 1906 earthquake and became a thriving community; its streets overflowing with traffic and tourists.

After the United States and China became allies during World War II, President Roosevelt signed a measure in 1943 repealing the Exclusion acts, allowing Chinese people to

become American citizens and setting a modest yearly quota for Chinese immigration. This was the first of several policies that opened doors to Chinese students, to women and to refugees from political turmoil. San Francisco's Chinatown flourished under these conditions, and today it is estimated that some 70,000 Chinese live within the 24-block radius that makes up the current boundaries.

Old SF Mint

On Commercial Street, the **Pacific Heritage Museum** ⓬ Number 698 (tel: 415-399-1124; open Tues–Sat until 4pm, guided tours) is located on the site of the old San Francisco Mint built in 1854. Tours include a look at the old vaults, in addition to an historical display detailing the building's history.

An important part of Chinatown's commerce and community is made up of what Americans refer to as The Six Companies, also known as the **Chinese Consolidated Benevolent Association**. The Six Companies, a far-reaching organization formed around the turn of the 20th century, became the central government of Chinatown, and acted under a coordinating board of control (made up of representatives from disparate organizations, community groups and clubs). The Six Companies act as a sort of embassy to Chinese visitors, arbitrate disputes within the community, and operate one of the largest Chinese language schools in the country, as well as playing a major role in organizing the massive and colorful Chinese New Year's Parade.

The Chinese New Year is celebrated, usually in February, with a noisy three-hour parade downtown and into the very heart of Chinatown. People from all over the Bay Area flank the streets for the procession, which is tailed by a huge 60-ft (18-meter) dragon carried by at least a dozen men. Often, the ceremonial dragon is made in Hong Kong and shipped over expressly for the New Year's parade. The dragon is on display every year after the parade, usually at 383 Grant Avenue. Firecrackers are every-

Fortune cookies are not part of Chinese food culture. In 1993, the US-based Wonton Food Company began producing them in China for the first time, marketing them as "Genuine American Fortune Cookies."

Map on page 108

BELOW: Kong Chow Temple has fine wooden carvings.

Map on page 108

Many Chinese temples are located at the top of buildings, in order to put them closer to heaven and the gods.

BELOW: the Golden Gate Fortune Cookie Factory.

where during New Year's week, and even four- and five-year-olds can be seen throwing them into gutters and cupping their ears in anxious anticipation of the blast.

Temple tour

Temples in Chinatown representing Taoism, Buddhism and other Asian religions function not only as places of worship but also as providers of community services such as schools, meeting rooms, dormitories and eating places for the elderly and the poor. Most of these temples are located at the tops of buildings – this is in order to place them closer to heaven and the gods. The temples tend to be lavishly decorated with hanging lanterns and other ornaments, and are heavy with the scent of the exotic incense burned in ceremonial offerings.

West of the Pacific Heritage Museum is **Waverly Place** ⓭, which is often called the "Street of Painted Balconies." An alley that runs parallel to Grant Avenue between Clay and Washington streets, Waverly is what might be

called the "real" Chinatown – the Chinatown that most visitors don't see. Here, stores sell lychee wine, pickled ginger, rice threads, dried lotus and powdered antler horns, reputed to restore male virility. Traditional Chinese roofs of turned-up jade and terra cotta tiles mark the edges of apartment house roofs.

At 125 Waverly is the **Tin Hou Temple** ⓮ (open daily), the Queen of the Heavens and Goddess of the Seven Seas. Tin Hou is said to protect travelers, sailors, artists and prostitutes and is believed to be the oldest Chinese temple in the United States. The most popular deity is Kuan Yin, a goddess of mercy, or "one who hears prayers." There's a temple dedicated to her in **Spofford Alley**.

From the Tin Hou temple, walk south on Waverly to Clay, turn right and walk west one short block to 855 Stockton to see another temple – this one with particularly fine wood carvings – called the **Kong Chow Temple** ⓯, (open daily).

Going north on Stockton will lead you toward tiny **Ross Alley**, where the fortune cookie is said to have been invented (although another claimant to fortune cookie fame is the Japanese Tea Garden in Golden Gate Park). These tiny treats are still made at the **Golden Gate Fortune Cookie Factory** ⓰ (tel: 415-781-3956; open until 8.30pm), in Ross Alley. The job is done in the blink of an eye, as a worker pulls a hot cookie off a rotating press and folds a fortune inside. Samples hot off the press to eat as you walk around can be bought for a few pennies.

Fortune cookies have moved with the times and now come in several varieties: there are adult versions with X-rated messages inside, and cookies containing lottery numbers or quotations from the Bible.

RESTAURANTS

Restaurants

Bix
56 Gold St. Tel: 415-433-6300. Open: D. **$$$**.
San Francisco's renewed taste for martinis requires swank digs and upscale munchables. Bix is a revival of the 1920s supper club, with tasty bites and live jazz. It's also is a regular stopover for the Swing Set on their way to the clubs on Broadway near North Beach.

Chef Jia's
925 Kearny St. Tel: 415-398-1626. Open: L, D. **$**
It's easy to overlook this place because it is next door to another, hugely popular restaurant, but you'll save time and be pleasantly surprised by this delicious food with unique specials. Be sure to try the yummy honey-chili prawns.

Empress of China
838 Grant Ave. Tel: 415-434-1345. Open: L, D. **$**
The only restaurant in Chinatown with a truly spectacular view gives diners a very good perspective on the neighborhood. The cocktail lounge overlooks Grant Street, while the dining room towers above Portsmouth Square. If you don't eat here, at least stop by for a drink and enjoy the ambience.

Far East Café
631 Grant Ave. Tel: 415-982-3245. Open L, D. **$$**
The Far East is a great place to take a small group to enjoy traditional Chinese food. Here you can have your own curtained-off booth for privacy. The food is decent and the deep wood interior and century-old chandeliers are a sight to behold, reminiscent more of a mansion than a restaurant.

Gold Mountain
644 Broadway.
Tel: 415- 296-7733. Open: Br, L, D. **$$**.
Authentic Hong Kong-style dim sum is served from roving carts in this cavernous room. Don't be intimidated by the language barrier; this is where local Chinese families eat, which is always a good sign.

House of Nanking
919 Kearny St. Tel: 415-421-1429. Open: L, D. **$**.
Expect long lines at this popular and acclaimed Chinese restaurant, where the cramped seating and pushy service are all part of the charm. What the restaurant lacks in atmosphere and cleanliness, it makes up for in deliciousness. Avoid crowded weekend evenings, but don't miss the opportunity to dine here before leaving town.

Lucky Creation
854 Washington St. Tel: 415-989-0818. Open: L, D. **$**.
Visiting vegetarians rejoice to discover this meatless Chinese eatery. The Lucky Creation specializes in imitation meat dishes, so it's easy to satisfy a hankering for sweet & sour pork *sans* pig.

Tommy Toy's
655 Montgomery St.
Tel: 415-397-4888.
Open: L, D. **$$$**.
Upscale, creative Chinese restaurant catering to the society set. Order the lobster, the minced squab or, better yet, the *prix-fixe* tasting menu to sample multiple courses – all served by impeccable and impeccably dressed wait staff. The décor is muted pink and jade tones. Sinatra ate here, so shouldn't you?

Yuet Lee
1300 Stockton St. Tel: 415-982-6020. Open: Br, L, D. Closed Tues. **$**.
The perennial champion of late-night nosh. Serving way after last call, the huge menu can satisfy any craving, especially seafood, but be aware the lighting is harsh and the atmosphere non-existent.

RIGHT: Chinatown's restaurants are good value.

UNION SQUARE TO THE FINANCIAL DISTRICT

The best shopping in the city is by the Theater District and near the soaring skyscrapers that make the money to spend on both

Though San Francisco is anything but an old-fashioned village, **Union Square** still fulfills to some extent the role that plazas and public squares once played in small towns. All walks of life gather in and around here: socialites find their gowns for debutante balls, the business-minded plot their corporate moves, residents come to see plays and to shop, and tourists board a cable car for a ride over Nob Hill or to visit the city's main **Visitor Information Center** on the lower level of Hallidie Plaza (on Market Street, tel: 415-391-2000; open Mon–Fri 9am–5pm, Sat, Sun and hols until 3pm).

Bordered by Geary, Post, Powell and Stockton streets, the square anchors an active commercial area – one of the best retail centers in the city – with a colorful history. First deeded for public use in 1850, Union Square acquired its name during the Civil War years, when pro-Union sympathizers rallied here. At the center of the square is a 90-ft (27-meter) Corinthian column, topped with a bronze *Victory* commemorating Commodore George Dewey's successful Manila Bay campaign during the Spanish-American War. Neither the 1906 earthquake nor the 1942 installation of the world's first underground parking lot-cum-bomb shelter rattled the venerable column.

A renovation unveiled in 2002 changed Union Square from a hangout for the homeless to a sleek spot for visitors to take a break or sip lattes in between shopping excursions.

Shop till you drop

A good place to watch the passing street parade is from the oversized steps. From this vantage point, you'll notice the bronze nude atop the memorial to President William McKinley (who died in San Francisco in 1901), by sculptor Robert

Map on page 108

LEFT: the Transamerica Pyramid
BELOW: ACT stands for the American Conservatory Theater.

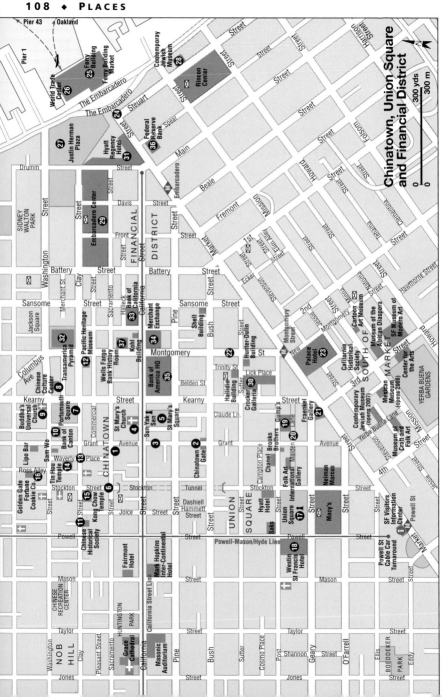

Chinatown, Union Square and Financial District

0   300 yds
0   300 m

Aitken. As his model, Aitken used a teenager, Alma de Bretteville, who become famous at 22 for marrying Adolph Spreckels, the much older and well-to-do president of the San Francisco Parks Commission. But Union Square is best known for the stores and hotels that have grown up around it. Fronting the west side is the **Westin St Francis Hotel ⓲**, which since 1904 has provided lodgings for countless dignitaries and celebrities. The plaza of the more modern **Hyatt on Union Square** is adorned with a Ruth Asawa fountain that literally embodies San Francisco. The bronze friezes of typical city scenes were cast in molds made from bread dough by some 250 schoolchildren and other local residents.

An important part of the scenery here are the "big three" department stores: **Macy's, Saks Fifth Avenue** and **Neiman-Marcus**. The latter is crowned by an exquisite stained-glass rotunda *(see photo on page 225)* which was salvaged from the City of Paris, San Francisco's first department store and the original occupant of the site.

Around the corner from Union Square at 135 Post Street is **Gump's ⓳**. Gump's started in business years ago by selling frames and mirrors to bars and bordellos during the Gold-Rush era, then moved steadily upscale to the present-day store, which is more akin to a museum-selling the best in jade, glassware, Oriental rugs, silks and antiques. Also on Post Street are classy establishments like **Brooks Brothers, Chanel** and other venerable names.

Maiden Lane

Running east to west parallel to Post Street is **Maiden Lane ⓴**, a tiny pedestrian-only alleyway lined with interesting stores and cafés – many with outdoor seating – that are perfect for a lunchtime snack away from the hustle of the square. Not to be missed

is the **Folk Art International Gallery** at 140 Maiden Lane. The gallery sells unique home accessories and ethnic textiles from all over the world, while the building itself was designed by Frank Lloyd Wright in 1948 and is a smaller version of his Guggenheim Museum in New York.

As well as theater, the Union Square area is known for its visual arts. The **Fraenkel Gallery ㉑** (49 Geary Street, tel: 415-981-2661; www.fraenkelgallery.com) is among the best of the many galleries on the surrounding streets.

Despite its commercial bias, the flavor of old San Francisco can still be found. **Montgomery Street ㉒**, east of Post Street (at the junction of Post and Montgomery is the Montgomery Street Metro station), is hallowed in city lore. Sam Brannan ran the length of Montgomery Street when he announced the discovery of gold in 1848, and soon the boulevard was overrun with '49ers. Mark Twain found inspiration here in a local fireman named Tom Sawyer, and Black Bart, Lotta Crabtree and Jack London have all paced the avenue.

Map on page 108

Take a trolley to the Theater District; for a list of theaters, see page 220.

BELOW:
Union Square has had a brand-new facelift.

The farmers' market at the Ferry Building happens Tues and Sun 10am–2pm, Sat 8am–2pm and Thur 4–8pm; fewer hours in winter.

BELOW: Ferry Building Marketplace.

The Financial District

The original '49ers sailed into San Francisco Bay, dropped anchor and set off north to pursue their dream of striking gold. It wasn't long before the city's original shoreline began to burgeon, contributing to the birth of today's soaring **Financial District**. Brokers, bankers and insurance agents now pursue wealth on several acres of landfill on and around Montgomery Street, nicknamed "Wall Street West." The interiors of many of these buildings are just as interesting as their facades, and most are open for public viewing.

The **Garden Court** of the lovely **Palace Hotel** ❷❸ (2 New Montgomery, tel: 415-512-1111) is replete with old-world opulence. Its magnificent dining room (*see photo on page 52*), opened in 1909, is surrounded by 16 marble Ionic columns and an intricate iron framework that supports a leaded glass skylight 48 ft (15 meters) above the floor, in addition to 10 crystal chandeliers.

Art Deco, Romanesque and the Chicago School are just a few of the styles that contribute to the architectural kaleidoscope of the Financial District, but the city's older facades also provide countless surprises. Some of the features to look for are: the Gothic styling of the **Hallidie Building**'s glass wall curtain (130 Sutter Street); the terra cotta carvings of ox-heads, eagles and young nymphs on the **Hunter-Dulin Building** (111 Sutter Street); the geometric designs of the **Shell Building** (100 Bush Street); and the winged gargoyles on the portico of the **Kohl Building** (400 Montgomery Street), a survivor of the 1906 quake.

An important and successful component of the Financial District is the **Embarcadero** ❷❹, an area built on land mostly reclaimed from the sea. Condominiums, restaurants and stores close by give the area its economic vitality.

The heart is the **Ferry Building** ❷❺ at Market and Embarcadero. Opening in 1898, it also survived the earthquake of 1906, with no more consequence than a stopped clock – the first time it had ceased to tick. The 230-ft (70-meter) tower is a near copy of the campanile of Seville's Cathedral. Before the construction of the bay bridges, the Ferry Building was the second busiest passenger terminal in the world, and even now ferries from here carry commuters to Tiburon and Sausalito.

Today it is home to the **Ferry Building Marketplace** (Mon–Fri, 10am–6pm 9am–6pm Sat, 11am–5pm Sun; tours and tastings Tues, Sat and Sun, noon; free), a rapturously received marketplace of food merchants, and a popular dining destination with signature suppliers and eating places. Outside on the pavement is a farmers' market, which a reporter for the *New York Times* says "many consider to be the best of the 3,700 farmers' markets in America."

The Embarcadero is more than just the Ferry Building Marketplace, however. **Covarrubias' mural** lights

with color the ramp to the **World Trade Center ㉖**; the mural was preserved from the 1939 Golden Gate International Exposition. Walking south on **Justin Herman Plaza ㉗**, which on sunny days is filled with picnicking office workers, leads to Steuart Street and the emerging **City Front District**. At 121 Steuart Street is the **Contemporary Jewish Museum ㉘** (tel: 415-344-8880, www.jmsf.org; Sun–Thur noon–6pm; charge). In 2007 it will move into premises in SoMa, which will incorporate part of the long-abandoned Power Substation. The new museum is designed by Daniel Libeskind, the man responsible for Freedom Tower on the site of the former World Trade Center in New York.

Looming above the area is the **Embarcadero Center ㉙**, a massive retail and office complex. The Embarcadero Center's only rival for this kind of variety in the Financial District is the **Crocker Galleria ㉚** shopping arcade, between Post and Sutter streets, which straddles the geographical divide between Union Square and the Financial District.

The Garden Court's modern architectural counterpart is the Embarcadero's immense **Hyatt Regency Hotel ㉛**, (Embarcadero 5, tel: 415-788-1234), a veritable microcosm where guests do not even need to leave the building to enjoy nature: the indoor atrium is 20 stories high and houses over 100 trees and 15,000 hanging plants.

Birds flit about the overhead skylight, while 170 ft (52 meters) below, visitors sink into the plush conversation pits that line the lobby. Even Charles Perry's geometric sculpture – rising only four stories above the pool of water that reflects it – is huge.

City within a city

The Hyatt Regency is just part of the "city within a city" that John Portman envisioned when he designed the Embarcadero Center – it is well-planned, uniform and self-contained. The 8½-acre (3.5-hectare) development consists of four high-rise office towers, the aforementioned plaza and an interwoven complex of restaurants and retail stores, all linked by pedestrian bridges and outdoor courtyards

Map
on page
108

TIP

The Embarcadero Center has two of the best high-rise viewing spots in the city. On the 41st floor of One Embarcadero is The Skydeck, open every day from noon until 9pm (charge) with a 360° panorama. The spinning restaurant, Equinox, at the top of the Hyatt Regency Hotel, is great for cocktails or dinner.

BELOW:
Downtown living.

Map on page 108

The Transamerica Pyramid is the tallest building in the city.

BELOW: taking a break in Maiden Lane.

filled with displays of sculpture. The center can feel a little sterile, especially at night, but is undoubtedly impressive nevertheless.

Exiting the plaza at the northwest corner on Clay Street, walk five blocks up Clay to the corner of Montgomery where the **Transamerica Pyramid** ㉜, (not open to the public), commands attention because of its great size and unusual shape.

The pyramid pierces the sky at 853 ft (260 meters), making it the tallest building in the city. Its aesthetic appeal was debated endlessly when it was first constructed in 1972, but now almost everyone seems to agree that its singular shape adds a welcome distinction to the San Franciscan skyline. At ground level, flanking the building, may be its most surprising feature – one of the world's rare urban groves of redwood.

Wall Street West

Turning left on Clay Street and three blocks down Sansome is the **Bank of California** ㉝ (400 California Street), the oldest banking hall in the district.

Crossing California Street and heading west leads to the **Merchant Exchange** ㉞ (tel: 415-421-7730; open weekdays). Another notable marker of San Francisco's history, the Exchange's heyday was early in the 20th century, when excited traders awaited news of arriving merchant ships – relayed from towers along the coast. Inside are fine paintings by the Irish artist William Coulter.

One block west, between Montgomery and Kearney, is the **Bank of America Headquarters** ㉟ at 555 California Street. Visitors to the 52nd floor of the Bank will find another stunning bird's-eye view of San Francisco in the **Carnelian Room** (tel: 415-433-7500), a cocktail lounge/restaurant that's open to the public after 5pm. On the way out, take a second look at the building's exterior and notice the red carnelian granite facade and the outdoor plaza's centerpiece sculpture *Banker's Heart*, a huge stone of polished granite.

A few blocks south is the **Federal Reserve Bank** ㊱ (101 Market Street, www.frbsf.org, tel: 415-974-3230). Inside, the **World of Economics** gallery explains financial principles through hands-on computer games and even cartoon stories. Tours (most weekday mornings) must be scheduled two weeks in advance.

Leaving the Bank of America building at the California exit, head east back toward Montgomery Street. Turn left to cross California Street and go north one block to the **Wells Fargo Bank History Room** ㊲ (tel: 415-396-2619; free), which offers a look at some hefty gold nuggets as well as insights into San Francisco's financial and Gold Rush history. There are banking articles, miners' equipment and dioramas. A fine **Wells Fargo Overland Stage**, once used on the coaching trails of the old West and now part of the bank's logo, forms the centerpiece of the museum. ❑

RESTAURANTS

Restaurants

Aqua
252 California St. Tel: 415-956-9662. Open: D. **$$$$**
Reservations are required at this seafood restaurant that is consistently rated as the best in San Francisco. The presentation and service are top-notch and chefs from around the world vie for opportunities to work here.

Asia de Cuba
495 Geary Street. Tel: 929-2300. Open: B, L, D. **$$$**
See and be seen at this Philippe Starck designed restaurant in the Clift Hotel. Chino-Latino fusion is served as diners sit in lush mahogany and leather banquettes. Hipper than thou.

Equinox
5 Embarcadero Center Tel: 415-291-6619. Open: D. **$$$**
Equinox, at the top of the Hyatt Regency Hotel, is the place to be for revolving rooftop fine dining and 360° views of the city. The food is a mix of American and California cuisines and is known for good steaks.

Fleur de Lys
777 Sutter St. Tel: 415-673-7779. Open: D. **$$$$**
The premier traditional French restaurant, with an elegant dining room and superior service.

Kokkari
200 Jackson St. Tel: 415-981-0983. Open: L, D. **$$$**
Warm and sumptuous, rustic yet sexy, Kokkari's blend of traditional Greek and California cuisine makes for a unique meal of bold flavors. Settle by the hearth for a glass of ouzo.

Le Colonial
20 Cosmo Place. Tel: 415-931-3600. Open: D. **$$$**
Upscale French Vietnamese fare amid gentle, swirling ceiling fans and leafy palm trees, transports diners to another world. A great respite, with creative cocktails and appetizers.

Masa's
468 Bush St. Tel: 415-989-7154. Open: D. **$$$$**
Perhaps the most expensive and critically lauded restaurant in San Francisco. A perennial winner in "top restaurant" lists, Masa's serves French and California cuisine.

Sam's Grill
374 Bush St. Tel: 415-421-0594. Open: L, D. **$$$**
Although the three-martini business lunch may be a thing of the past, this old-school grill is still going strong after 125 years. Choose either the high-ceiling dining room or a private booth, and enjoy American cuisine free from pretension and impervious to change.

Scala's Bistro
432 Powell St. Tel: 415-395-8555. Open: L, D. **$$**
Located at the base of the Sir Francis Drake Hotel, this Italian and French bistro features an open kitchen, intimate seating and an impressive selection of wines. The service is perfect and the location, in the heart of Union Square, can't be beat. Go dancing afterwards at the Starlight Room upstairs.

The Slanted Door
1 Ferry Building #3 (The Embarcadero). Tel. 415-861-8032. Open: L, D. **$$$**
Opened just a few years ago, this place instantly became one of the premier restaurants in the city serving wholesome, flavorful Vietnamese food. Make reservations long before you come to San Francisco.

Waterfront Restaurant
Pier 7 (The Embarcadero). Tel: 415-391-2696. Open: L, D. **$$$**
East-West fusion capitalizing on fresh seafood. The Bay Bridge is stunning from most tables, but unlike some restaurants, the food at the Waterfront Restaurant is just as good as the view.

PRICE CATEGORIES

Prices for three-course dinner per person with a half-bottle of house wine:
$ = under $20
$$ = $20–45
$$$ = $45–85
$$$$ = more than $85

RIGHT: Californians go crazy for fresh food.

CIVIC CENTER TO SOMA

Civic duty, ardent opera fans, edgy atmospheres,
excellent dining opportunities, and museums
of elegance and whimsy define
these downtown areas

San Francisco's collection of historic public buildings is the **Civic Center**, a downtown complex bisected by Van Ness Avenue, the city's widest street. Arthur Brown, Jr, the most celebrated architect of his era, was responsible for many of the Bay Area's outstanding buildings, including Sproul Hall on the University of California's Berkeley campus, several buildings (with his partner John Bakewell) on the Stanford University campus and Coit Tower.

Architectural ensemble

Brown's City Hall, and the adjoining **Veterans Auditorium Building** ❶ (which houses the **Herbst Theater**, tel: 415-392-4400), have been acclaimed by one historian as the greatest architectural ensemble in America.

Built in 1914, **City Hall** ❷ (tel: 415-554-6023; one afternoon tour a week) is a magnificent Beaux Arts structure, honeycombed with municipal offices and both civil and criminal courts running from a central rotunda. The building sits where Van Ness crosses McAllister Street, and was the scene of the famous murders in 1978, when Harvey Milk and Mayor George Moscone were shot by Supervisor Dan White.

City Hall was again the scene of controversy when same-sex mar-

riages were performed here in 2004.

The **War Memorial Opera House** ❸ (tel: 415-864-3330 for box office), which sits opposite City Hall and was the birthplace of the United Nations, has a drama or two of a different sort. San Franciscans are not only passionate about the arts, but energetic, too. For many years a loosely organized group of about 50 flower throwers – mostly men – known as the Opera Standees Association was tolerated by, but not formally associated with, the San

Map
on page
116

LEFT: City Hall's interior was restored to its former glory after a recent refurbishment
BELOW: San Francisco Museum of Modern Art (SFMoMA).

Emily Sano is the director of the Asian Art Museum.

BELOW: City Hall was built in 1914.

Francisco Opera. "Opera-throwers", as they were called, are fans who hurl bouquets at beloved divas during encores. Sometimes they brusquely push aside ushers and patrons alike to take advantage of the mere 30 seconds during which they can perform their self-appointed task of homage.

It requires more than a little skill to send flowers 35 ft (10 meters) over the heads of the orchestra so that they land perfectly at the desired singer's feet. The Standees' record was held for some time by one successful "member" who hurled some 300 bouquets in a single season, each one hitting its mark.

Flanking Arthur Brown's Opera House and the Veterans Auditorium is the **State Building** ❹ and, mirroring its curving exterior, the lavish **Louise M. Davies Symphony Hall** ❺, home of the San Francisco Symphony. Tours (tel: 415-864-6000) are conducted around the hall, whose highly regarded architects –

Skidmore, Owings & Merrill – also designed the State Building.

At the northeastern end of the Civic Center buildings is the former public library, built in 1916, which now houses the **Asian Art Museum** ❻ (tel: 415-581-3500, www.asianart.org; open Tues–Sun 10am–5pm, until 9pm on Thur; charge). This is one of the largest collections of Asian art in the world, and contains not only Chinese art, but Indian, Persian, Southeast Asian, Korean and Japanese objects. There are over 15,000 pieces in the collection (with approximately 3,000 showing at any one time) spanning 6,000 years of history. Highlights of the permanent collection include the oldest dated Chinese Buddha in the world, from AD 336.

The **Public Library** ❼ is next door at Larkin and Grove streets. Behind are the **Federal Building** ❽ and **United Nations Plaza** ❾. This triangular space, occupying the area between Fulton, Hyde and Market

streets, commemorates the birth of the United Nations in 1945 when the charter was signed.

The last structure in the Civic Center complex is the **Bill Graham Civic Auditorium** at 99 Grove Street (tel: 415-974-4060), named after the irascible impresario responsible for so many of the city's rock concerts during the 1960s.

The Tenderloin

East of Civic Center toward Union Square and bordered by Market and Sutter streets is **The Tenderloin** ⓫, or the "loin" as some locals call it. Known in the past as a den for drugs, crime, grime and the shadier sides of life, the neighborhood also has unique architecture, wonderful and inexpensive ethnic restaurants and clean, affordable hotels just a hair off-the-beaten path. But don't be fooled by the hip hotels and bars, as this neighborhood can still be dangerous: during the day keep your eyes open and at night, be extra alert.

The Tenderloin is not without its gems, however. While sketchy playgrounds, dingy streets, young street hustlers and transsexuals are part of the ever-happening landscape, there are still many places to visit. Crowds line up outside almost every night to hear live music in the historic **Great American Music Hall** (tel: 415-885-0750), once a Barbary Coast bordello with a voluptuous rococo interior, now a venue hosting musicians from all over the world.

The former brothel is by the Mitchell Brothers O'Farrell Theater – the most notorious strip club in San Francisco. The O'Farrell Theater was created on the lot of a former car dealership and has been open since 1969, minus a few hiccups for trafficking obscenity and the death of one of the brothers (a story that was made into the feature film *Blood Brothers.*)

On the corner of Taylor and Ellis streets at **Glide Memorial Methodist Church**, the charismatic Reverend Cecil Williams and his devoted staff and volunteers have been feeding and caring for the poor and homeless for more than 40 years. For an uplifting and unforgettable experience, check out a Sunday service or "celebration," and worship with the Glide Ensemble, a 140-member choir that sings and sways to blues, jazz, gospel and spirituals every week.

Also don't miss the **Shooting Gallery** (839 Larkin Street, tel: 415-931-8035) a noteworthy place that showcases offbeat art exhibits, and **Shalimar** (*see page 121*) one of the best Indian/Pakistan restaurants in the city. Stop into any number of other inexpensive and tasty eateries of the Vietnamese, Cambodian and Indian varieties, or head for one of the ubiquitous diners. You'll also find lots of neighborhood gay bars and "dives" to quench any thirst for a drink and local 'loin color.

Map on page 116

TIP

The Public Library at Civic Center has free internet access in 15-minute intervals. For a map of WiFi cafés go to: www.cheesebikini.com/wifi-cafes. For other information about email and the internet: *see page 235*.

BELOW: the interior of the Great American Music Hall.

TIP

The largest city-owned solar installation in the US sits on top of SoMa's Moscone Convention Center. In 2005, San Francisco was named one of the Top 10 "greenest cities" in America, in a survey conducted by *The Green Guide*.

BELOW: 1906 carousel by Zeum in Yerba Buena Gardens.

SoMa

On the other side of Market Street from Civic Center lies a very different kind of neighborhood. Whereas Civic Center is stately, dignified and elegant, **SoMa** (**So**uth of **Ma**rket Street) is one of the city's most forward-looking districts. Once a colorless, quasi-industrial neighborhood of warehouses and factory outlets, SoMa is now better known as "two square miles of hot nightclubs, fashionable restaurants, experimental theaters, museums, lofts and galleries," as a local brochure puts it.

After the millennium, the gentrification extended, particularly towards the east, from SoMa proper to the bay. With the opening of the baseball stadium, SBC Park, and new, cool neighborhoods like South Beach and McCovey Cove *(see page 158)* enjoying the prosperity that followed, the rehabilitation of this part of the city became complete.

The largest structure in the heart of SoMa is the **Moscone Convention Center ⑫**, home to most of the major (and many) conventions that are held in the city each month. Above Moscone Center South is a well-funded **Children's Center**, one of the few civic sites in the nation dedicated to children and youth.

If any delegate should hanker after a little culture during breaks from the convention floor, the Moscone is surrounded by a dazzling array of museums – some prestigious and prosperous; others constructing glittering new buildings to move into.

SoMa's biggest attraction is the fantastic **San Francisco Museum of Modern Art ⑬** (151 3rd Street, tel: 415-357-4000, www.sfmoma.org; open summer: 10am–6pm; winter: 11am–6pm; closed Wed; charge) with its collection of 15,000 works of art. Designed by Swiss architect Mario Botta and costing over $60 million when completed, the museum opened to the public in 1995. Although many

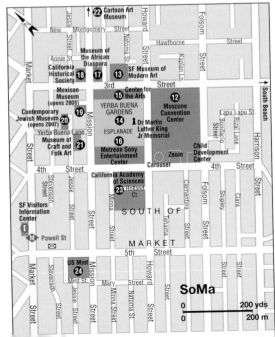

SoMa

0 ___ 200 yds
0 ___ 200 m

think the building overshadows the collections, it's worth visiting if only to admire the effects of sunlight on the entrance hall below the five-story glass-roofed staircase (see photo on page 56).

Inside, however, there is much to contemplate: works by American and European Expressionists such as Max Ernst, Picasso, Paul Klee and the Californian painter Richard Diebenkorn shouldn't be missed. Just inside the entrance is a good coffee shop, while the gift shop is perfect for classy presents to take back home.

Arts and entertainment

West of the Moscone Center is **Yerba Buena Gardens** ⓮, a 22-acre (9-hectare) site occupying the entire block between 3rd and 4th streets. Yerba Buena is an arts and entertainment complex interspersed with tranquil patches of greenery.

One of Yerba Buena's most innovative venues is **Zeum** (tel: 415-777-2800, open Wed–Sun 11am–5pm; charge), a visual arts facility geared toward young people. This being California, Zeum has its own anima-

tion studio, next to a production studio where kids can make and star in their own music videos. International touring companies give performances at Yerba Buena's theater, in the **Center for the Arts** ⓯ (tel: 415-978-2700; gallery closed Mon), where art exhibitions, movie showings, dance and other events are also staged throughout the year.

The complex overlooks the **Esplanade**, a pretty downtown park that includes terrace cafés, an outdoor performance area with lawn seating for 5,000, and a walk-through waterfall leading to the **Dr Martin Luther King, Jr**. **Memorial**.

Next to the Esplanade is an entertainment complex, sponsored by Sony, called the **Metreon** ⓰ with a 15-screen movie theater; an IMAX theater, an excellent food court, and interactive exhibits of all things bright and shiny. It is at 4th and Mission.

Mission Street, might, in fact, be the most cultural thoroughfare in San Francisco, with six museums hovering around its periphery. At No. 685, near the Center for the Arts, is the **Museum of the African Dias-**

Map on page 118

Femme au Chapeau *by Henri Matisse, on show in SFMoMA.*

BELOW:
Yerba Buena Gardens.

Map on page 118

Zuni martini.

BELOW: fresh food and friendly service keeps fans flocking to Zuni.

pora **17** (www.moadsf.org) which explores African-American culture and history. MoAD, is aiming for a late-2005 opening. On the other side of the street is the downtown branch of the **California Historical Society 18** (678 Mission Street, tel: 415-357-1848; open Tues–Sun; charge), which probes the past with art collections and exhibition galleries.

Much development is taking place around Mission between 3rd and 4th streets. By 2008, this will be the dramatic new location for the **Mexican Museum 19**, currently headquartered in Fort Mason *(see page 131)*. The new building is designed by Mexican architect Ricardo Legorreta, known "for his signature use of traditional colors and natural light to create geometric forms that are welcoming yet mysterious."

Another signature building is being constructed as the new home of the **Contemporary Jewish Museum 20** *(see page 111)*. Designed by Daniel Libeskind, it incorporates part of the historic Jessie Street Power Substation.The proposed completion date for the Jewish Museum is 2007.

The second transplant from Fort Mason (late 2005) is the **Museum of Craft and Folk Art 21**, located on a new "street" of attractions, stores and cafés that links Mission and Market Street, called **Yerba Buena Lane**.

Farther down Mission are the premises of the **Cartoon Art Museum 22** (814 Mission Street, tel: 415-227-8666; open Wed–Sat; charge), one of only three in the US dedicated to the preservation, documentation and exhibition of cartoons.

At Howard Street are the temporary premises of the **California Academy of Sciences 23** (875 Howard, tel: 415-321-8000, www.calacademy.org, open daily 10am–5pm; charge). Its permanent home in Golden Gate Park is being remodeled and is scheduled to re-open in 2008. The Academy features interactive science exhibits and the **Steinhart Aquarium**, filled with exotic fish and other sea creatures.

At the western end of SoMa is the imposing facade of the former **US Mint 24**. Although empty at present, the building will soon be put to use as – yes, a museum. ❏

RESTAURANTS

Restaurants

Ananda Fuara
1298 Market St. Tel: 415-621-1994. Open: L, D. $
Inexpensive and delicious, this is the perfect change of pace for non-carnivores tired of veggie burritos and Caesar salads. There is much to order here, from veggie "meatloaf" to mushroom ravioli.

Ar Roi Thai Cuisine
643 Post St. Tel: 415-771-5146. Open: D. $$
Flavor-packed dishes, including delicious soups like *Tom Kai Gai* (coconut chicken with lemongrass and cilantro), Thai beef salad and pan-fried noodles, are served here in a cool, Art-Deco style atmosphere.

Asia SF
201 9th St. Tel: 415-255-2742. Open: D. $$$–$$$$
Reservations are required for this nightclub and restaurant where the entertainment – "gender illusionists" – double as your waitstaff. This place is outrageous, only-in-SF fun for big groups and people who don't mind a bit of gender bending with their Asian cuisine.

La Suite
100 Brannan St. Tel: 415-593-5900. Open: Br, L, D. $$$
San Francisco's French *enfant nouveau* has exploded on the scene,

demanding attention, and has impressed the critics and the public. The cuisine manages to be authentic and contemporary, with a stellar wine list and epic cheese cart. Beautiful Bay Bridge views.

Le Charm
315 5th St. Tel: 415-546-6128. Open: L, D. $$
French food's greatest hits, reasonably priced. Ratatouille, escargot, duck confit, crème brûlée, and classic French onion soup all share this comfortable, unpretentious stage.

LuLu
816 Folsom St. Tel: 415-495-5775. Open: L, D. $$$
Tremendously trendy SoMa spot, especially good for big group lunches and dinners. Lulu's specializes in wood-fired and rotisserie-style delicacies, and the cocktails are potent.

Patisserie Café
1155 Folsom St. Tel: 415-703-0557. Open: Br, L, D $$
This gallery space serving "exotic cuisine" has an outdoor patio, primarily French-inspired dishes and the best fried *beignets* this side of New Orleans. See and be seen by the neighborhood's population of artists and epicurians.

Ponzu
410 Taylor St. Tel: 415-775-7979. Open: B, L, D. $$
A good bet for pre- or

post-theater drinks and dining, Ponzu blurs the lines of Asian cuisine, delivering tasty tidbits from Malaysian satay to Vietnamese prawns. The specialty cocktails are potent and heady.

Shalimar
532 Jones St. Tel: 415-928-0333. Open: L, D. $
Delicious Indian and Pakistani food made just the way it is back in the home country. Natives of India and Pakistan who live in the Bay Area drive hours to eat in this hole-in-the-wall and listen to Bollywood-inspired soundtracks. The best of many Indian eateries in the Tenderloin area.

Town Hall
342 Howard St. Tel: 415-908-3900. Open: L, D. $$$
Regional American classics like New Orleans-style smoked chicken gumbo are served up nicely in this remodeled, historic building in SoMa. Try the shrimp *etouffée* or the San Francisco favorite, *cioppino* (a type of fish stew).

Tu Lan
8 Sixth St. Tel: 415-626-0927. Open: L, D. $
This Vietnamese hot spot is known for its cramped, hot and sketchy location. It's a hole in the wall, but people love it, waiting patiently for memorably tasty noodle dishes.

XYZ
181 3rd St. Tel: 415-817-7836. Open: Br, L, D. $$$$
A popular spot with directors, actors and wannabes. The excellent, creative dishes combine fine local and seasonal vegetables, plus meat and fish in modern Californian style. There's also superb service and a wine list featuring over 500 different varieties.

Yank Sing
Rincon Center, 101 Spear St. Tel: 415-957-9300. Open: Br, L, D. $$
Dim sum place using fresh ingredients in a sparkling clean interior. Perfect for first-timers.

Zuni Café
1658 Market St. Tel: 415-552-2522. Open: Br, L, D. $$$
Floor-to-ceiling windows, sidewalk tables, a copper-topped bar and an upstairs loft contribute to Zuni's allure. But it's great food – from freshly shucked oysters to organic burgers from the famed Neiman Ranch – that keeps patrons and critics buzzing.

PRICE CATEGORIES

Prices for three-course dinner per person with a half-bottle of house wine:
$ = under $20
$$ = $20–45
$$$ = $45–85
$$$$ = more than $85

NOB HILL

The robber barons of the Gold Rush era vied to build the most beautiful mansions possible, creating a lavish, luxurious "hill of palaces"

Nob Hill is a tiny but exclusive neighborhood dominated by a few grand hotels, Grace Cathedral and Huntington Park. Three blocks in any direction will find you in a different neighborhood – Chinatown to the north, the Financial District to the east, Union Square to the south and Russian Hill to the west.

Hill of palaces

From a historic perspective there is no better place to start a relationship with San Francisco's gracious homes than at **Nob Hill**. The cable car lines cross at **California** and **Powell** streets, and from here there is a magnificent view of the bay, crossed by the Bay Bridge and framed by the pagodas of Chinatown and the distinctive spire of the Transamerica Pyramid. The climb up California Street ends atop what the author Robert Louis Stevenson called the "hill of palaces."

In a fevered rush to outdo each other in opulence, the railroad "robber barons" of the 19th century built palatial homes on this fine hill. Although many of the houses that remain have been converted into condos or multi-dwelling apartment buildings, there has been little diminishing effect on the overall allure.

The highest of the city's seven major mounds, Nob Hill was not a desirable residential area until the invention of the cable car in 1873. Only then did the influential railroad barons agree to locate their colossal mansions here, after running cable car tracks down California Street to the Central Pacific (now Southern Pacific) headquarters on Market Street. The **Cable Car Barn and Powerhouse ❶**, nerve center of the present cable car system, can be inspected in a handsome 1910 structure at the corner of Mason and Washington streets on the flank of the hill *(see page 128)*.

Map on page 124

LEFT:
the Ritz-Carlton.
BELOW:
the Pacific Union Club was built in 1855.

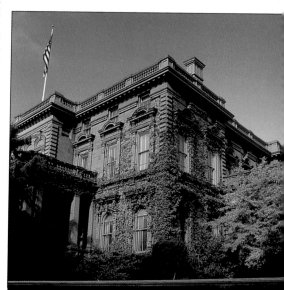

A dog-day afternoon in Nob Hill.

Architectural exuberance

San Francisco's architectural style has always been exuberant. Two years after gold was discovered in 1848, the population exploded from a humble community to nearly 25,000 people. In a short time, San Francisco became a sprawling, teeming mass of speculators bent on striking it rich.

At first, there wasn't time to build proper accommodations. Each day, more tents appeared and shacks were flung up with whatever materials were at hand. Even the schooners that hauled the precious supplies of food and tools around the Cape were pressed into service. Dragged ashore, doors were cut in the hulls, and the ships were transformed into houses, stores and even hotels.

But the new-found wealth pouring in from the gold fields created a community that wouldn't be satisfied with "tent-city" status. Real houses were built, spreading westward from the bay, at a rate unprecedented for the 19th century – from 15 to 30 a day in 1852. The favored material for construction was wood, cut and shipped in vast quantities from the virgin pine forests of the Oregon Territory farther up the West Coast. But even with the modern advances of balloon framing and manufactured nails, little could keep pace with the housing demand, and some homes and hotels were shipped as prefabricated kits from the East and assembled on site.

James Ben Ali Haggin was one of the first to build a mansion, a home of around 60 rooms. The "Big Four" – banker William C. Ralston, grocer Leland Stanford, hardware merchant Mark Hopkins and dry goods purveyor Charles Crocker – quickly followed suit. The real Gold Rush fortunes were made, not from mining, but from the hard-earned dollars of the miners, by those who supplied the tools, goods and services.

Techniques that allowed for the mass production of wooden orna-

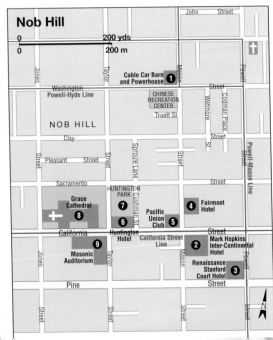

mental shapes gave even common houses a splendid aspect. Every architectural fashion of the day was fair game, from Victorian Gothic to Queen Anne, from French Renaissance to Turkish towers. Throughout the city, the result is a dazzling architectural eclecticism. In San Francisco, Moorish cupolas can be found on an Italianate facade, perhaps accompanied by an Egyptian column or two. For the very rich, no expense was too great, no splendor too excessive. And this reached its zenith on Nob Hill.

Grand hotels

The best-known landmark on the "hill of palaces" is the **Mark Hopkins Inter-Continental Hotel ❷** (999 California Street, tel: 415-392-3434), which occupies the site of the former Mark Hopkins mansion. The original home had lavish stables with rosewood stalls, silver trimmings and mosaic floors covered with Belgian carpets. Hopkins saw much of this luxury destroyed in the fire that raged for five days and nights following the earthquake of 1906, but the house was soon rebuilt. Today, enjoying a cocktail or a meal at the **Top of the Mark** (tel: 415-392-3434), the Art Deco-style restaurant in the sky, is a romantic, time-honored custom for visitors to the city, whether to savor the view for the first time or to renew an acquaintance from a previous trip.

The **Renaissance Stanford Court Hotel ❸** (905 California Street, tel: 415-989-3500) is also a beautiful testament to San Francisco's history. The illuminated glass-domed ceiling and extensive marbling are features of the lobby, and many of the rooms offer stunning vistas of the city.

Even more opulent is the elegant **Fairmont Hotel ❹** (950 Mason Street, tel: 415-772-5000) with its gilded lobby and faux-marble pillars. It, too, was built on the ashes of a great mansion, and retains an aura of original splendor. The Fairmont is the perfect place for afternoon tea – hats and gloves optional.

The Mark Hopkins, the Stanford Court and the Fairmont hotels are, for many people, the essence of San Francisco glamour.

Map on page 124

The Top of the Mark, with its near-360° view, has 100 martinis on the menu and jazz most evenings. A dress code is in effect from 8pm.

BELOW: the Top of the Mark, in the Mark Hopkins Hotel.

TIP

The Nob Hill Spa may be the most luxurious day spa, but the city has an entire menu of healing and beauty arts on tap, from walk-in yoga classes to nail salons. One of the most exotic spas is lavender-scented Kabuki Springs in Japantown, with candlelit baths perfect for tired tourists. Tel: 415-922-6000.

BELOW: the doors and windows of Grace Cathedral are worth studying closely.

Snob Hill

San Francisco lore has it that the contraction of the word *nabob* – meaning Moghul prince – gave rise to the name Nob Hill. Given the concentration of wealth to be found here, and the exclusiveness that such riches have been known to inspire, Nob Hill soon earned itself another nickname from the less affluent of the city's denizens: "Snob" Hill.

But the nabobs of the late 19th century no longer wield unlimited power in the neighborhood, and while the Pacific Union Club may not be opening its doors to the masses, the general public can be seen everywhere. And there is much to see.

Even at the height of their influence, the nabobs were – just occasionally – kept in check. Charles Crocker, the only one of the Big Four not to have a luxury hotel named for him today, owned a sprawling mansion that occupied most of the street on California between Taylor and Jones streets.

Crocker's desire to own the entire block was thwarted by a Chinese undertaker named Nicholas Yung who declined to sell his corner lot to Crocker for a generous, even exorbitant price. Infuriated, Crocker proceeded to erect a 40-ft (12-meter) "spite fence" around three sides of the property. An outraged mob marched onto Nob Hill in protest, demanding that the fence be torn down and that Charles Crocker be lynched.

Neither event happened in the end: Yung never did surrender his property and, when Crocker's mansion was destroyed in the 1906 earthquake, the site was taken over by the Episcopal Diocese. Today Crocker's property is the site of Grace Cathedral.

The **Pacific Union Club** ❺ (1000 California Street), directly opposite the Fairmont Hotel, is one of the few surviving buildings from the 1906 earthquake and fire. Constructed for silver magnate James Flood in 1855, the sturdy brownstone structure, with its pine-framed entrance, is now a private club, and can only be admired from the outside.

Last word in luxury

More welcoming is the 12-story **Huntington Hotel** ❻ (1075 California Street, tel: 415-474-5400), refreshingly not owned by a hotel mega-chain, which began life in the 1920s as the 140-room Huntington Apartments, and was described at the time by San Francisco's *Illustrated Daily Herald* as the last word in luxury. After World War II, when the building was converted into a hotel, the enormous rooms were retained and subsequently embellished with fine antiques, imported silks and original artwork.

Most of the suites today are individually decorated, and some have kitchens. The Huntington's Big 4 restaurant celebrates Messrs Crocker, Hopkins, Huntington and Stanford and evokes the robber baron era with its woody, masculine interior, while it's easy to feel like one of the hill's pampered residents in the Hunting-

ton's **Nob Hill Spa** (tel: 415-345-2888). The spa's indoor jacuzzi and infinity pool have one of the most spectacular views in the city.

During the Christmas season, the Nob Hill hotels host free choral concerts in their festively decorated lobbies. And, of course, as in bygone days, the *nabobs* still descend from the heights to patronize the opera.

The late columnist Herb Caen's description of a particular opening night at the Civic Center's Opera House highlighted the persistent and still-present gap between the city's haves and have-nots. "All the well-worn contradictions of capitalism were very much in evidence," Caen observed. "Limos purring, ladies preening, guys groaning, beggars supplicating from their positions on the icy sidewalks… [but] the really rich carry no cash."

State of grace

Huntington Park ❼ is one of the best maintained and most pleasant public spaces in the city. The park sits across Taylor Street from stately **Grace Cathedral ❽** at the top of

Nob Hill. The cathedral, started in 1928 but not consecrated until 1964, is unremarkable in its overall architecture, but the doors and windows are worth a closer look. The doors are cast from Lorenzo Ghiberti's original *Doors of Paradise* in Florence, while the Rose Window was inspired by the blue glass of Chartres Cathedral. Other windows in the cathedral depict modern heroes like Albert Einstein and astronaut John Glenn.

Located diagonally from Huntington Park at Taylor and California streets is the **Masonic Auditorium ❾** (tel: 415-776-4702 for a schedule of concerts and events), a multifunctional performance and event space with perhaps the city's best acoustics outside the Symphony Hall or the Opera House.

With performances ranging from Van Morrison to comedian George Carlin, to a slew of dates for the San Francisco Jazz Festival, the auditorium is a wonderful, comfortable sit-down venue. The lobby has a two-story mosaic laced with Masonic imagery, but no secret handshakes are needed for admittance. ❑

Afternoon tea in a Nob Hill hotel is a leisurely and sophisticated affair.

Restaurants

Big 4 Restaurant
1075 California St. Tel: 415-771-1140. Open: B, Br, L, D. $$$
The Big 4 is a manly place, named after the four "robber baron" railroad tycoons whose photos and memorabilia line the walls. Dark wood paneling adds to the men's-club ambiance and the menu is suitably heavy on meat and game – from filet mignon and rack of lamb to wild boar chops. Eat heartily and enjoy.

Fournou's Ovens
Renaissance Stanford Court Hotel, 905 California St. Tel: 415-989-1910. Open: B, L, D. $$
Enjoy Mediterranean-inspired dishes in the open-kitchen dining area, or have breakfast or lunch in Pavillions, a sun-drenched atrium that looks down the cable-car line.

Laurel Court
Fairmont Hotel, 950 Mason St. Tel: 415-772-5260. Open: B, L, D, no dinner Sun. $$$
After a spectacular restoration in 1999, the

Laurel Court is the centerpiece of the Fairmont's public areas; try the afternoon tea from 2:30–4:30pm daily.

Nob Hill Café
1152 Taylor St. Tel: 415-776-6500. Open: Br, L, D. $$
A small, delightful neighborhood spot that's actually more restaurant than café. Sip wine or espresso at a sidewalk table and enjoy Northern Italian cuisine with an emphasis on pasta and pizza at this classy yet casual family-owned establishment.

Tonga Room
Fairmont Hotel, 950 Mason St. Tel: 415-772-5278. Open: D. $$
Tiki-bar kitsch. Go for expensive rum drinks in coconut-shaped cups, a happy-hour buffet of fried finger food, cover-song singers, and an indoor rainstorm for good measure. Pacific-rim dinners also served.

● ● ● ● ● ● ● ● ● ●
Prices for three-course dinner per person with a half-bottle of house wine: **$$$$** *$85 and up,* **$$$** *$45–85,* **$$** *$20–45,* **$** *under $20*

SAN FRANCISCO'S CABLE CARS

They're much more than a means of transportation and have been designated a National Landmark

Operating three routes – the Mason-Taylor, Powell-Hyde and California lines – San Francisco's cable cars are among the last in the United States, at least 100 cities having abandoned them for buses. Underestimating the draw of this tourist attraction, San Francisco tried to get rid of the cars in 1947, but a vigorous local campaign saved them by a City Charter.

Today, the cable cars take nearly 10 million passengers a year, more than half of them local commuters. It is the visitors, of course, who buy the engraved knives, belt buckles, posters and T-shirts emblazoned with pictures of the beloved cars, or dig into their wallets for genuine cable car bells and walnut music boxes playing Tony Bennett's song *I Left My Heart in San Francisco*.

After a $65 million, 21-month refurbishment took the cars out of service, a citywide party celebrated their return in 1981. Colored balloons bore the message, "They're Back," and customers waited from dawn to be among the first passengers. In their absence, visitors to Fisherman's Wharf fell by 15 percent. Rudyard Kipling visited in 1889 on his way to India, and wrote, "They turn corners almost at right angles, cross over other lines and for aught I know run up the sides of houses." *For cable-car tips and etiquette, see page 134.*

Cable Car Barn & Powerhouse, 1201 Mason Street, tel: 415-474-1887. Apr–Sept 10am–6pm, Oct–Mar 10am–5pm, closed holidays; free.

ABOVE: Cars are pulled by a wire rope running beneath the track's route, passing through the machinery in the Cable Car Barn at Mason and Washington streets, also a working museum *(see below, left)*.

ABOVE: This old photograph from 1890 shows the California Street cable car passing railroad magnate Mark Hopkins' mansion, on the far right of the picture with the tower. The home is now the Mark Hopkins hotel, where a well-dressed doorman *(left)* greets each guest with a smile.

LEFT: "gripmen" who drive the cable cars stay fit on the job. At the beginning and ends of some routes, the cars are still rotated by the manually-operated turntables.

ANDREW SMITH HALLIDIE

The cable car system was created in 1873 by Andrew Hallidie, a British-born engineer with a reputation for building suspension bridges and experience in mining engineering. Seven years before, it's said, he saw a horse slip, causing the chain to break on an overloaded streetcar it had been pulling uphill. Hallidie set about devising a system that would eliminate such accidents. Although Hallidie and his friends put up the $20,000 to get the cable cars operating, he was anticipated in 1870 by Benjamin Brooks, son of a local lawyer, who had been awarded a franchise to operate a similar system, but had failed to raise the necessary financing.

When the Hallidie plan came to fruition, scepticism was the order of the day. "I'd like to see it happen," said realtor L.C. Carlson, "but I don't know who is going to want to ride the dang thing."

Critics of the system abide to this day. Some say that the cars, which are on a fixed track and have no ability to duck potential collisions, are inherently unsafe. Columnist Dick Nolan called the braking system "unimprovable" or "blacksmith shop crudity at its worst." And one family living at Hyde and Chestnut streets initiated an (unsuccessful) law suit against the loud noise, which measures 85 decibels at street level.

BELOW: At the beginning of the 20th century, 600 cars rolled over 115 miles (185 km) of track. But a fleet of electric trolleys powered by overhead wires hastened their demise. Today, the system has only 30 cable cars and a mere 17 miles (25 km) of track.

ABOVE: This 1848 image of a Powell and Mason cable car on the turntable at Powell and Market streets shows how little has changed on these 19th-century rides.

CENTRAL NEIGHBORHOODS

The Marina hugs the waterfront, Pacific Heights scales
the hills. Japantown has parades and a peace pagoda
while Hayes Valley has chic shopping

In 1860, **Fort Mason** became one of the earliest residential districts in San Francisco. The US Army took over the area at the start of the Civil War, retaining it throughout World War II, when the fort served as an embarkation point for more than a million soldiers. Decommissioned in the 1970s, this seafront area is now one of the city's premier art centers, where every day of the month there is a program of shows, lectures, meetings, readings and other events.

Art for everyone

The **Fort Mason Center** is home to a number of museums and galleries. The **Museo ItaloAmericano** (tel: 415-673-2200; open Wed–Sun; charge), is the only museum in the United States devoted exclusively to the art and culture of Italy and Italian-Americans.

Two museums that will soon move to SoMa *(see page 120)* are the **Museum of Craft and Folk Art** (tel: 415-775-0991; open Wed–Sun; charge), a collection of inventive cultural exhibits, from utilitarian objects to fine art; and the **Mexican Museum** (tel: 415-202-9700; open Wed–Sun; charge), which celebrates the soul of Mexican art and Latino culture with a collection of more than 12,000 objects representing

thousands of years of Mexican history. The **SFMoMA Artists Gallery** (tel: 415-441-4777; open Tues–Sat; free) is a lofty, light-filled space and home to an innovative program that offers rentals of artwork (sculpture, paintings, photography, mixed media, etc.) with an option to buy. The scheme is to allow art aficionados the opportunity to experience art in their own environments. The gallery also stages 11 annual, well-attended exhibitions that showcase Californian artists.

Map on page 132

LEFT:
Pacific Heights.
BELOW:
enjoying a cappuccino
on a chilly day.

TIP

A four-block zone of the *über*-cool Marina District is now immersed in free Wi-Fi. The wireless zone covers Chestnut Street between Fillmore and Scott streets.

The **Magic Theatre** (tel: 415-441-8001, box office tel: 415-441-8822), a long-time resident of Fort Mason, has earned recognition and prominence as one of the few theaters in the US dedicated solely to developing and producing new plays. The roster of playwrights who have debuted their work here includes Sam Shepard, David Mamet, Michael McClure, Nilo Cruz and Rebecca Gilman.

The Fort Mason Center also houses numerous offices for non-profit arts and environmental organizations, in addition to **Greens** (tel: 415-771-6222, *see page 139 and 173*), a waterfront eatery with a fantastic view and delicious vegetarian food. A favorite walk in a city of walkers is the pathway that joins Fort Mason to Aquatic Park, which abuts Fisherman's Wharf.

Heading in the opposite direction is another waterside walk, one that winds all the way to the Presidio.

The Marina District

The waterfront **Marina District** ❷, popular with young urban dwellers, encompasses the area all the way west over to the edge of the Presidio, and passes the grassy space known as **Marina Green**, where people gather on the Fourth of July to watch fireworks, and kite-flyers and joggers gather year-round.

Meander to the end of the jetty near the Golden Gate Yacht Club to inspect the unique **Wave Organ**, where the unearthly "music" is the product of waves gurgling through an undersea sculpture consisting of 25 pipes jutting into the ocean. As waves crash against them, each pipe produces a diffferent sound.

Continue walking the Golden Gate Promenade for an invigorating route that skirts the Presidio and leads along **Crissy Field** – a shoreline park popular with picnickers, sunbathers and nature lovers – to the famous bridge (*see page 161*). For a

BELOW:
privacy in a city corner.

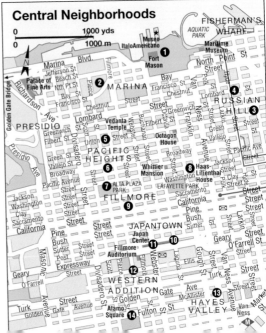

Map on page 132

different, more residential, flavor of San Franciscan charm, the city's inland neighborhoods are also nearby for exploration.

Russian Hill

The first neighborhood is **Russian Hill ❸**, southeast of Fort Mason and serviced by the Powell-Hyde cable car line. Russian Hill is known for magnificent views, stately homes, hidden bistros and a labyrinth of secret streets, stairways and alleys like Macondray Lane, which connects Taylor and Jones streets. Macondray Lane was the inspiration for Barbary Lane, the setting of much of the action in Armistead Maupin's *Tales of the City* books and TV series.

Russian Hill is also home to **Lombard Street ❹**, known as "the crookedest street in the world." Between Hyde and Leavenworth streets, this one-block stretch of Lombard takes cars on eight hairpin turns along a cobblestone roadway. As if lining up for some urban rollercoaster ride, tourists drive up to the top on sunny afternoons and

wait their turn to traverse this unique slalom course. Although stories vary, one theory for the curves is that they were carved in the 1920s in order to allow horses to negotiate the hill. To each side are beautifully landscaped homes, tucked precariously into the slopes of Russian Hill. Anyone on foot might have an easier time strolling down Lombard's less famous footpath, admiring the architecture, the views and the gardens along the way.

The **San Francisco Art Institute** (800 Chestnut Street, tel: 415-771-7020), located in a gorgeous 1920s Spanish Revival building, was responsible for the education of American talents like Annie Leibovitz, Mark Rothko, Ansel Adams and Dorothea Lange. It's worth stopping in to see the Diego Rivera murals, and to admire the view of the bay from the courtyard adjacent to the school's café.

Union Street

Four streets south of Lombard is the **Union Street ❺** area, the first neighborhood in the city to convert

San Francisco was named the No 1 city for running in a recent Runner's World *survey.*

BELOW:
Lombard is "the crookedest street in the world."

The Haas-Lilienthal House in Pacific Heights is open to the public for tours.

BELOW:
the Vedanta Temple
was built in 1905.

many of its gingerbread Victorian houses into boutiques, art galleries and restaurants. Appreciating Union Street's charm is a delightful way to spend an afternoon, but be sure to take plenty of money along – the coffee shops and stores are pretty upscale. Lovely mansions are a feature of this area, although many are not open to the public. Be sure to note an eight-sided oddity, the **Octagon House** (2645 Gough, tel: 415-441-7512; free) built in 1861. Furnished with Colonial and Federal period antiques, the house is open to the public about three times a month; call for details.

Turning left on Green Street leads to the **Vedanta Temple** (2963 Webster, tel: 415-922-2323). This building is a tribute to religious tolerance – an analgam of architectural styles meant to convey that all religions stem from common roots – and the effect is spectacular. Joined in architectural harmony are Queen Anne turrets, Moorish arches, medieval turrets, parapets and a Russian onion dome. At 2727 Pierce is the **Casebolt House**. This massive Italianate

edifice dates from 1865 – near the end of California's silver era – and forms a link with the days when San Francisco was a young city with a glittering future.

Pacific Heights

Southwest of Russian Hill is the neighborhood of **Pacific Heights ❻** which, for the most part, escaped the 1906 earthquake and fire. An address here still denotes position and power. **Alta Plaza Park ❼** is a good starting point for an architectural stroll, for the view is magnificent: to the south, Twin Peaks, Buena Vista and Potrero Hill are visible in one commanding sweep while, in the other direction, turning toward the bay, the ships appear dwarfed by the unfolding panorama below. Most of the houses here are not open to the public.

At 2600 Jackson, across the street from the park, is the **Smith House**, a Jacobean-style brick structure built by shipyard tycoon Irving Murray in 1895 for his daughter. That the house is built of brick is noteworthy: not indigenous to this part of Cali-

Cable Car Tips

Russian Hill, known for its magnificent views, is just one of the neighborhoods serviced by the city's famous cable cars. To enjoy the best from these mobile historic landmarks, here are a few tips.

The Powell and Market Street turnaround is both the most popular and the worst place to board. As the point of origin for more than one line, waiting to get on can take a long time, especially in the tourist season. The area is also the haunt of panhandlers and scam-artists who see out-of-towners as good targets. It's a much better idea to board at the other end of the line, or at one of the less frequented stops along the route. Riding the cars at night is a very romantic experience. Few people realize they run as late as 10pm, when the nocturnal view is superb and the cars are uncrowded.

• Never attempt to board a moving cable car, and be ready to squash in tight. Hold packages on your lap.

• Do not hang off the sides; this is extremely dangerous.

• Never refer to cable cars as "trolleys" unless you are ready to be corrected by a local.

Map on page 132

fornia, bricks had to be brought in, making it a rare and costly material. The mansion was also the first fully electrified house in the city. Down the street at 2622 Jackson is the **Gibbs House**. This copy of a Roman villa, built in 1894, was the first commissioned work of the celebrated designer Willis Polk, who was later honored for his contributions to the city by having a street named after him. Don't miss the bas-reliefs of the muses that decorate the entrance.

At 2421 and 2415 Pierce Street is the **James Irvine Home**, designed by Edgar Matthews. Notice the windows with their graceful pane designs. Inside, the house is beautifully executed – a piece of architectural trickery makes the building seem to be much larger than it is by reducing the inner scales of the house. In fact, much of San Francisco was built in this manner, to overcome spatial restrictions.

To the left along Pacific is the **Monteagle House**, designed by Lewis Hobart, the architect of Grace Cathedral. It is French-Gothic in style, and was built in 1923. The oldest house in Pacific Heights is the **Leale House**, at No. 2475. It was built in 1860 as a farmhouse, part of a 25-acre (10-hectare) dairy farm. In time, it became the home of a retired sea captain who wrote a book called *Tule Sailor*.

On the corner of Pacific and Webster is a gorgeous view of the bay, one that includes Alcatraz and Angel islands. At 2550 Webster is the **Bourn Mansion**. This was the townhouse and office of the richest man in San Francisco during the 1920s and 1930s. William B. Bourn was president of the Spring Valley Water Company and inherited one of California's mines.

Heart of the Heights

The two blocks of Broadway and Webster are the heart of Pacific Heights. When the cable car lines were being laid, they covered the whole of the city, but didn't run down Broadway. It was believed that the residents of this area were wealthy and resourceful enough to provide their own transportation.

TIP

Most mansions in Pacific Heights are privately owned; nevertheless, enjoying the architecture from outside, and the views of the bay, is a pleasant way to spend an afternoon.

BELOW: Pacific Heights living.

At 2120 Broadway is the **Flood Mansion**, a "palace," as it was called then, commissioned by Comstock mine owner James Flood. It is a magnificent neoclassical Revival building, its interior rich with red lacquer, bamboo, a maple library, a walnut and mahogany staircase and Tiffany skylights. After the earthquake, Mrs Flood expressed fears about the largely wooden-built house. Her husband told her not to fret, because "I'll build you a marble house on a granite hill."

There is no granite in San Francisco, let alone a granite hill. So Mr Flood had a granite slab brought in from outside the city, on which he built the house at **2222 Broadway**. This is a copy of a three-story Italian Renaissance villa and was completed in 1912, six years after Mrs Flood expressed her fears. The building now contains offices.

After continuing down Broadway for two blocks to Laguna, turn left on Jackson. At 2090 Jackson is the **Whittier Mansion**, commissioned in 1894 and completed in 1896. From the outside, the house presents an odd conglomerate of styles, but the Roman temple entranceway abuts the Queen Anne tower with a harmony that attests to the skill of the architect, Edward Swain.

Architecture and romance

At Jackson and Octavia Street, the back of the **Spreckels Mansion** can just be seen. This is one of San Francisco's most elegant mansions, originally commissioned by the wealthy sugar magnate Adolph Spreckels. The gate on the Jackson Street side is the old delivery entrance, and behind the window in the wall was where the gatekeeper lived. The low-rise building behind the mansion houses a covered pool. The Spreckels Mansion is the current residence of romance novelist Danielle Steele.

At 1925 Jackson is the massive, baroque **Grenlee Terrace** apartment building. The **Haas-Lilienthal House 8** at 2007 Franklin Street is straight ahead and to the right. This huge, furnished Victorian house, built in 1886 in Queen Anne style, is one of the few homes in Pacific

In the mid 1960s, the Fillmore Auditorium was arguably the most famous club in the States. Promoter Bill Graham not only showcased local bands, he also booked the best of the rest, like the Doors and Jimi Hendrix. The club still packs in the crowds.

BELOW: the Fillmore promoted the careers of Jefferson Airplane and the Grateful Dead.

Heights that is open to the public (tel: 415-441-3004; one-hour docent tours Wed, Sat and Sun; charge). If, after all this, your feet are tired from climbing, you can turn back here to rest in **Lafayette Park**, drinking in the crisp scent of eucalyptus trees and watch ships sail by on the bay.

The Fillmore District

Fillmore Street cuts across Union Street through the **Fillmore District** ❾, which came to fame in the mid-1960s with the rock concerts staged at the **Fillmore Auditorium** (tel: 415-346-6000; www.thefillmore.com). It was from here that promoter Bill Graham helped launch the careers of Jefferson Airplane, Janis Joplin and the Grateful Dead.

Today, the area is also known for an art-house movie theater, good restaurants, and stores selling both new and vintage clothes. Smaller than the Fillmore, but jumping most nights, the **Boom Boom Room** at 1601 Fillmore Street, tel: 415-673-8000, has live blues, boogie, soul and funk, in addition to dance grooves from DJs most nights.

Japantown

Adjacent to the Fillmore District between Octavia and Fillmore streets is **Japantown** ❿, known to locals as J-Town and home to many of the 12,000 Japanese San Franciscans. The neighborhood is dominated by the **Japan Center** ⓫, an enormous complex of stores, theaters, sushi bars and restaurants. Its distinguishing feature is a **Peace Pagoda** 100 ft (30 meters) high, with five tiers (odd numbers bring good luck) donated by Japan. The Webster Bridge midway in the Japan Center evokes the Ponte Vecchio in Florence.

At 1625 Post Street is the 14-story Miyako Hotel (tel: 415-9223200), offering accommodations in both Eastern and Western style. On Bush Street is the **Konko Kyo Temple**. Founded as a religion in 1859, Konko-Kyo (faith) developed as a sect of Shintoism, a form of ancestral worship in Japan. The interior of the church is beautiful.

At the intersection on the north side of Sutter is **Super Koyama Market**. Specializing in fresh, prepared fish, it sells *sashimi*, *gobo* and

Map on page 132

Japantown's distinctive Peace Pagoda.

BELOW: marching musicans in Japantown.

Map
on page
132

*Stylish shopping in
Hayes Valley.*

daikon, too. A *torii* gate marks the entrance to **Nihonmachi Mall**, a cobblestoned pedestrian shopping and eating area. The mall, designed by Ruth Asawa, is meant to resemble a small Japanese village. Silk-embroidered kimonos, books on Japanese art, tea ceremony utensils and calligraphy scrolls are just some of the treats on sale.

Just south of Japantown is the **Western Addition** ⓬, where the **African Orthodox Church of St John Coltrane** at 930 Gough Street, (tel: 415-673-3572) may well be the only church in the world dedicated to a jazz musician. Coltrane had no connection with the church, and was not canonized so far as we know, but he certainly knew how music could enrich the spirit.

After rising rents forced the church out of the Divisadero storefront it had occupied for 30 years, the congregation found temporary premises at Gough Street, and draws a mixed crowd of Christians, novelty seekers and jazz lovers on Sunday mornings. The service may be long and untraditional, but the sentiments expressed are heartfelt, and deserve to be treated with respect. The Western Addition is an area where you should stay alert while walking around.

Hayes Valley ⓭ has undergone gentrification and transformation during the past decade. Bordering the Western Addition and Civic Center, today you'll find swanky boutiques and shoe stores, hip restaurants, cafés and artsy design stores, where prostitutes and drug dealers once worked. The changes coincided with the removal of a freeway on-ramp that sustained damage during the 1989 earthquake.

Alamo Square

Although San Francisco contains scores of Victorian houses, those most popular on postcards are the ones beside **Alamo Square** ⓮, which is bordered by Fulton and Hayes streets at Scott. It's a pleasant little hillside park (but be careful after dark), with a view not only of the brightly-colored homes and Downtown's skyscrapers, but also within sight of the Civic Center. ❏

RESTAURANTS & BARS

Restaurants

Amici's
2033 Union St. Tel: 415-885-4500. Open: L, D. **$**
With exceptional New York style pizza baked in brick ovens, Amici's is a must for thin-crust lovers. Kid-friendly.

Betelnut
2030 Union St. Tel: 415-929-8855. Open: L, D. Closed Mon. **$$**
A pan-Asian bar specializing in dumpings and noodle bowls with bold, exciting flavors.

Elite Café
2049 Fillmore St. Tel: 415-346-8668. Open: Br, L, D. **$$**
This tried-and-true locals' fave serves Cajun and Creole inspired seafood dishes in a cheery atmosphere. An excellent raw bar beckons and the Cajun brunch, with perfectly seasoned Bloody Marys, is worth getting up for.

Greens
Fort Mason, Building A (Buchanan St at Marina Blvd). Tel: 415-771-6222. Open: Br, L, D. **$$$**
Organic produce, seasonal specials and a mesquite grill are the cornerstones of this vegetarian cuisine. Add to this one of the most spectacular views of the Golden Gate Bridge and Marina, and Greens becomes memorable.

Mifune
1737 Post St (Japan Center). Tel: 415-922-0337. Open: L, D. **$**
Noodles of every type here, from *ramen* to *soba* to *udon* are served both hot or cold and in many variations. A good options for veggies and carnivores alike.

Powell's Place
1521 Eddy St (Fillmore Center). Tel: 415-409-1388. Open: Br, L, D. **$**
Soul food that sticks to your ribs. Opened by gospel singer Emmit Powell, the award-winning fried chicken, smothered pork chops and sweet-potato pie are served in generous and inexpensive portions.

Rasselas
1534 Fillmore St. Tel: 415-346-8696. Open: Br, L, D. **$$**
A simple but exciting Ethiopian menu entices diners to this jazz supper club. First timers might like to try the dinner sampler for variety.

Seoul Garden
22 Peace Plaza (at Laguna). Tel: 415-563-7664. Open: L, D. **$$**
Savory meats cooked right at your table, with successful but unobtrusive flair. The meat is tender and succulent, but the spiciness is up to you. Never tried Korean? This is the place to start.

Suppenkuche
601 Hayes St. Tel: 415-252-9289. Open: Br, L, D **$**
One of the few German restaurants in the city, updated German classics – *spaetzle*, shnitzel, potato pancakes and wonderful, hearty soups – are served to diners sitting family style on long spartan benches. Around 20 beers (mostly German) on tap.

Zarzuela
2000 Hyde S. Tel: 415-346-0800. Open: D. **$$$**
A sophisticated Spanish restaurant on the top of Russian Hill along the cable car route. This is a great place to drink sangria and share tapas or steaming plates of flavorful paella with a group of hungry friends.

Bars

Bus Stop
1901 Union St. Tel: 415-567-6905.
A slightly dingy sports bar, but good for catching a game on TV or a happy hour beer.

Matrix Fillmore
3138 Fillmore St. Tel: 415-563-4180.
The Matrix has a rock 'n' roll history; it was opened by Marty Balin of Jefferson Airplane in 1965.

PRICE CATEGORIES

Prices for three-course dinner per person with a half-bottle of house wine:
$ = under $20
$$ = $20–45
$$$ = $45–85
$$$$ = more than $85

RIGHT: vivacious baker in Hayes Valley.

Haight-Ashbury is for following the hippie tr
but also for post-millennium modernis
in search of cutting-edge boutique
Golden Gate Park is for everyone

For many people, a visit to San Francisco wouldn't be complete without some time spent around **Haight-Ashbury ❶**. For several hot months in the first summer of love, 1967, life became a costume party in a wonderland setting of brightly painted Victorian buildings. The neighborhood was a swirl of colors as flower children painted storefronts, sidewalks, posters, cars, vans and, of course, themselves. The days and nights were filled with sex, drugs and a pot-laced breeze, with music provided by Janis Joplin, Jefferson Airplane and the Grateful Dead – all of whom lived in Haight-Ashbury pads.

Upper and Lower Haight

Things change, of course. Today there are more homeless on the streets than hippies, and the color scheme on some Victorians has been toned down. Bus-riding tourists snatch up Summer of Love T-shirts. Nevertheless, upscale boutiques in the Upper Haight also draw shoppers to avant-garde fashions found nowhere else in the city.

Haight-Ashbury is really two parts: Upper Haight, bright, shiny and closest to Golden Gate Park, and Lower Haight *(see page 147)*, seedier, funkier and to some people more exciting. The Upper Haight has the hippie legacy; the Lower Haight is more hip-hop than hippie.

Upper Haight is a good shopping destination, with great boutiques and secondhand shops. Some of the best vintage stores are Aardvark's Odd Ark (1501 Haight Street, tel: 415-621-3141), Buffalo Exchange (1555 Haight Street, tel: 415-431-7733) and La Rosa Vintage (1711 Haight Street tel: 415-668-3744). The people at Kweejibo (1612 Haight Street, tel: 415-552-3555) design and make their own men's shirts, with *über-*

Map on pages 158–59

LEFT: hanging out in the Haight.
BELOW: vivid Victorian.

hip mini versions for kids. Wasteland (1660 Haight Street, tel: 415-863-3150) is the biggest and most extensive clothing store, featuring new and used clothes for all genders and gender-benders.

There are also heaps of shoe stores, T-shirt shops, and one of the city's best children's stores, Kids Only (1608 Haight Street, tel: 415-552-5445),with a killer selection of kid-size rock 'n' roll apparel.

At the end of the street is San Francisco's Taj Mahal of record stores, Amoeba Music (1855 Haight Street, tel: 415-831-1200). Housed in a former bowling alley, Amoeba has a huge selection of new and used CDs and vinyl, in addition to vintage and modern music posters. If you're a music fan, expect to spend at least an hour here, maybe more, and be sure to bring a credit card. Prices are great at Amoeba, but you might have trouble keeping the volume down.

Then and now

Haight-Ashbury's 1960s Psychedelic Shop, which hawked concert tickets and rolling papers, is now a pizza parlor. Diggers, a street theater commune, is an organic food café. And at the center of what was once the hippie universe – the corner of Haight and Ashbury streets, where Joplin, the Airplane and the Dead performed – a clothes store and a Ben & Jerry's ice-cream parlor are the primary attractions, aside from the nonstop sideshow of street people, of course.

Not everything has changed. There is still an ample representation of head shops, where a variety of drug paraphernalia can be bought, and the Haight continues to offer in abundance the tolerance that it proposed in 1967. The denizens of the post-millennium years owe something to the 1960s mind-expansion movement – in addition to a hippie culture all its own, the Haight

For reservations call:
Baseball: 831-5510
Bowling: 753-9298
Boating: 752-0347
Fly casting: 386-2630
Football: 831-5510

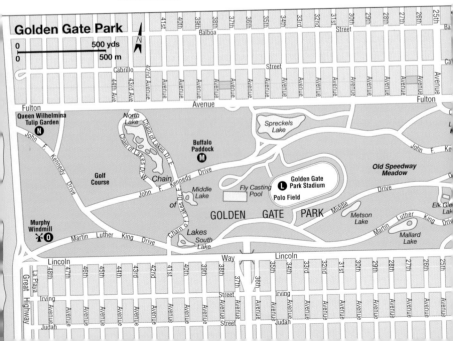

became in its time a haven for new ideas in alternative medicine, ecological preservation, conceptual art and natural foods.

To relive all this, walking tours of around two hours' duration are offered by Flower-Power Haight-Ashbury (tel: 415-863-1621) with tours departing at 9.30 am Tuesday and Saturday. To continue the hippie trail on your own, follow Haight Street west, where it runs into that famous playground of the 1960s: Golden Gate Park.

Golden Gate Park

Adjoining Haight-Ashbury and leading all the way to the Pacific Ocean, **Golden Gate Park** is eight blocks wide and 52 blocks long, covering an enormous 1,040 acres (420 hectares). This outdoor playland of wind-swept dunes was the project of the park's designer, William Hammond Hall. His dream was to create a public space using natural topography instead of imposing artificial forms. With a combination of deep-rooting sea grasses, lupine and trees, he began the arduous task of creating a park by tacking down the sand dunes in the eastern park.

Credit for his effort, however, eluded Hall, mostly because his work was overshadowed by his successor, the canny Scotsman "Uncle John" McLaren. From the little house at the park's eastern edge, **John McLaren Lodge** (501 Stanyan Street), the short, gruff Scot managed his outdoor empire with diligence and endurance. Off Kennedy Drive in the Rhododendron Dell is a lifesize **statue of McLaren**, who detested the monuments that the city fathers insisted on placing. Not by accident, many of the statues in Golden Gate Park are virtually hidden by foliage.

The park, although big enough to offer ample opportunity for seclusion, is a busy place: a popular way

Maps:
Park 142
City 158

For reservations call:
Golf: 751-8987
Horses: 668-7360
Picnics: 831-5500
Soccer: 831-5510
Tennis: 753-7001

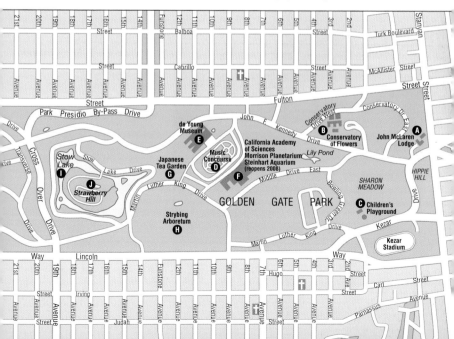

Dance mask from the de Young Museum.

BELOW: gallery in the newly rebuilt de Young Museum.

to experience the diversity it offers is to cover the terrain on a mountain bike. Start at the Panhandle (a narrow strip of parkland at the park's eastern edge bounded by Fell and Oak streets) and end at the ocean a few miles westward. Bicycle and in-line skate rentals are available along the park's periphery – and also at the ocean, if you want to start from the other direction and end up back in the Haight. The following is a short tour of the park, starting from the east and ending in the west.

Conservatory Drive's most famous attraction is, of course, the **Conservatory of Flowers** Ⓑ (tel: 415-666-7001; open Tues–Sun 9am–4.30pm; charge.) An extensive renovation program has repaired the damage done in a 1995 winter storm that blew away 40 percent of its glass tiles. This glass "palace" is believed to have been modeled after a conservatory in London's Kew Gardens, and was the property of a San Jose businessman. It opened to the public in Golden Gate Park in 1879. Housing wonderful collections of rare palms and other tropi-

cal flora, the atmosphere inside is one of color unleashed and an energetic, vibrant mood pervades.

A seasonal flower bed in front is a natural announcement to its entrance, and the grounds around the conservatory have fine collections of fuchsias and azaleas.

Oldest playground

Head west along Conservatory Drive to John F. Kennedy Drive and east to Kezar Drive, which curves by the **Children's Playground** Ⓒ, the oldest playground in a public park in America. Up the hill is a carousel (open daily). Built in 1912, it has richly decorated steeds, a turning tub, rockers and two chariots for aspiring Ben Hurs. The carousel giftshop is open at the same time, so you can buy a picture of your favorite horse to take home.

Hippie Hill, on the north side of the field opposite the Children's Playground, was renowned in the 1960s for its gatherings of long-haired young people playing music and smoking pot. It was here that they brought the idea of Golden Gate Park to the rest of the world, inspiring many in the process.

Take MLK Jr Drive at the southwest corner of the playground, head west through the park, then stroll north up to Concourse Drive. Take the second right to the cultural center of Golden Gate Park, where major museums flank the 20,000-seat outdoor **Music Concourse** Ⓓ, a formal area of trees, fountains and benches where musical performances are held in the summer.

The area surrounding the Music Concourse is undergoing massive reconstruction, which started with the demolition of the existing de Young Museum because it was seismically unfit. The new **de Young Museum** Ⓔ, a bold, monolithic structure with a copper skin designed to slowly green into patina,

is in stark contrast to the Mission Revival structure it replaced. The new museum is scheduled to open in late 2005; meanwhile, many of its exhibits are on display at the California Palace of the Legion of Honor *(see page 162)*. The de Young Museum has one of the finest collections of American paintings in the US.

Gardens and fish

On the opposite side of the Music Concourse is the **California Academy of Sciences ⑦**, feauring interactive science exhibits and also housing the **Steinhart Aquarium** and **Morrison Planetarium**. It, too, is closed for reconstruction, and not due to reopen until 2008. The museum and aquarium are temporarily housed in SoMa *(see page 120)*, but the planetarium could not be moved and its stars must remain dark for awhile.

West of the concourse is the **Japanese Tea Garden ⑨** (tel: 415-668-0909; charge), the most visited site in the park. Devised by George Turner Marsh, a successful dealer in Asian art, the garden was originally intended to represent a Japanese village. Marsh hired a renowned Japanese gardener, Makoto Hagiwara, who planted traditional dwarf bonsai conifers, elms and cherry trees. Hagiwara (whose family is said to have invented the fortune cookie – a claim hotly disputed in Chinatown) also designed the winding brooks with their moss-covered rocks, irises and carp pond. A large bronze Buddha cast in Japan in the 1790s overlooks the garden.

The **Tea House** offers rice cookies and green tea on its menu, while a wishing bridge, a wooden gateway and a five-story pagoda add to the garden's Japanese aura.

Heading south, on the other side of MLK Jr Drive, is the **Strybing Arboretum ⑪** (tel: 415-661-1316; weekdays until 4:30pm, weekends until 5pm; charge), with over 70 acres (28 hectares) of gardens, fountains, a bookstore and a library. The Strybing is really a park within a park. There is a Garden of Fragrance dedicated to the visually impaired, a Succulent Garden and a Conifer

Most of Golden Gate Park was originally covered in sand dunes, but by 1879 the park's designer William Hammond Hall and his assisant John McLaren had organized the planting of more than 155,000 trees.

BELOW: the Conservatory of Flowers opened to the public in 1879.

Garden. A biblical garden contains plants mentioned in the Old and New Testaments. Visitors can learn planting techniques at the demonstration gardens, or take classes, lectures and "theme walks."

In the vicinity of Strybing is the **San Francisco Botanical Garden** (free, open daily, guided walks at 1.30pm) with 7,500 varieties of plants from all over the world, including some that are no longer found in their native habitats.

Not are away is the lovely, sweet-smelling **Garden of Shakespeare's Flowers**, with "lady-smocks," rosemary and 150 other species mentioned in Shakespeare's writings. The bust of the bard is one of only two copies cast in 1914 by George Bullock. Match the flora and the folio, comparing your guesses with the botanical quotes on the plaques provided by the park.

Strawberry Hill

Exiting the arboretum at MLK Jr Drive, follow the road north, then west until you reach **Stow Lake ❶**, the largest of the park's 11 lakes,

Golden Gate's master gardener, John McLaren – a gruff Scot who ruled with an iron will and refused to retire – made would-be applicants identify and spell the names of 100 plants before offering them a job.

which offers boating, scenic picnicking and hiking. **Strawberry Hill ❷** (459 ft/140 meters), located in the center of the lake, is the highest point in the park. Anyone who climbs its slopes is rewarded with a spectacular view – on a clear day, you can see the Farallon Islands, 26 miles (42 km) out to sea, and Mount Diablo, 30 miles (48 km) inland to the east. Mount Tamalpais or "Mount Tam," can be seen to the north across the Golden Gate Bridge.

In addition to its many lakes, gardens and millions of plants, Golden Gate Park offers sports lovers of every kind a satisfying weekend workout (main park roads are closed to traffic on Sundays to make this easier). There are football, baseball and soccer fields; *bocce*, basketball, tennis and handball courts; and lawn bowling greens.

There are also horseshoe and barbecue pits, marble chess tables, a golf course, a running track, jogging, bike and bridle paths and hiking trails. Dog owners can even train their pets here. Swarms of in-line skaters take over much of the roadways and hold races during the summer, while others keep the lost art of roller disco alive. After-work or weekend games of "ultimate frisbee" are often in progress on the large grass fields. If fishing lures you, head for the charming, old-fashioned Fly Casting Pool.

West of Transverse Drive is **Lloyd Lake ❸**, celebrated for its stately Portals of the Past. These six white marble columns formed the portico of the A.N. Towne home on Nob Hill before the big quake and fire of 1906, and were moved here some time later to lend a dignified air to this part of the park.

As sunset approaches, plan to end your visit to Golden Gate Park out by the ocean. It was this more secluded western end of the park that was the favorite gathering spot for the outdoor-loving hippies – including the Human Be-In during the famous "Summer of Love" in 1967.

At the **Polo Fields** a match might be in progress, fans craning their necks in the stadium, but more likely the space will be occupied by joggers or equestrians from the riding stables nearby.

Heading west on JFK Drive, you'll come to a surprise. On the northern side of the road, evocative of the 18th century, is the **Buffalo Paddock** . The buffalo here trace their lineage not to the Great Plains, but to the Bronx Zoo of New York City, where the species was bred in captivity and saved from extinction around 1900. Admiring visitors often find themselves feeding these serene beasts the bread they brought to feed the birds.

Following JFK Drive to the end, the **Old Speedway Meadow** is a lovely expanse of land at the western edge of the park. North is the **Queen Wilhelmina Tulip Garden**, where the renovated **North Dutch Windmill** and the **Murphy Windmill** in the park's southwest end

loom forlorn in the wind. These windmills once pumped water from the streams that flowed nearby; today they stand tall in the sun as it sets slowly over the ocean. Linger over the sunset awhile, or stroll back through the park to Haight-Ashbury.

Lower Haight

The Lower Haight is completely different to the Upper Haight. Heading east on Haight Street, the two neighborhoods are separated by several residential blocks. From the Upper Haight, the transition is marked by **Buena Vista Park**, a shabbily maintained and steeply sloping urban space with beautiful stone masonry that references its long-gone glory days, but today's park is more likely to highlight a parade of pit bull dogs or beer cans. On the brighter side, it does have spectacular views, including a panorama of the downtown area from the two tennis courts.

Walking the downward slope of Haight Street, some beautiful Victorian architecture can be admired, with more and more being restored all the time. In particular, the block

Maps:
Park 142
City 158

Serenity in the city – the fragrant Japanese Tea Garden.

BELOW:
painting the park.

Map on pages 158–59

For the best in vinyl and CDs, cruise to 1855 Haight Street.

BELOW:
the Dead of the day.

between Divisadero and Scott Street display opulent examples.

East of Scott Street marks the real beginning of Lower Haight, a ragtag huddle of cafés, bars, vinyl record shops, hair salons and medical marijuana dispensaries. Gallery 683 (683 Haight Street, tel: 415-861-1311) is a good bridge between the two neighborhoods. Run by two authentic hippies, the shop specializes in tribal art, drums, masks and genuine 1960s rock 'n' roll posters. It's probably the best place in the Lower Haight to buy unique gifts.

Across the street, Mickey's Monkey (214 Pierce, tel: 415-864-0683) sells vintage decor that you would not be able to find elsewhere, some of it fantastic, some of it fantastically tacky, and all of it inexpensive. To find funky duds for wacky parties, try Costumes on Haight (735 Haight Street, tel: 415-621-1356).

Modern beat

For a more modern beat, step into the headquarters of Future Primitive Sound (597 Haight Street, tel: 415-551-2328), a B-Boy gallery celebrating and selling hip-hop music, urban fashion and street art.

For the DJs in your life, two all-vinyl music shops are Groove Merchant (687 Haight Street, tel: 415-252-5766) for the hippest of the hip, and Rooky Ricardo's (448 Haight Street, tel: 415-864-7526) with LPs and 45s from all genres and generations.

Cafés down here are a far cry from the see-and-be-seen establishments elsewhere, anchored by Café International (528 Haight Street) and The Horse Shoe Café (566 Haight Street). Here you can see people actually reading and writing, not just posing and sipping soy chai lattes on their lunch hours.

If you're in need of more robust libation, beer is the norm in the Lower Haight, and Toronado (547 Haight Street) leads the pack with a menu of brews from all around the world. Mad Dog in the Fog (530 Haight Street) is a semi-British establishment that smells like an authentic pub and broadcasts non-American football games most of the hours it is open. ❑

RESTAURANTS & BARS

Restaurants

All You Knead

1466 Haight St. Tel: 415-552-4550. Open: B, L, D. **$**

From *über*-carnivores to hard core vegans, from families with kids to hipsters still up from the night before, this diner delights. The menu is encyclopedic, prices seem to be stuck in the 1980s, and portions are gigantic. Standouts include tofu peanut sauce scramble and the French onion soup.

Canvas Café

1200 9th Ave. Tel: 504-0060. Open: Br, L, D. **$**

This is café culture evolved. Cheap and tasty food, beer and wine, live music and spoken word performances, and tons of great art that you might actually imagine hanging in your home. Off Golden Gate Park, it's perfect for lunch.

Cha Cha Cha

1801 Haight St. Tel: 415-386-5758. Open: L, D. **$$**

Smack dab in the middle of Haight-Ashbury, Cha Cha Cha is a fun place for tapas, Caribbean-inspired entrees and sangria. The crowd is young, hip and noisy.

Chow

1238 9th Ave. Tel: 415-665-9912. Open: Br, L, D. **$$**

Eclectic, casual dining after a day in Golden Gate Park. Excellent salads (try the Cobb)

and mouthwatering flat-iron steaks. Gets busy with the college crowd around dinner time.

Japanese Tea House

Japanese Tea Garden, Golden Gate Park. Tel: 415-752-1171. Closes 6pm. **$**

Enjoy tea in this most serene of spots, inside the beautiful Japanese Tea Gardens of Golden Gate Park.

Kan Zaman

1793 Haight St. Tel: 415-751-9656. Open: D. **$**

Kan Zaman is a perennial favorite with locals. Expect a loud and fun night with belly dancers (Thur–Sat) and hookahs filled with apple-scented treats to smoke at the tables, while sitting on floor cushions and sipping spiced wine.

Naan 'n' Curry

642 Irving St. Tel: 415-664-7225. Open: L, D. **$**

So much flavor for so little cash. The Inner Sunset location is one of several Indian/Pakistani eateries known for its delicious food and low prices. Short on decor but long on spiciness, the chicken vindaloo, tikka masala and tandoori all hit the mark.

Okina Sushi

776 Arguello St. Tel: 415-387-8882. Open: Wed–Sat D. **$$**

No soup, fancy rolls or anything fried at this traditional sushi restaurant, which as been open for

25 years. Okina's secret is generous pieces of fresh fish providing a serene, healthy meal.

Park PJ's Oyster Bed

737 Irving St. Tel: 415-566-7775. Open: L, D. **$$**

A delicious and fun seafood restaurant in the heart of the Inner Sunset neighborhood, where an open kitchen and occasional Mardi-Gras nights keep the place hopping. No gimmicks here – just fresh and flavorful food.

Pork Store Café

1451 Haight St. Tel: 415-864-6981. Open: B, L. **$**

First opened in 1916 as a butcher shop, the Pork Store is now a classic diner, with a good lunch but an epic breakfast. Window seats provide amusing people-watching in the Haight; avoid the crowded weekends.

Rosamunde Sausage Grill

545 Haight St. Tel: 415-437-6851. Open: L, D. **$**

This tiny storefront grill just sells sausages – but what a variety! Wild boar, duck, chicken, smoked lamb – and, of course, spicy vegan sausage.

Bars and Clubs

Hobson's Choice

1601 Haight St. Tel: 415-621-5859.

This corner bar is the Haight's best for people-watching with booze. Sit near the window and sip

the cocktail of the day, probably a sweet concoction that will be ladled into your glass from a fruit-filled barrel.

Martin Mack's

1567 Haight St. Tel: 415-864-0124.

A beloved local pub where Americans, Brits, and Irish all get along until the subject of football arises. It's a good place to stop by for a Guinness on a cool day or a cider on a hot one. Irish chow is served.

Milk

1840 Haight St. Tel: 415-387-MILK.

The Upper Haight's only dance club, with DJs specializing in hip-hop, soul and funk. Many of the nights are free if you arrive before 10pm.

Nicki's BBQ

460 Haight St. Tel: 415-621-6508

A fun and funky DJ dance club in the Lower Haight featuring Grateful Dead Monday, reggae Tuesday, and other music Wednesday–Saturday. Free before 10pm, except on Tuesday.

PRICE CATEGORIES

Prices for three-course dinner per person with a half-bottle of house wine:

$ = under $20
$$ = $20–45
$$$ = $45–85
$$$$ = more than $85

MISSION AND CASTRO

Gays, artists, tourists and Latinos do a salsa mix in
these vibrant neighborhoods. The music
is loud and their residents are proud

he Mission and the Castro districts of San Francisco are both vibrant elements of the city's culture. Their respective Latino and gay communities would seem to have little in common, but a visit to Dolores Park, the geographical meeting point of the two neighborhoods, shows how proximity has bred familiarity: families gather for birthday celebrations alongside gay sunbathers, from whom the park gets its tongue-in-cheek nickname: Castro Beach.

The Mission District

The **Mission** ➋ is San Francisco's Latino neighborhood, and "Latino" is as specific as anyone can get. The demographics of the Mission have changed in tandem with the politics of Latin America, as Central Americans fleeing political turmoil in their own countries joined Mexican immigrants here. In the latter part of the 20th century, due to lower rents and accessibility, artists and musicians moved in, too, earning the Mission the easy-going reputation of being the city's new bohemia.

With a wealth of good, reasonably priced restaurants, trendy cafés and hip nightspots, the face of the neighborhood has gone from one that was predominantly Latino to include an energetic and eclectic mix of people.

The Mission takes its name from

Mission Dolores (3321 16th Street, tel: 415-621-8203; small charge), San Francisco's oldest building and the sixth mission in a chain of Spanish settlements that stretched 650 miles (1,050 km) from San Diego to northern California.

Captain José Moraga and Fray Francisco Palóu founded the mission with a handful of settlers in 1776, just days before the signing of the Declaration of Independence on the opposite side of the country. The church was dedicated to San Francisco de

LEFT: Mission Dolores, founded in 1776, is the city's oldest building.
BELOW: keeping the peace in the Mission.

Dolores Park, between the Mission and the Castro, is one of the sunniest spots in the city, and perfect for sunbathing.

BELOW: Mission accomplished.
RIGHT: pooch in (silk) boots.

Assisi, but became known as Mission Dolores, probably because of the small lagoon on which it was built, Nuestra Senora de los Dolores.

Over the centuries this building's 4-ft (1-meter) thick adobe walls have withstood several natural disasters. The original bells, cast in the 1790s, hang from leather thongs above the vestibule, and most of the original craftwork is intact. Over 5,000 nameless Costanoans are buried in the small cemetery next to the mission, along with several notable figures from San Francisco's early years, including the first governor of Alta California and the first *alcalde* (mayor) of Yerba Buena.

Salsa and savvy people

The neighborhood's main strip is **Mission Street**, lined with discount shops, outlets for inexpensive clothes, pawn brokers, poolrooms, bars, diners and produce stands. This is the place to check out the *cholos* cruising the neighborhood in low riders or to listen to salsa and lively Mexican folk songs blasting from the bars. Four blocks west of Mission Street is

Dolores Street, a palm-lined boulevard bordered by brightly painted homes with bay windows. Just off Dolores on Liberty Street, between 20th and 21st, are some of the city's beautifully restored Victorian houses. Nestled between Dolores and Mission streets is **Valencia Street**, the city's hip epicenter lined with cafés, bars and boutiques.

The Latino community's identification with *la raza* (the race, or the people) is reflected in the many **murals** scattered throughout the neighborhood: painted on bare walls, on buildings, inside or outside restaurants. Of particular note is **Balmy Alley**, which has gained world recognition for its many political murals. It's worth strolling around the area just to see what you can see, or take one of the guided walking tours that can cover 40 murals or more.

The **Galería de la Raza** (2857 24th Street, tel: 415-826-8009; open Wed–Sun) has been hailed as one of the most important Chicano art centers in the country, and presents a series of exhibits featuring both local artists and photographers. Also worth

looking inside is the **Women's Building** (3543 18th Street, tel: 415-431-1180; open weekdays), with its own set of inspiring murals.

Dolores Park, up by the Castro, is a sloping green square fringed at the top with a stately row of Victorian houses. This is one of the sunniest spots in the entire city, with an impressive view of the East Bay.

The Castro District

San Francisco is often referred to as the gay capital of the world, a title its residents wear with pride. The active lesbian and gay community that has made its home in the **Castro ❸** has contributed significantly to every area of San Francisco's culture: economic, artistic and political.

Recent years have brought a calming effect on the once-turbulent community. Angry rhetoric has cooled as activists who once railed against the establishment have become a part of the establishment themselves. There are fewer raucous marches, as there are fewer local injustices for mass anger to be directed at – whatever the situation

in other parts of the world. And yet there are still struggles to overcome: equal rights and/or wedded status for long-term single-sex partners is currently the hottest topic (*see page 51*).

The residents of the Castro are among the most forward-looking in the city. It came as little surprise to anyone who lives or plays here that, in 2005, Castro Street became the second neighborhood to be covered by wireless internet access. Now, up and down the street – in bars, in cafés, indoors and out – anyone with a wireless enabled laptop computer can sit down and connect.

The entrance to all this fun is the Market Street MUNI station (or take the Market Street trolley). Just outside the station in **Harvey Milk Plaza** is a plaque remembering the city's first openly gay politician, who was murdered in 1978 (*see page 51*).

Castro Street, between 17th and 19th streets, is the neighborhood's compact business section, and in these two blocks are plenty of stores, bars and restaurants offering opportunities for an afternoon or two of browsing, imbibing and dining.

Map on pages 158–9

TIP

J-Church: take this streetcar line from anywhere Downtown toward Noe Valley. Sit with your back to the driver and on the right-hand side of the car for incredible views at the top of Dolores Park.

BELOW: the Mission and the Castro host most of the city's best parades.

Map on pages 158-9

The Castro Theater was built in 1922. On special evenings, an organist ascends out of the stage floor.

BELOW: nightclubs and bars feature cabaret and dancing queens.

The **Castro Theater** is a beautiful work of Spanish baroque design. This revival house with great movies sometimes features a live organist who plays on an ascending platform, a nostalgic reminder of childhood movie-going days.

Another stroll, this time down Market Street between Castro Street and Church Street will also give a feel for the vibrancy of the neighborhood.

A recent addition to the Castro is the Charles M. Holmes Campus at The Center, locally known as **The Center** (1800 Market Street, tel: 415-865-5555; open Mon–Sat). Dedicated in 2002, it is located at the edge of Hayes Valley and is closer to the Mission than the Castro, but has become the nexus for community events, classes, support groups and information regarding the local LGBT (Lesbian, Gay, Bisexual, Transgender) community.

Be sure to stop by the 3 Dollar Bill Café for a cup of coffee or to study the recent **Psychiatric Survivors Memorial Skylight**, dedicated to the people who suffered under damaging psychiatric care.

Fairs and festivals

By timing your visit, it's possible to catch one of several special events that are staged throughout the year. The International Lesbian & Gay Film Festival in June, which began in 1977, receives worldwide attention each year for the films that are screened at the Castro Theater, the Yerba Buena Center for the Arts and at other venues around town.

San Francisco Pride, also in June, attracts over half a million participants who answer its call to "Stand Up, Stand Out, Stand Proud." After a series of events, including a tea dance usually held at City Hall, the celebrations culminate in a parade of floats and high-stepping frivolity.

The Castro Street Fair takes place the third week of August, while each Halloween the neighborhood hosts a highly entertaining, night-long spooky parade attended by residents from all over the city. The costumes are fabulous, darling.

Harvey Milk's birthday is celebrated on May 22, while on November 27, a candlelight march is held to commemorate his murder. ❏

RESTAURANTS

Restaurants

Blowfish Sushi To Die For
2170 Bryant St. Tel: 415-285-3848. Open: L, D. **$$$**
An unconventional sushi restaurant catering to a western palate, (you'll find appetizers and rolls made with sirloin, in addition to the standard nigiri selections), Blowfish Sushi has tasty and whimsical sake cocktails served in a swank atmosphere. It's loud, and fun. For *fugu* fans, the restaurant is licensed to serve the Northern Pufferfish.

Bissap Baobab
2323 Mission St. Tel: 415-826-9287. Open: D. **$$**
A funky, international café with a diverse clientele, serving West African fare and refreshing but potent cocktails made from homemade juice. Standout dishes include the spinach pastele pastry, the mafe with tofu in a peanut sauce, and the oniony chicken dibi with couscous.

Café Gratitude
2400 Harrison St. Tel: 415-824-4652. Open: B, L, D. **$**
Vegan, vegetarian and raw food is served here, including soups, salads, pizzas, smoothies and organic coffee made with the finest ingredients. The setting is comfortable and easy-going. Occasional live music and a friendly staff make this off-the-beaten-path gem a perfect spot any time of the day.

Delfina
3621 18th St. Tel: 415-552-4055. Open: D. **$$$**
Ultrafresh, seasonal ingredients are used in the creative Italian fare at this crowded Mission hot spot. Save room for the excellent desserts, and don't share.

Foreign Cinema
2534 Mission St. Tel: 415-648-7600. Open: D. **$$$**
Dinner and a movie gets a new spin at this popular, industrial-chic eatery. Diners can choose to sit inside to enjoy the innovative California cuisine, or better yet, dine on the heated outdoor courtyard where films are screened nightly on a concrete wall in back.

Luna Park
694 Valencia St. Tel: 415-553-8584. Open: L, D. **$$**
You get to make your own s'mores at your table if you order them here for dessert. This hot-spot near 18th Street has a fun, party-like atmosphere, excellent mussels and *pomme frites* in addition to a delectable burger and other well-prepared dishes. Be sure to make a reservation.

Orphan Andy's
3991 17th St. Tel: 415-864-9795. 24hrs. **$**
One of only a handful of 24-hour spots in the city, this tiny diner has fabulous shakes, malteds and tuna melts on rye any time you need them.

Panchita's 3
3115 22nd St. Tel: 415-821-6660. L, D. **$$**
Enjoy this mix of California and Salvadorian semi-fine dining. A great place for small groups or intimate, off-the-beaten path romantic dinners.

We Be Sushi
1071 Valencia St. Tel: 415-826-0607. Open: L, D. **$$**
Some of the finest sushi in the smallest space possible. This tiny spot makes you wait for a table and pay cash, but it's worth it. The bigger and newer version down at 16th and Valencia is just as good, just not as fun, as its predecessor.

The Mission is the place for burritos. Slipping into any tacqueria with its open-grill kitchen and casual atmosphere will yield cheap eats with high-class flavor – one way people in the know save money in the city.

RIGHT: a feast for the palate and the eye.

AROUND SAN FRANCISCO

From bridge to shining bridge: a tour around the city's outer fringes, from the Bay Bridge in the east to the Golden Gate in the west

lthough it is the Golden Gate Bridge that features on all the postcards, San Franciscans are particularly fond of its less glamorous neighbor, the **Bay Bridge** ❹. The Bay Bridge (correct title: San Francisco-Oakland Bay Bridge, although few refer to it as this) is the longest steel high-level bridge in the world, 8¼ miles (13.5 km) in length. Built in 1936 with great difficulty *(see page 30)*, it is actually two different types of bridge – a cantilever bridge on the Oakland side and a suspension bridge on the city side – connected via a tunnel through Yerba Buena Island.

Treasure Island

Sitting just off the Bay Bridge in the middle of the bay is 403-acre (163-hectare) **Treasure Island** ❺. At the new millennium, several hundred San Franciscans, most of them teachers, firefighter, police officers and students, took up residence here, their stay probably limited to ten years – an interim period between the US Navy's departure and the city's plans for development and renewal. The existing **Nimitz House** (which once housed navy top brass) is used as a venue for special events and to accommodate important guests.

Man-made Treasure Island was created in the late 1930s and attached to the middle of the just-completed

bridge, its purpose being to house the Golden Gate International Exposition that brought 17 million visitors in 1939 and 1940. The Expo's central landmark was a 400-ft (122-meter) Tower of the Sun, designed by the acclaimed architect Arthur Brown Jr, who was also responsible for Coit Tower and much of Civic Center.

Now that the navy has moved out, the city has inherited 1,011 housing units formerly occupied by its personnel, two vast hangars, a jail, movie theater and marina, and sports

Map on pages 158–9

LEFT: boat parade in the bay.
BELOW: the Cliff House has new restaurants and great views.

You're never too old to be a Giants fan.

fields, bowling alley and tennis courts. There is also a museum in the horseshoe-shaped **Administration Building** with 20,000 artifacts and displays depicting the history of the navy, marines and coast guards, the history of the Bay Bridge and the China Clipper flying boats.

Bayside developments

In the last few years, far-reaching developments have taken place on the city's eastern waterfront within sight of the Bay Bridge. Along the Embarcadero, south of the Ferry Building, is a wonderful promenade that stretches from the Financial District, underneath the Bay Bridge all the way to SBC Park.

For now (but probably not for long), it's possible to stumble on a couple of throwbacks to the old waterfront days – a few sailors' bars and Red's Java Hut where you can get a cheap burger and a beer along with one of the best views in the city.

The area is a sunny refuge from the rest of the often fog-shrouded city, and it's easy to understand why this is fast becoming a popular spot for new housing developments, high-rises, food stores and restaurants.

South of the Bay Bridge, the neighborhood of **South Beach** ❻ was transformed by the opening of whizzy baseball stadium **SBC Park**, (formerly PacBell Park), the home of the mighty San Francisco Giants. The area is a perfect example of the marriage of old and new San Francisco. Formerly crumbling warehouses now house fine dining establishments, bookstores and chic furniture galleries.

Desolate streets have been transformed into palm-tree lined walkways, and a once barren bay front is now **McCovey Cove** (named after Willie McCovey, a baseball Hall of Fame member and former San Francisco Giant). At McCovey Cove is an historical **baseball walk** that

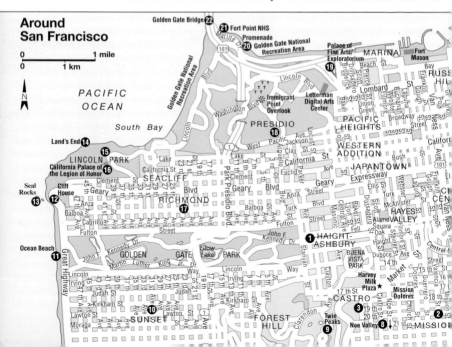

some foreign tourists find useful to educate themselves on the mysteries of this sacred American pastime.

South Park, between 2nd and 3rd and Brannan and Bryant streets, is a small neighborhood that, at the turn of the millennium, was the home of San Francisco's dot-com elite (*Wired* and its web counterpart *HotWired* began here).

Now, after most of these companies have come and gone, or just moved to larger offices elsewhere, South Park is a lovely place to enjoy a meal at one of the cafés lining the park in the middle of the grand circle.

The gentrification of the South Beach area has spread down 3rd Street with the introduction of a new MUNI rail line. Forgotten parts of the city, like **China Basin**, **Dogpatch** and **Hunter's Point**, are now accessible to the city by rail, and with more people and small businesses moving in, the social and cultural landscape continues to evolve.

Potrero Hill

Continuing south, the next destination is **Potrero Hill** ❼, a former working-class neighborhood of colorful houses and utilitarian stores that has been discovered by the new gentry. Not far away is San Francisco's old and beloved sports park. Although it now goes by the name of **Monster Park**, die-hard fans will always call the famous sports arena Candlestick Park. One of the reasons the 1989 mid-afternoon earthquake, which collapsed the Bay Bridge, did not result in more casualties is because most locals were either in Candlestick Park or at home watching baseball's World Series rather than in transit on the bridge itself. Monster Park is where the San Francisco 49ers play football.

South of the **Mission** (*see page 151*) and the **Castro** (*see page 153*) is low-key **Noe Valley** ❽ whose main thoroughfare, 24th Street, is sometimes called "Stroller Alley" due to the number of young mothers

Map on pages 158–59

Tours of SBC Park are available: go to www.sbcpark.com

BELOW: wheel me out to the ball game.

Map on pages 158–59

Follow the 49-Mile Scenic Drive through Golden Gate Park to the Pacific Ocean.

BELOW: jogging past Fort Point; the fort was built during the Civil War.

pushing baby carriages. The street resembles a miniature village with its array of offbeat stores and interesting restaurants. Noe Valley is a pleasant place to stroll around without meeting many other tourists and is evocative of the city's residential neighborhoods, completely different in character from hustling, bustling **Haight-Ashbury** *(see page 141)*.

Twin Peaks

A winding scenic drive leads to the top of **Twin Peaks** ❾, translated into Spanish as El Pecho de la Chola (the Bosom of the Indian Girl). The hills (910 ft /227 meters in height) are dominated by television towers but offer a wonderful panoramic view of the city and surrounding bay *(see photo, page 68)*. Both parking and viewing points can be found along Twin Peaks Boulevard. Well-heeled San Franciscans clamor to live at the top of Twin Peaks. Once they've made their expensive house purchases they discover – come moving day – another price to pay for the view: the streets are too narrow to accommodate removal vans.

A pleasant way to reach the next destination overlooking the Pacific Ocean, is to follow the **49-Mile Scenic Drive** as it meanders down Laguna Honda and 7th Avenue to and through Golden Gate Park. Alternatively, head west on Taraval through the **Sunset District** ❿, home to the **San Francisco Conservatory of Music**, and pick up the Great Highway northwest of **Lake Merced**.

At the far western end of Golden Gate Park is **Ocean Beach** ⓫. Although the beach has dramatic ocean views, only the hardiest souls dip their toes into the ice-cold water. Farther north along the coast is the **Cliff House** ⓬. Once a magnificent building fashioned to resemble a French chateau, after a series of fires, remodeling and owners, the present structure is part of the Golden Gate National Recreation Area. At **Seal Rocks** ⓭, sleek and playful sea lions frolic in full view, while up on the cliff are the **Sutro Baths**. Little remains of the swimming complex built to enchant the city's inhabitants when it opened in 1896, but the views are wonderful.

Golden Gate Bridge

When sailing under the Golden Gate Bridge today, it is interesting to consider that at one time engineers felt that it would be impossible to build a span at this point because of the depth of the water (318 ft/97 meters, at its deepest point), and the powerful tidal rush.

The city authorized studies for a bridge in 1917, but it was 1933 before the first shovelful of earth turned under the gaze of master engineer Joseph B. Strauss (no relation to the famous waltz composer). Four years later it was finally opened, at a cost of $35 million and the lives of 11 construction workers. Today the bridge serves the more than 40 million vehicles a year that drive between the city and regions to the north.

San Franciscans think of the Golden Gate Bridge as their own, of course, but the unwieldy administrative board that runs it consists of 19 members, some from as far away as Mendocino and Humboldt counties, 350 miles (563 km) north.

Without a lengthy detour around the bay, the bridge provides the only direct route to these outlying regions, and that gives a clue to the reason for the association. These two counties, along with the other five with seats on the board (San Francisco, Marin, Sonoma, Del Norte and Napa), helped to pay for the bridge's construction back in the 1930s by buying into the bond issue.

The initial investment has been recouped many times over: Marin and Sonoma counties alone receive at least $27 million a year as their share of bridge tolls. More than 17 million southbound cars cross the bridge each year to head to other parts of California. Nobody counts the northbound cars, because no toll is collected from them; it's one-way toll fees only.

Romantic as the bridge is, some people are more concerned about the hard facts: including its freeway approaches, the Golden Gate Bridge is 1.7 miles (2.7 km) long, with the suspension section stretch-

ing for 6,450 ft (1,966 meters). The towers stand 746 ft (227 meters) above the water. The total length of wire on both main cables is 80,000 miles (129,000 km).

The bridge was built so sturdily that it has closed only three times due to high winds. Crews work continually from one end of the bridge to the other and back, sandblasting rust and repainting the bridge orange – not red, as is often thought – using 10,000 gallons (38,000 liters) of paint a year.

Offering magnificent views and cooling, often frigid breezes, the bridge has always been popular with walkers, more than 200,000 of whom turned out to celebrate its opening in 1937. When it was again closed to motorists in honor of its golden anniversary, four times as many pedestrians turned up – so many fans, in fact, that their combined weight caused the bridge's central span to sink measurably.

Perhaps the best Golden Gate tale will remain in the fog of Hollywood myth, and may never be confirmed. According to legend, Alfred Hitchcock wanted as his final scene in *The Birds* (filmed in nearby Bodega Bay), his heroine driving to safety, toward San Francisco – only to find the Golden Gate Bridge covered in birds. The scene was deemed too scary an ending to release. ❏

RIGHT: the Golden Gate is having a seismic retrofit to strengthen it against earthquake damage.

BELOW: the Palace of Fine Arts dates from 1915. The dome received a massive renovation in 2004.

Land's End

Near the Palace of the Legion of Honor is a path that leads to **Land's End** , the wildest part of San Francisco's coast. Be sure to check the tides before setting off as walkers have been known to become stranded. This part of the Golden Gate National Recreation Area is called **Lincoln Park** , and was designed by John McLaren, the longtime czar of Golden Gate Park.

The **California Palace of the Legion of Honor** (tel: 415-863-3330; open Tues–Sun 9.30am–5pm; charge) opened in 1924 as a memorial to California's war dead. There is a peculiar and moving grandeur to the museum's architecture, with its courtyard and columns and porticoes. Inspired by the Palais de la Légion d'Honneur in Paris, it is also a showcase for European art. One of five original castings of Rodin's *The Thinker* resides in the palace's Court of Honor; almost 70 of his other sculptures are on display in the **Rodin Gallery**, where weekend organ recitals are sometimes held. Included in the museum's collection is El Greco's *St John the Baptist* and Monet's moody *The Grand Canal, Venice*. From the palace are also some of the finest views of the city and the Golden Gate Bridge.

Richmond District

Lincoln Park is part of the interesting **Richmond District** , which has undergone a transition: in recent years it's become a new Chinatown. Located between Golden Gate Park and the Presidio, Richmond was previously little but sand dunes stretching down to the Pacific Ocean. The well-known landscape photographer Ansel Adams used to play here as a boy, and a number of his photographs evoke the area as it looked around the end of the 19th century.

In the 1970s, second- and third-generation Chinese familes began moving here from the crowded downtown Chinatown, to settle next to the Greeks, Russians and Irish who were already in residence. Today, the Richmond area is made up of family dwellings, brick and cement row houses, and low-rise apartment buildings. The main avenue is **Clement Street**, crammed full of restaurants, groceries, clothiers and bookstores.

The **Presidio** , which for more than 200 years housed the military guardians of the region, is one of the most desirable pieces of land in America, commanding the wooded heights overlooking the Pacific Ocean and the approach to the Golden Gate Bridge. So when it was decommissioned in 1993, there were endless discussions as to what was to become of it.

Fortunately, the real estate vultures were kept at bay and the entire complex is now managed by the Golden Gate National Recreation Area, the National Park Service and the controversial Presidio Trust; the trust's aim is to make the Presidio self-sustaining. This involves building business parks and other attrac-

tions that maintain the historic character of the grounds. One of these projects is the massive complex next to the Lombard Street entrance that houses filmmaker George Lucas's **Letterman Digital Arts Center** (not open to the public). Fortunately for San Francisco, Lucas left a view of the Palace of Fine Arts.

Northbound travelers can exit the road before reaching the Golden Gate Bridge and drive around a tranquil, wooded hillside dotted here and there with the now-deserted white clapboard homes that once housed the military personnel.

Palace of Fine Arts

At the Presidio's eastern end is one of the city's most admired buildings, the **Palace of Fine Arts** ⓭, whose domed rotunda and lagoon-reflected arches were designed by Bernard Maybeck for the 1915 Panama-Pacific International Exposition. The structure was modeled after the mysterious edifice in the painting, *The Island of the Dead.*

Housed inside the romantic neo-classical facade is a very modern museum: the **Exploratorium** (tel: 415-563-7337; open Tues–Sun 10am–5pm; charge), subtitled "the museum of science, art and human perception." Hands-on exhibits emphasize perception as the means to explore our relationship to light, color, sound and hearing, touch and heat. The Exploratorium was founded by Frank Oppenheimer, the brother of Robert Oppenheimer, known as "the father of the atomic bomb."

The **Golden Gate Promenade** ⓴, which extends from the bridge past the palace and onward through the Marina District to Fisherman's Wharf, is a scenic way to approach Fort Point, at the northern end of the Presidio. **Fort Point National Historic Site** ㉑ is a brick guardhouse, built around1860, that was used as a base of operations during construction of the **Golden Gate Bridge** ㉒. Close by is the **Roundhouse** (open daily 8.30am–7.30pm summer, 9am–5pm in winter) housed in an attractive 1938 building where information and souvenirs can be found to amplify enjoyment of the most fabulous sight in San Francisco. ❏

Rodin's The Thinker, *outside the California Palace of the Legion of Honor.*

Restaurants

Al-Masri
4031 Balboa St. Tel: 415-876-2300. Open: D. **$$$**
Dinner at Al-Masri is an all-evening affair of unique dishes and belly dancers, all in a fantasy courtyard atmosphere.

Angkor Wat
4217 Geary Blvd. Tel: 415-221-7887. Open: L, D. **$$**
Beautiful carvings of the Buddha, and the wait-staff are truly gracious. Cambodian food; Richmond area.

Aziza
5800 Geary Blvd. Tel: 415-752-2222. Open: D. **$$$**
It takes a lot to get SF foodies to outer Richmond, but Aziza delivers with its Moroccan-influenced cuisine.

Beach Chalet
1000 Great Highway. Tel: 415-386-8439.
Open: B, Br, L, D. **$$**
Great for sunset cocktails and brunches with beach views. Kid-friendly.

Chez Papa
1401 18th St. Tel: 415-255-0387. Open L, D. **$$**
The owners grew up in the South of France and strive to recreate the everyday food culture of Provence in Potrero Hill. The result is superb.

Cliff House
1090 Point Lobos.
Tel: 415-386-3330.
Open: B, Br, L, D. **$$$**
An unparalleled view of the Pacific Ocean, Marin Headlands, Sutro Baths and the entrance to the Golden Gate. Recently renovated, it has a swank restaurant, a casual bistro, a bar and a brunch terrace, all sharing the grand vista.

Java Beach Café
1396 La Playa Blvd. Tel: 415-665-5283. Open: B, L. **$**
Sunny days are made for sitting out front drinking a beer, a mere block from the ocean. Foggy days are made for lingering inside, drinking lattes.

Khan Toke
5937 Geary Blvd. Tel: 415-668-6654. Open: D. **$$**
This restaurant is reminiscent of a Bangkok temple, with low tables and an orchid garden. The Thai food is worth the trip to Richmond.

• • • • • • • • • • • • •
Prices for three-course dinner per person with a half-bottle of house wine: **$$$$** *$85 and up,* **$$$** *$45–85,* **$$** *$20–45,* **$** *under $20.*

OAKLAND AND BERKELEY

Oakland has Jack London landmarks and speedy access
to Silicon Valley, while Berkeley has long been
a pioneer of social experimentation

D espite all the hard knocks – especially author Gertrude Stein's infamous quip that "there is no *there* there" – Oakland is emerging from the shadow cast by its older sister to the west. Lower rents, easier access to Silicon Valley and the Marin County-based movie post-production companies, and a slightly slower way of life have, in the last few years, attracted many would-be San Franciscans.

These urban dwellers, in turn, have created a demand for better restaurants and more sophisticated facilities generally. And things are looking pretty good – especially for women: according to a recent US census, Oakland ranks third in the number of businesses owned by women. More than half a century after Stein's disparaging observation, visitors might reconsider: there is a there here.

Jack London's legacy

Oakland's version of Fisherman's Wharf is the restaurant and shopping pedestrian walk called **Jack London Square and Village** ❶. The Oakland native and author of *The Sea Wolf* and *The Call of the Wild (see pages 27, 64 and 167)*, who died in 1916, might not be impressed to see the over-priced restaurants and T-shirt stores, but he would be able to munch crab, listen to good music and watch sail-boats pass by. The **First and Last Chance Saloon**, a place London used to frequent, is popular with tourists, while nearby is London's sod-roofed Yukon cabin, which was moved from Alaska to the waterfront, in tribute to the city's most famous son.

Moored in the harbor is the **USS Potomac**, President Franklin D. Roosevelt's "floating White House," now a National Historic Monument (open Mon and Tues 9am–1pm, Wed and Fri 9am–5pm; dockside tours: tel: 510-627-1215; charge). Oakland's

Map
on page
166

LEFT: preservationists
are campaigning for
the Oakland Fox
to be restored.
BELOW: Jack
London Village.

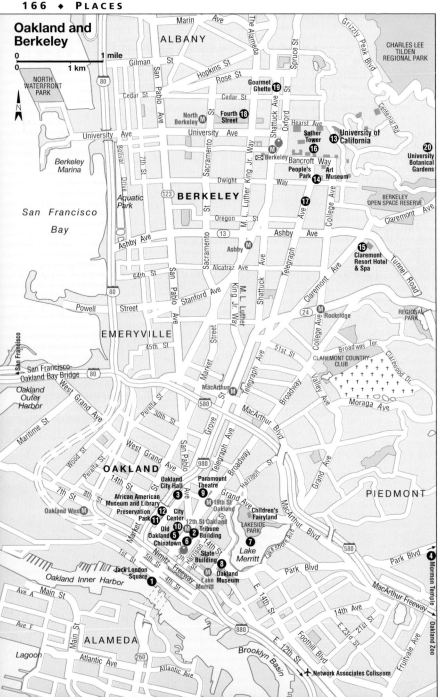

Oakland and Berkeley

0 _____ 1 mile
0 _____ 1 km

ALBANY

CHARLES LEE
TILDEN
REGIONAL PARK

NORTH
WATERFRONT
PARK

Marin Ave

Gilman St

Hopkins St

Rose St

Cedar St

Gourmet
Ghetto ⑲

Fourth
Street ⑱

North
Berkeley Ⓜ

University Ave

Sather
Tower ⑯

University of
California ⑬

⑳
University
Botanical
Gardens

Berkeley
Marina

Aquatic
Park

BERKELEY

Dwight Way

People's
Park

Art
Museum ⑭

BERKELEY
OPEN SPACE RESERVE

Oregon

⑰

Ashby Ave

San Francisco
Bay

Ashby Ⓜ

Alcatraz Ave

Claremont Ave

64th St

Stanford Ave

Claremont
Resort Hotel
& Spa ⑮

Tunnel Road

Powell Street

EMERYVILLE

45th St

Rockridge Ⓜ

REGIONAL
PARK

CLAREMONT COUNTRY
CLUB

Broadway Ter.

San Francisco-
Oakland Bay Bridge

Oakland
Outer
Harbor

West Grand Ave

MacArthur

Moraga Ave

Maritime St

30th St

MacArthur Blvd

PIEDMONT

OAKLAND

14th St

Oakland
City Hall ③

Paramount
Theatre ⑨

African American
Museum and Library ⑫

Preservation
Park ⑪

City
Center

Children's
Fairyland

Oakland West Ⓜ

19th St
Oakland Ⓜ

Grand Ave

12th St Oakland Ⓜ

Old
Oakland ⑤
Chinatown ⑥

Tribune
Building ②

⑩

LAKESIDE
PARK

State
Building ⑦

Lake
Merritt

Mormon
Temple ④

Jack London
Square ①

Oakland Inner Harbor

Oakland
Museum ⑧

Lake
Merritt Ⓜ

Park Blvd

MacArthur Freeway

Oakland Zoo

ALAMEDA

Atlantic Ave

Brooklyn Basin

Foothill Blvd

Network Associates Coliseum

other landmarks include the **Tribune Building** ❷, with its distinctive tower; **Oakland City Hall** ❸, complete with wedding-cake cupola; the recently restored **Rotunda Building**, and, in the hills above, the five-towered, white granite **Mormon Temple** ❹, the only Mormon temple in California. From its lofty heights are wonderful views of the bay.

On Sunday mornings, there's a **farmers' market** in the area called **Old Oakland** ❺. Not far away is **Chinatown** ❻, smaller and more negotiable than its big brother across the bay. Visible from the Nimitz Freeway, if you're driving toward the airport, is the **Network Associates Coliseum**, which is the home of the Oakland A's baseball team, the National Basketball Association's Golden State Warriors and the Oakland Raiders AFC football team.

On the eastern edge of town is a natural landmark, **Lake Merritt** ❼. This large salt-water lake and wildlife refuge, rimmed by Victorian houses and a necklace of lights, is the location of **Children's Fairyland**, touted as the country's first "3-D" theme park. The lake is also popular for sailing or picnicking year-round. At the **Oakland Zoo** (tel: 510-632-9525; open daily 10am–4pm; charge), visitors can ride in the sky in gondolas overlooking some of its 440 animals.

Architectural delights

Not far from the lake are two contrasting architectural delights – the **Oakland Museum** ❽ (1000 Oak Street, tel: 510-238-3401; Wed–Sat 10am–5pm, Sun noon–5pm; charge) and the Art Deco **Paramount Theatre** ❾ at 2025 Broadway.

The Oakland Museum, landscaped with terraces and gardens, occupies three levels, and is considered by many to be the finest museum in the state for information on California's art, history and natural science. The **Cowell Hall of California History** has a huge collection of artifacts, while the **Gallery of California Art** is known for its oil paintings.

The beautiful Paramount Theatre is the home of the Oakland Ballet and the Paramount Organ Pops. The theater also screens old movies, complete with newsreels. Campaigners

Map on page 166

In the books Martin Eden *(1909) and* John Barleycorn *(1913), Jack London wrote about the Oakland waterfront where he grew up.*

BELOW:
the Claremont Resort was completed in 1915.

Currently, there are seven Nobel Prize-winners on the faculty at Berkeley. Since 1939, there have been a total of 19 Nobel laureates on the staff.

are hoping to renovate another Art Deco gem, the **Oakland Fox Theater**, located on Telegraph Avenue between 18th and 19th streets.

Other Oakland attractions include **City Center** , a mall with restaurants, jazz concerts and art exhibits; **Preservation Park** ⓫, a restored Victorian village with 19th-century street lamps and lush gardens; and the **African American Museum & Library** ⓬ (125 14th Street and Martin Luther King, Jr Way, tel: 510-637-0200; open Mon–Sat noon–5.30pm). For many black Americans, Oakland has a special significance; it was here in the 1960s that the Black Panther Movement was founded. The Panthers' politics spread from here to college campuses around the country.

Berkeley

Just north of Oakland is **Berkeley**, a city famous for social experimentation. The city grew up around the **University of California** ⓭ (www.berkeley.edu), considered one of the country's finest public universities. Berkeley began as a humble prep school operating out of a former fan-

dango house in Oakland, and eventually became part of the nine-campus University of California system.

It was the Free Speech Movement of 1964 that put Berkeley on the map. At issue was a UC Berkeley administration order limiting political activities on campus. This touched off massive student protests and, in turn, similar protests on campuses nationwide. For several years the campus remained a smoldering center of protest and political action.

In 1969, students again took to the streets to stop the university's expansion in an area they wanted to preserve as **People's Park** ⓮. They ultimately prevailed, despite the intervention of 2,000 National Guard troops and violence that led to the death of an onlooker. Years later, People's Park began to draw more drug dealers and drifters from the city's homeless than it did students. But today, student unrest has turned more to rest and recreation, so the city has added basketball and volleyball courts to People's Park, which is also used as a site for festivals and concerts. Another attempt in the 1990s to

reclaim the park for commercial purposes was met with resistance, proving the spirit of the '60s lives on.

On the approach to Berkeley from Oakland, two buildings catch the eye. On a hillside toward the south is a fairy-tale white palace, the **Claremont Resort Hotel and Spa** ⓯ (tel: 510-843-3000), which, like San Francisco's Palace of Fine Arts, was finished just before the Panama Pacific International Exposition of 1915. The other landmark is a pointed structure, the university's bell tower. Its official name is **Sather Tower** ⓰, but it is known to everyone simply as the "Campanile" because the tower is modeled after St Mark's Campanile in Venice, Italy.

To get the feel of Berkeley at its liveliest, take a walk down **Telegraph Avenue** ⓱ from Dwight Way to the university. Here students, townspeople and visitors pick their way between stores that hark back to the '60s (think jewelry and pottery) interspersed with those catering to the needs of modern students (think tracksuits). Music fans should head for Rasputin, one of the

biggest independent record stores in the Bay Area. More shopping can be found in the neighborhood north of University Avenue called **Fourth Street** ⓲, where boutiques sell bijou crafts and designer kids' clothes.

Gourmet ghetto

The people who shop in Fourth Street are often to be found dining in Upper Shatuck Avenue, known locally as the **Gourmet Ghetto** ⓳. Spearheaded by Chez Panisse (see below and page 55), the restaurant's success lead to other eating establishments opening up nearby. As it's necessary to book a month ahead for dinner at Chez Panisse, the overspill is no doubt great.

Berkeley's climate (it can be foggy in San Francisco but sunny across the bay) produces sweet-smelling results for the **University Botanical Gardens** ⓴ (tel: 510-643-2755; open daily 9am–5pm, closed first Tues of each month; charge, but free on Thur) in Strawberry Canyon, where more than 12,000 species thrive in this research facility. ❑

Map on page 166

The People's Park protests of 1969 lead to singer Joni Mitchell writing a hit song about "They paved paradise, and put up a parking lot."

Restaurants	Chez Panisse	Le Cheval	Yoshi's
Breads of India	1517 Shattuck Ave, Berkeley. Tel: 510-548-5525.	1007 Clay St, Oakland. Tel: 510-763-8495.	510 Embarcadero West, Oakland. Tel: 510-238-9200. Open: Br, L, D. **$$**

Breads of India
2448 Sacramento Ave, Berkeley. Tel: 510-848-7684. Open: L, D. **$$**
High marks from both the student population and East Bay foodies. The key is freshness. Cash only.

Chef Edward's Bar-B-Que
1998 San Pablo Ave, Oakland. Tel: 510-834-9516
Open: L, early D. **$**
This barbeque shack is known for its "Piggly Wiggly Sandwich," pulled-pork dripping with sauce.

Chez Panisse
1517 Shattuck Ave, Berkeley. Tel: 510-548-5525.
Open: D Mon–Sat. **$$**
Alice Waters never strayed from her commitment to serving the freshest locally-grown and pedigreed ingredients. The grand dame of California Cuisine has inspired imitators, but this is where it all started. Menus change nightly, all meals are *prix-fixe* and reservations must be made a month in advance. The Café at Chez Panisse offers a more moderately-priced a la carte menu.

Le Cheval
1007 Clay St, Oakland. Tel: 510-763-8495.
Open: L, D. **$$**
For 20 years, this classic Oakland restaurant has packed them in, who come for Le Cheval's menu of Vietnamese delights.

Spenger's Fresh Fish Grotto
1919 4th St, Berkeley. Tel: 510-845-7771.
Open: L, D. **$$$**
Specialties here include Yellowtail Jack pan seared with hazelnut crust, mashed potatoes, and spicy Jamaican hot rum butter. Arrive hungry.

Yoshi's
510 Embarcadero West, Oakland. Tel: 510-238-9200. Open: Br, L, D. **$$**
This classy Japanese on Jack London Square doubles as one of the Bay Area's best jazz venues. Superfresh sushi makes the perfect date night, but Sunday matinees are kid friendly – as are the *udon* noodles. Call for reservations.

● ● ● ● ● ● ● ● ● ● ● ●
Prices for three-course dinner per person with a half-bottle of house wine: **$$$$** *$85 and up,* **$$$** *$45–85,* **$$** *$20–45,* **$** *under $20.*

From the high sequoias of Muir W
the high-tech spark of Silicon Val
Bay Area is happy, v
and in consta

Outside San Francisco are at least as many fascinating sights and delights as there are in the city. Mountains, redwood forests and wonderful Pacific beaches beckon, as well as sparkling Sillicon Valley. Travel is easy: three bridges span the bay; an underground train system (BART) links up the East Bay with the city; ferries criss-cross the water; and trains run up and down the peninsula. Getting around by car, though, is the most attractive way to explore these coasts, hills and valleys.

Marin County

Starting north from San Francisco on US 101, the route to Marin County begins by crossing the fantastic Golden Gate Bridge. Directly ahead, the Marin Headlands are wild and lonely cliffs, standing in contrast to the metropolis left behind across the bay.

At the northern end of the bridge is the **Marine Mammal Center** ❶ (tel: 415-289-SEAL; open daily 10am–4pm; free but donations welcome), a non-profit organization that rescues sick or injured marine mammals stranded along the coastline. Volunteers help to rehabilitate the seals and sea lions before returning them to the sea at this unusual wild animal hospital. The Mammal

Center is part of the **Golden Gate National Recreation Area**.

The town of **Sausalito** ❷, accessible by ferry (tel: 415-773-1188, from Pier 41 or the Ferry Building, approximate 30-minute crossing) from San Francisco, is known as the "French Riviera" of the West Coast because of its Mediterranean climate, art galleries and restaurants. After a stroll beneath the palm trees along the curved main street, visitors can sense some of the changes of the past century in the gracious Victorian homes

Map on page 172

LEFT:
aerial view of
Sausalito and Tiburon.
BELOW:
ferries are frequent.

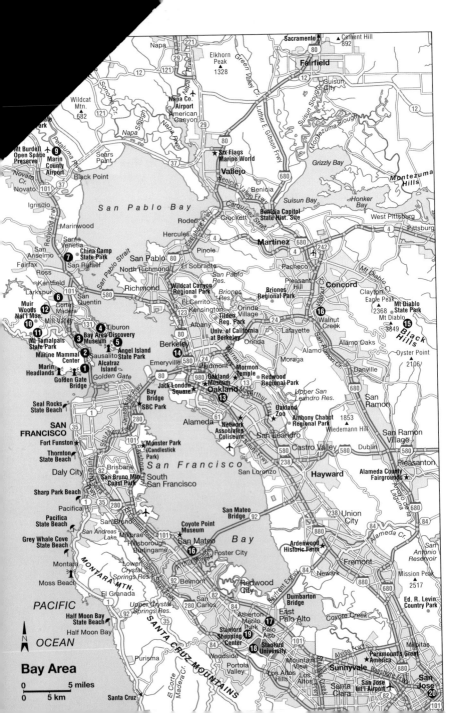

that hug the hill. In the 1870s, when California fruit and vegetables were shipped to Europe, English captains sometimes set up homes here. Quaint, tree-lined walkways, small, carefully manicured gardens and specialty stores attest to the British influence.

When Sausalito became an important shipping link between other parts of California and San Francisco, the main street sprouted innumerable saloons, brothels and gambling houses, with the town serving as a base for liquor boot-leggers who supplied the speak-easies of San Francisco.

As recently as the 1950s, the late Sally Stanford, restaurateur and madam, crossed the bridge after she shut down her San Francisco bordello to drive to her restaurant (now closed) on Bridgeway Drive. Stanford ran for Sausalito's town council in the early 1960s, and became mayor of the town in 1973.

Stop by the **Green Gulch Zen Center** (1661 Shoreline Highway, tel: 415-383-3134), a meditation community offering a pastoral contrast to San Francisco, only 12 miles (19 km) away. Extensive vegetable gardens, lovingly cultivated by Green Gulch residents, cater to the Zen Center's restaurant, Greens, in San Francisco's Marina District (*see page 139*).

Visitors are welcome to enjoy the tranquil grounds, to attend morning instruction or simply to sample some homebaked bread with tea. The Zen Center offers classes in Buddhist philosophy, meditation retreats and workshops, and they offer special Sunday programs that are open to the public.

Just north of town is the delightful **Bay Area Discovery Museum ❸** (557 McReynolds Road, East Fort Baker, tel: 415-339-3900; open Tues–Sun; charge) with hands-on exhibits focusing on natural sciences, art and multimedia.

Tiburon

East of Sausalito and also just a ferry ride from San Francisco, is **Tiburon ❹** – well-known for **Ark Row**, a winding street of art galleries, restaurants and specialty stores. But Tiburon was not always so appealing. Before 1930 the town was a marsh, and people lived in rough and often shabby "arks." When entrepreneur Fred Zelinsky filled in the swampy land, he constructed a street where people once had to paddle to get to the grocery store. Tiburon has now developed into a wealthy residential town, attracting San Franciscans who prefer the 20-minute ferry ride to freeway traffic jams.

In fact, Tiburon has been luring city dwellers for more than a century, ever since Dr Benjamin Lyford, a pioneering embalming surgeon, tried to start one of California's first utopian communities in the late 1800s. In his promotional brochure for Hygeia – named after the goddess of health – Doctor Lyford promised a community with "restrictions that will keep out the

Houseboat living in sunny Sausalito.

BELOW: hot-tub heaven, Marin County.

vices and vampires common to all communities." At the northern exit of town, his Victorian home and **Lyford's Tower**, once the gateway to the Hygeia, are reminders of this eccentric experiment.

Isolated hideaway

A ferry ride from Tiburon (or from San Francisco) takes visitors to **Angel Island ⑤**, an uninhabited isle of protected parkland where deer and other wild animals graze. This triangular-shaped island draws picnickers to enjoy its panoramic views of San Francisco and the Golden Gate Bridge. A stroll around the island's perimeter trails takes only about an hour, but an ambitious climb up to the top of **Mount Livermore** delivers breathtaking views, literally.

Angel Island hides many secrets. It has been home to the Coast Miwok, to Spanish explorers, Russian otter hunters, American soldiers, and many others. In the 1840s the island belonged to Antonio Osio, who grazed his cattle here and cut timber for the Presidio at Yerba Buena. In 1853, the United States assumed ownership and for more than a century, the island was used by the military.

First tagged *Isla de los Angeles* by the crew of the Spanish ship *San Carlos*, for thousands of Chinese immigrants interned here it became the dreaded "Ellis Island of the West." The ruins of stations used for processing immigrants and holding World War II prisoners are on the island's northeast side. The buildings near the ferry landing were once a quarantine station during a 19th-century smallpox epidemic. **Fort McDowell**, on the eastern side, was used to process soldiers as early as the Spanish-American War. Later, the fort became a missile base.

To the south, an area near the Coast Guard station at **Point Blunt** was once a favorite dueling spot for San Franciscans. In 1858, a crowd of 1,000 came here to witness a duel between a state senator and a United States commissioner, but these days the crowds are more low-key, arriving mainly to relax, sail, picnic and ride mountain bikes.

Back in Tiburon, continue on

TIP

For information on ferries to Sausalito, Tiburon and Angel Island, see page 213. For organized tours, see page 231.

BELOW: abandoned Army barracks on Angel Island.

Map on page 172

Paradise Drive, a road that winds along the eucalyptus-scented **Ring Mountain Preserve** before opening onto some lovely views of the bay. Paradise Drive leads to another bay town, **Larkspur ❻**, popular with commuters to San Francisco and the East Bay. Larkspur is a quiet town nestled against the foot of Mount Tamalpais and is best known for its award-winning restaurant, the **Lark Creek Inn** *(see page 178)*. The downtown area is listed with the National Register of Historic Places.

Farther north is Marin County's largest town, **San Rafael ❼**, still only 17 miles (27 km) from San Francisco. Its main point of interest is the **Marin Civic Center** (tel: 415-499-6400), designed by Frank Lloyd Wright and host to concerts, lectures and performances, from symphonies to political and speaking programs. For years, the headquarters of the award-winning visual-effects company, Industrial Light & Magic (not open to the public), founded by movie director George Lucas, has had studios here.

Straight up US 101, near the **Mt Burdell Open Space Preserve ❽**, is the **Marin County Airport ❾**.

West coast

North of Sausalito, off Highway 1, are **Muir Beach** and **Muir Woods ❿**. The beach is a pretty, open area with sheltered coves for picnicking. Nearby, a nude sunbathing area is protected from the wind by a cluster of rocks.

Both the beach and the woods are named after naturalist John Muir, and known for the grove of sequoia trees that have thrived in the damp, foggy climate. Hikers and strollers begin their journey on a paved walkway that winds through eucalyptus and tall columns of red-tinted trees leading eventually to a high, open path that drops to the ocean.

Steep Ravine, the rocky beach at the foot of the trail, offers the dramatic sight of the waves meeting the rock wedges straight on, frothy spray sent high into the air. Look for the unusual albino redwood; its bark is a pale, sinewy green and its needles are actually white.

Campaigner and environmentalist John Muir.

BELOW: the tiny skyscrapers of San Francisco, seen from Mount Tamalpais.

Just past Muir Woods is **Stinson Beach**, the most popular beach in the Bay Area. Students study while sunbathing, families picnic and build sandcastles, and brave souls splash in the chilly water.

Continue north on Highway 1 for Point Reyes and Mendocino *(see page 183)*. To stay local, turn right off Highway 1 onto Panoramic Highway and follow the signs to **Mount Tamalpais** ⓫. Once home to the Miwok tribe (whose members never ascended its peak because they believed their gods lived there), Tamalpais actually has three peaks. The east one (2,571 ft/784 meters) is popular for its trails leading to the fire-lookout tower at the summit. Cyclists enjoy riding along **Corte Madera Creek** up to the top of Mount Tam.

At the foot of Mount Tamalpais is the little town of **Mill Valley** ⓬, on whose south side is Old Mill Creek. In 1836 John Reed built the US's first sawmill here. The streets of Mill Valley spread out from the old railroad depot and provide shady avenues for walking and shopping.

East Bay

The Bay Bridge leads to **Oakland** ⓭ *(see page 165)* and **Berkeley** ⓮ *(see page 168)*. Over the Berkeley ridge and east of the town of Walnut Creek is **Mount Diablo** ⓯, a central landmark in California. The name ("mountain of the devil") stems from the occasion when the US government tried to usurp it from the Native Americans and a strange spirit was said to have intervened to scare off the soldiers. The peak's panoramic vista of the jarring, craggy summits of the Sierra Nevada mountains, bordering the fertile Central Valley, is a sight to remember for some time to come.

South and Silicon Valley

South of San Francisco, two other bridges cross the bay. The first is at **San Mateo** ⓰, a suburban residential community with a wildlife habitat and picnic facilities. The **Coyote Point Museum for Environmental Education** (1651 Coyote Point Dr, tel: 650-342-7755; charge) is a learning center to inspire commitment to environmental responsibility. Coyote Point features a huge walk-through aviary, home to more than four dozen native California birds in an up-close, natural setting, in addition to an enlarged walk-through honeycomb that is part of an exhibition on honeybees.

The second bridge, the Dumbarton Toll Bridge, is just before **Palo Alto** ⓱, the wealthy college town 33 miles (53 km) from San Francisco. Palo Alto is a major player in the Silicon Valley tech scene, mainly through its association with nearby **Stanford University** ⓲ *(see page 179)*.

When the railroad tycoon Leland Stanford turned over the bulk of his fortune to the college in the 1890s, he included an 8,200-acre (3,320-hectare) horse farm that gave the

BELOW:
Mill Valley's Village Music is for collectors of vintage and vinyl.

Map
on page
172

campus its nickname, "the Farm," which is still in use. Frederick Law Olmsted (architect of New York's Central Park) had a hand in designing the campus, handsomely dotted with cloisters and yellow sandstone buildings with red tile roofs. The university's first president wrote that the campus itself was "an integral part of a Stanford education."

The observation deck of the 250-ft (76-meter) **Hoover Tower** (open daily until 4pm; small charge), gives spectacular views of Silicon Valley, and rooms in the tower display documents from the Herbert Hoover presidency.

Also worth visiting are the **Rodin Sculpture Garden** (tel: 650-723-4177) and the **Stanford Linear Accelerator Center** that generates pulsating, high-energy electron beams. Six private tours are given every month by reservation only (tel: 650-926-2204 or visit www.standford.edu for tour schedules).

Between Stanford and **Menlo Park** is the **Stanford Shopping Center** ⑲, a handsome, upscale plaza of stores and eating places.

Tech central

About one hour's drive south of San Francisco on US 101 is the Silicon Valley "capital" of **San Jose** ⑳. Although the town has much to offer anyone in the tech industry, its main attraction for casual visitors is its classy museums. Combining the two interests is the **Tech Museum of Innovation** (201 South Market Street, tel: 408-294-TECH; open Tues–Sun 10am–5pm; charge) or "The Tech" to computer geeks and locals, which is focused on technology and the way it is changing all aspects of how society works, lives, learns and plays.

A huge space is packed with interactive exhibits, an IMAX theater and an educational center for workshops and labs. Exhibitions range from the application of technology to the science of genetics to the art of robotics.

The **San Jose Museum of Art** (110 South Market Street, tel: 408-294-2787; open Tues–Sun 11am–5pm, Fri 11am–10pm; free) is dedicated to 20th- and 21st-century art, and the diversity of the Bay Area.

Hands-on heaven: the Tech Museum of Innovation.

BELOW: the San Jose Museum of Art has free admission.

Map on page 172

Exhibit from San Jose's Rosicrucian Egyptian Museum.

The collection houses nearly 1,500 works of art, including new media and installations. Among many treasures are blown-glass sculptures by Dale Chihuly and photographs by Ruth Bernard.

The **San Jose Historical Museum** (1650 Senter Road, tel: 408-287-2290; open Tues–Sun noon–5pm; charge) consists of 25 acres (10 hectares) on which are 27 original and reconstructed homes, businesses and landmarks showing the history of San Jose and the Santa Clara Valley. The museum has paved streets, running trolleys and an ice-cream parlor. Tours and interactive programs include music, art and the panning of gold.

The **Rosicrucian Egyptian Museum and Planetarium** (1342 Naglee Avenue, tel: 408-947-3636; open Mon–Fri 10am–5pm, Sat and Sun 11am–6pm; charge) is architecturally inspired by the Temple of Amon at Karnak and houses the largest collection of Egyptian artifacts exhibited in the western US. The collection includes tombs, mummies and thousands of ancient objects. The "tomb tour" is a favorite with children. The planetarium in Rosicrucian Park at Park and Naglee avenues presents shows Tuesday through Sunday.

Kids are also entertained by the interactive hands-on exhibits at the **Children's Discovery Museum** (180 Woz Way, tel: 408-298-5437; charge) but what fascinates the entire family is the **Winchester Mystery House** (525 South Winchester Boulevard, tel: 408-247-2101; open summer 9am–7pm, winter until 5pm, different tours available; charge), the 160-room mansion of the heiress to the Winchester rifle fortune.

Up to her death in 1922, Sarah Winchester spent millions of dollars on bizzare building works. Staircases leading nowhere, doors opening onto blank walls and some ceilings too low to allow standing. All this construction was because she believed it was the only way to escape the spirits of all the people the Winchester weapons had killed. The gardens are interesting – and the giftshop is huge. ❑

Restaurants

Café Niebaum-Coppola
473 University Ave, Palo Alto. Tel: 650-752-0350.
Open: L, D. **$$**
A casual Italian eatery owned by director Francis Ford Coppola. The focal point is the wine bar, where selections from Coppola's own winery are available.

Joe's Taco Lounge and Salsaria
382 Miller Ave, Mill Valley.
Tel: 415-383-8164.
Open: L, D. **$**
Joe's is good for a quick Mexican lunch. Relax on the patio after your trip to Muir Woods or Mount Tam, or refuel in the fun and funky lounge.

Manka's Inverness Lodge
30 Calendar Way, Inverness.
Tel: 415-669-1045.
Open: D. **$$$**
A former sportsman's lodge, Manka's retains its woodsy charm but is also known for cutting-edge food; it has long been a destination for foodies far and wide.

Lark Creek Inn
234 Magnolia Ave, Larkspur.
Tel: 415-924-7766.
Open: Br, L, D. **$$$**

Inside a Victorian home, celebrity chef/restaurateur Bradley Ogden delivers seasonal fresh ingredients and American fare in a delightful setting. Enjoy a selection from the vast California-only wine list as you dine beneath the redwoods.

The Pelican Inn
10 Pacific Way on Highway 1, Muir Woods. Tel: 415-383-6000. Open: L, D (B for hotel guests). **$$**
The Pelican Inn is a British-style pub and restaurant; also a cozy hotel. Sit next to the fireplace and eat hearty UK food like Shepherd's Pie or bangers and mash.

Sam's Anchor Café
27 Main St, Tiburon.
Tel: 415-435-4527.
Open: Br, L, D. **$$$**
Drive or sail into this restaurant that's been slinging chowder and fresh seafood delights for more than 85 years. Lunch on the dock by the boats is terrific.

● ● ● ● ● ● ● ● ● ●
Prices for three-course dinner per person with a half-bottle of house wine: **$$$$** *$85 and up,* **$$$** *$45–85,* **$$** *$20–45,* **$** *under $20.*

Silicon Valley

Silicon Valley stretches about 20 miles (32 km) from the lower San Francisco peninsula to the town of San Jose. Clustered at first around Stanford University, eBay, Google, Yahoo, Electronic Arts, Apple Computer, Netscape and Intel are just a selection of the famous IT names founded here. A large part of any history of modern computing will list Silicon Valley milestones.

Formerly known as Santa Clara Valley and settled in the mid-1800s by farmers, it is bounded to the east by San Francisco Bay and to the west by the Santa Cruz mountains. It embraces nearly 15 cities, including Palo Alto, home of Stanford University, to whose engineering school America's brightest went to study radio, the Valley's first high-tech industry.

In 1938, two Stanford students, David Packard and William Hewlett, founded Hewlett-Packard on Palo Alto's Addison Street, now a state historical monument.

After receiving a Nobel Prize for the electronic transistor in 1956, Valley native William Schockley intended to build an empire, but the eight young engineers he hired all left to form Fairchild Semiconductor. It was here, in 1959, that Bob Noyce developed the miniature semiconductor set into silicon. Noyce, known to many as the mayor of Silicon Valley, co-founded Intel with Gordon Moore in 1968.

"The Homebrew Computer Club" was formed in 1967, with meetings held around the Stanford campus. This group really lit the fire of the microcomputer revolution. At 2066 Crist Drive in a Cupertino garage Steve Jobs and Steve Wozniac turned out their first computer for the club, and later formed Apple Computer. Apple's headquarters are still in the Valley town of Cupertino.

During the 1980s, personal computers replaced arcade games as the entertainment of choice. Then along came e-mail and the World Wide Web. At first these were mainly electronic notice boards for boffins;

now they are indispensable tools. When the internet started to catch on with an estimated 18 million users in 1995, a frenzy began. Entrepreneurs hunted for ways to exploit the value of the emerging market, and people flocked to Silicon Valley in much the same way they had to the Sierras when gold was discovered in 1848. But this time, instead of picks and pans, they carried business plans and floppy discs.

Through the tumult and excitement of the dot-com boom, many got burned and the industry suffered a high-profile crash in 2001, led by the over-valuation of the Time-Warner merger with AOL (neither of them Silicon Valley residents).

But plenty of life rose from the rubble. Yahoo wanted the world to use a branded verb for searching the internet. It did, but the brand was Google. On its stock-market floatation Google overtook Time-Warner as the world's most valuable media corporation; eBay has gobbled up many of the old "bricks and mortar" auction houses; and Apple Computer took a market out from under Sony, replacing the once-ubiquitous Walkman with the now-ubiquitous iPod.

With all these hard-working techies, the Valley is probably the best place in the world to own a delivery pizza company. ❑

RIGHT: Google's Silicon Valley headquarters. Other companies include eBay, Yahoo and Apple.

SAN FRANCISCO NORTH TO MENDOCINO

With vineyards, whale watching
and traces of Sir Francis Drake,
these Californian cliffs and beaches
are a delight to discover

The four-hour drive from San Francisco to the lovely town of Mendocino can easily provide four full days of travel and delight. It starts at the Golden Gate Bridge, then hugs the coast on spectacular Highway 1 before turning inland to pass by enticing wineries and towering redwoods. Attractive coastal towns, seductive diversions and awe-inspiring scenery are here for the taking, mile after mile.

Point of the Kings

From Muir Woods *(see page 175)*, the 45-minute drive to **Point Reyes National Seashore ❶** is particularly beautiful, especially the portion on Sir Francis Drake Highway, just off Highway 1. Drake landed here in 1579 and claimed the peninsula for the British, in the name of Queen Elizabeth I. He named the peninsula "New Albion" (New England), supposedly because he was reminded of the jagged cliffs and rugged shoreline of his homeland.

On January 6, 1603, Don Sebastian Vizcaino gave Point Reyes its current name, *La Punta de Los Reyes* (The Point of the Kings), in commemoration of the three Kings' visit to Jesus on the 12th day of Christmas. Like a blunted arrow, Point Reyes points into the Pacific, the narrow finger of Tomales Bay at its

base and Drakes Bay on its southern edge. Flocks of birds, a colony of sea lions and tidepool creatures flourish in this 65,000-acre (26,000-hectare) natural showcase. Thirty-two thousand acres (13,000 hectares) of the National Seashore are officially designated as wilderness.

Start at the **Bear Valley Visitor Center** (open daily 9am–5pm) for an introductory hike up to **Arch Rock** – from the trail a strange, rock/statue can be seen jutting from the water – or **Sculpture Beach**, where waves

Map on page 184

PRECEDING PAGES:
Highway 1.
LEFT: Mendocino.
BELOW: Point Reyes Lighthouse.

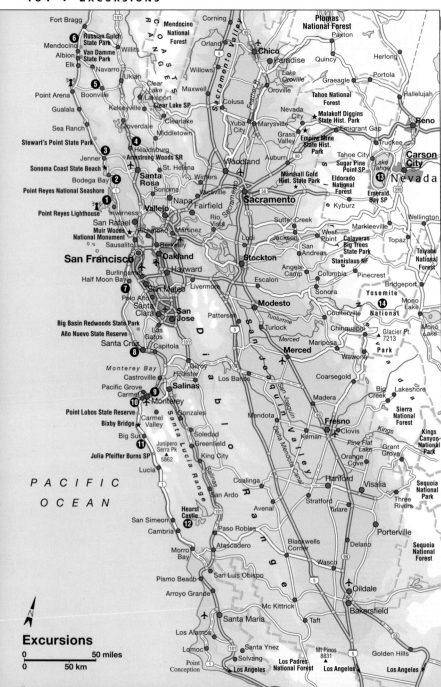

Excursions

0 ——————— 50 miles

0 ——————— 50 km

crash into coastal caves and tunnels. Another hike is along the **Limantour Trail** leading to the *Estero de Limantour*, a quiet wetland protected by dunes and tall grass – a delightful picnic spot. **Drake's Beach**, where Drake once grounded his ships for repairs, is a little farther down the coast. Hemmed in by **Tomales Bay** on one side and the park on the other, the little town of **Inverness** provides a charming stop. On the way out of town, look for the miniature royal palace on the dock, giving a whimsical twist to sleepy Inverness.

Just north of town is another place that might slow down your journey to Mendocino, the **Johnson Oyster Company** (17171 Sir Francis Drake Boulevard) – especially if you're hungry. Oysters are sold by the case on the premises and to many Bay Area restaurants or – for those who seek instant gratification – in small, inexpensive cocktails.

The drive along the coast is magnificent, with grazed, smooth fields flanked by the ocean at one side and the surreal, commanding **Drakes Bay** on the other. At **Point Reyes**

Lighthouse, gray whales can be spotted between December and May (peak period mid-Jan–Mar) as they head south toward warmer waters. The lighthouse, its revolving lens casting a powerful beam, was constructed in 1872 after 15 ships were destroyed off the point. It was built low on the precipice because winds at the top can reach 40 mph (64 kph). The beam is also visible beneath the frequent fog. Nearby is **Sea Lion Overlook**, where the sleek creatures sunbathe on rocks.

Russian River Valley

Beautiful as the vistas are, not everyone has the time to take Highway 1 all the way to Mendocino. Follow the coastal road through beautiful **Bodega Bay ➋**, and then turn inland at **Jenner ➌** to follow the equally gorgeous **Russian River Valley** across to US 101. Redwoods flank the Russian River, and the trees in 700-acre (284-hectare) **Armstrong Woods** (named for a 19th-century lumberman who donated the land) reach suitably impressive heights.

Where the Guerneville River

Map on page 184

Artists are attracted to this part of northern California, and you're never far from a sculpture or two.

BELOW:
a hard day in the Russian River Valley.

Road meets US 101 north of the town of Santa Rosa, head north for **Healdsburg ④**, where three valleys meet – Alexander, Dry Creek and Russian River. A beach on the river encourages swimming, fishing and canoeing. There's also a tree-shaded, Spanish-style plaza dating from the 1860s. The **Healdsburg Museum** on Matteson Street, housed in the old Carnegie Library building, displays Pomo tribal artifacts and 19th-century exhibits from the region.

Vineyards and sheep

There are more than 60 wineries within a half-hour's drive of Healdsburg, and the industry's growth and the concomitant rise in tourism have been bringing almost a million visitors a year to this pretty town. Opposite the 130-year old **Belle de Jour Inn** on Healdsburg Avenue is the tasting room of the **Simi Winery** (daily until 5pm; tours at 11am and 2pm). One entry in the 1942 guestbook is by Alfred Hitchcock, who drew a sketch of himself and noted "The port here is far too good for most people." There are numerous

other wineries in the area, especially in the picturesque **Alexander Valley**, east of US 101.

State Highway 253 snakes westward from US 101 just south of Ukiah to join northbound State Highway 128 at Boonville. This narrow, often-wooded country road meanders through the valley past grazing sheep, vineyards and orchards all the way to **Navarro** and thence to the coast.

Winemaking first began here more than a century ago, when many frustrated seekers after gold settled and planted vineyards. **Boonville ⑤** is a delightful little place. You can eat well and stay comfortably at the **Boonville Hotel** (tel: 707-895-2210), which calls itself a roadhouse, defined by *Funk & Wagnall's* dictionary as, "an inn or restaurant in a rural locality which caters especially to transient pleasure seekers."

Other worthwhile stops include the **Anderson Valley Historical Society Museum** (open Mar–Nov Fri–Sun 1–4pm), in a red, one-room schoolhouse north of Mountain View Road, and the **Buckhorn Saloon and Anderson Valley Brewing**

Between December and April, this portion of the California coast is part of the migratory path for whales. Whale-watching trips can be organized from Point Reyes or Mendocino.

BELOW: cruising the California coast.

From San Francisco

TIME BY CAR	MILES	KM
Carmel/Monterey		
2–3 hours	133	214
Hearst Castle		
3–4 hours	197	333
Lake Tahoe		
3.5 hours	211	340
Los Angeles		
11 hours (coast)	437	703
8 hours (inland)	389	626
Mendocino		
4 hours	156	251
Napa/Sonoma		
1 hour	44	71
Santa Cruz		
2 hours	74	119
Yosemite		
4 hours	210	338

Company (tours daily 1.30pm and 4.30pm). The selection of microbrews are made using water from its own well. There are coffee shops too.

Highway 128 accompanies the Navarro River all the way to the coast, skirting glorious **Redwood State Park**, before heading up through tiny **Albion** – named by a British sea captain, who in 1853 built a sawmill. The estuary here, one of half a dozen in the county that mark the transition between fresh water rivers and the sea, is popular with kayakers. Along with the legends of Sir Francis Drake roaming this coast in the 16th century is speculation that he may have built a fort here. The scenery can hardly have changed over the centuries, except for the bijou inns and high-end restaurants, especially around **Elk**.

Magnificent Mendocino

Mendocino ❻, 156 miles (251 km) north of San Francisco, is a cultured town with an active year-round arts center and many galleries. Gingerbread houses cling to windswept headlands, as a local writer put it,

and white picket fences and ancient wooden water towers abound. It's a lovely, low-key place, much of the pleasure coming from just strolling around. But with more than 20 bed-and-breakfast inns, be aware that the town becomes crowded on weekends.

Among the homes dating from the middle of the 18th century, the **Ford House** on Main Street and the **Kelley House** on Albion Street have been turned into historical museums. Blair House on Little Lake Road will be familiar to TV viewers of *Murder, She Wrote,* and the Hill House also appeared on the show. Both offer bed-and-breakfast.

Mendocino was all but deserted for the first part of the 20th century but underwent a cultural renaissance in the 1950s when artists and musicians moved in. The town stages a Whale and Wine Festival in March, when the migratory whales are seen off the coast, and a Music Festival in July. Just don't be fooled into thinking it will be hot in July; Mendocino and San Francisco share similar temperatures during the summer months.   ❑

Map on page 184

High-end restaurants in California are noted for tasty – and tall – food.

BELOW: art gallery near Mendocino.

SAN FRANCISCO SOUTH TO BIG SUR

**Highway 1 runs much of the length
of California's Pacific Coast. This stretch,
from Santa Cruz to Big Sur, is the most beautiful**

Highway 1 south from San Francisco may be the most spectacular route in America. The road is a series of razor-sharp switch-backs, climbing hills, plunging into valleys, and hugging the coast the entire time. Steep, rugged mountains loom on the left-hand side of the road, while on the right is nothing but a sheer drop to the wild, crashing waves below.

For a real West Coast experience, the best means of transportation is a motorcycle, or at least a convertible. Either can be rented in San Francisco, with a drop-off point arranged farther south. This way you can smell the scents, feel the fog, and play cruising music very loudly. However you travel, expect climate changes every few miles – from fog to rain to blinding sunshine. This is the *real* California.

Cruising to Santa Cruz

Assuming there are no traffic problems, around 35 minutes after leaving San Francisco, Highway 1 reaches **Half Moon Bay ❼**, a pretty spot known for weekend outdoor concerts, and perhaps the first blast of bright sunshine since arriving in foggy San Francisco.

The first community of any size is the beach town of Santa Cruz, 74 miles (119 km) from San Francisco.

At the northern end of Monterey Bay, the city of **Santa Cruz ❽** (population: 256,000) is cool, green and shimmers with redwoods. When the **University of California** opened a campus here a few decades ago, the influx of academic activity transformed what had previously been a quiet backwater into an activist community. Santa Cruz became rejuvenated with excellent restaurants, cafés, bookstores and a multitude of stores catering to the needs of students and visitors.

**Map
on page
184**

LEFT:
Julia Pfeiffer Burns
State Park.
BELOW:
tent cabins at an
eco-lodge near
Half Moon Bay.

Cans of fish in Cannery Row. Monterey was known for its sardines.

The University's campus plays a significant part in local life. The campus is responsible for the **Long Marine Lab**, a working marine studies laboratory (open Tues–Sat 10am–5pm, Sun noon–5pm); an arboretum containing plants from around the world, plus an outdoor Shakespeare festival and a wide-ranging series of performing arts (tel: 831-459-ARTS for a schedule).

Santa Cruz has sparkling clean air and is one of the sunniest spots around, usually unaffected by the chilly winds and blinding fog that can hover over the coast, both north and south. Be sure to bring your swimsuit, and oil up for some tan maintenance.

This is also a great place for surfing; not for nothing does the town have one of the few – perhaps the only – monument to a surfer on the promenade, looking out toward the breaking surf.

The **Santa Cruz pier** is the place for all things fishy – fish restaurants, fish markets and good facilities for fishing. Next to the pier is a wide, white, sandy beach, and nearby is the **Beach Boardwalk** (mid-May–early Sept daily, weekends only in winter; free), nearly 100 years old, with a carousel only a little younger and a Big Dipper built in 1924. Wednesday afternoons, rain or shine, the **Downtown Farmers' Market** is at the corner of Cedar and Lincoln streets, with stands overflowing with fruit, flowers, seafood, cheese and olive oil.

Leaving Santa Cruz, Highway 1 follows the coast in a beautiful arc around Monterey Bay. During the spring, the high sand dunes are covered in a carpet of marigolds. The road passes near the beach town of **Capitola** in a confusing manner, then dramatically chills out again. Peanut and agricultural produce stands make pleasant stops for picking up snacks.

Monterey

The city of **Monterey** ❾ (population: 33,000), at the northern end of the Monterey Peninsula, comes as a surprise after this peaceful journey. Thanks to writer John Steinbeck, a big attraction is the part of town now

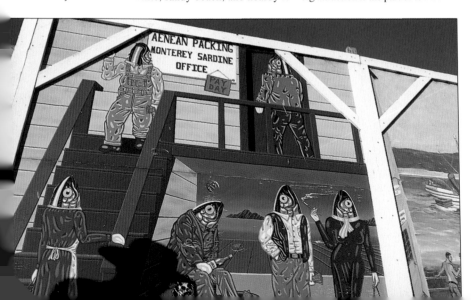

known as **Cannery Row**. During World War II, Monterey was a major sardine capital, and in Steinbeck's words, was "a poem, a stink, a grating noise, a quality of light, a tone, a habit, a nostalgia, a dream."

When the fishing boats came in, heavy with catch, the canneries blew their whistles, and the residents streamed down the hill to take their places amid the rumbling, rattling, squealing machinery of the canning plants. When the last sardine was cleaned, cut, cooked and canned, the whistle blew again, and the workers trudged back up the hill, wet and wreathed in the smell of fish.

After the war, for reasons variously blamed on overfishing, changing tidal currents and divine retribution, the sardines disappeared from Monterey Bay and all the canneries went broke.

But, as Steinbeck pointed out, it was not a total loss. In those early years of the industry, the beaches were so deeply covered with fish guts, scales and flies that a sickening stench covered the town. Today, the beaches are bright and clean, and the air is sparkling fresh. Cannery Row, located along the waterfront on the northwest side of town just beyond the Presidio, has become an impressive tourist attraction, the old buildings filled with bars, restaurants, a wax museum, stores, a carousel and food vendors.

Amazing aquarium

A trip to Cannery Row offers a visit to one of the world's premier aquariums, the **Monterey Bay Aquarium** (886 Cannery Row, tel: 831-648 4888; open daily but different hours, call for details; charge). The enormous building, with indoor dolphin tanks and outdoor pools overlooking the sea, stands on the site of what was Cannery Row's largest cannery, the Hovden Cannery.

More than 100 galleries and exhibits include more than 350,000 specimens, from sea otters, leopard sharks, bat rays and giant octopuses, to towering underwater kelp forests. Feeding time is particularly fascinating, when keepers in glass tanks talk to spectators through underwater microphones. Although always

Map on page 184

 TIP

The Monterey Jazz Festival, which introduced Jimi Hendrix to an American audience, is held in September. For tickets, tel: 925-275-9255 or go to www.trilogyticketing.com to book online.

BELOW: the Monterey Bay Aquarium is one of the finest in the country.

crowded, this fabulous sanctuary – one of the best in the United States – is worth an amount of waiting time, but be warned: it may spoil future visits to lesser aquariums.

In downtown Monterey, the main visitor attraction is **Fisherman's Wharf**. (The real working wharf is two blocks east.) Fisherman's Wharf is alive with restaurants, stores, fish markets and sea lions swimming around the pilings, noisily announcing their presence.

The Path of History

To see the rest of Monterey, a 3-mile (5-km) walking tour, called The Path of History, leads past the more important historical buildings and sites. These include the **Customs House**, the oldest public building in California, now a museum; **Pacific House**, a two-story adobe with a Monterey balcony around the second floor; and impressive historical exhibits from the Spanish, Mexican and early American periods.

Other attractions include **Colton Hall**, a two-story building with a classical portico, the site of the state's first (1849) constitutional convention; **Stevenson House**, a former hotel where the romantic (and sickly) Robert Louis Stevenson lived for a few months while courting his wife; and the **Royal Presidio Chapel**, in constant use since 1794. US President Herbert Hoover was married here.

The **Presidio**, founded in 1770 by Gaspar de Portolá, now serves as the **Defense Language Institute Foreign Language Center**. Other points of interest are the **Allen Knight Maritime Museum**, with relics from the era of sailing ships and whaling, and the **Monterey Museum of Art** (tel: 831-372-5477; open Wed–Sat 11am–5pm, Sun 1–4pm; charge).

In mid-September, the **Monterey Jazz Festival** attracts many of the biggest names in music to the Monterey Fairgrounds. It was here that Jimi Hendrix was brought to the attention of the United States.

Kayaking on Monterey Bay is growing in popularity, offering a delightful opportunity to get out among the otters and sea lions. A

TIP

Be aware that there is a charge to take the 17-Mile-Drive around the Monterey Peninsula, and that "some motorcyclists made trouble once," and so no motocycles are allowed on this private road. The drive takes approximately 3 hours.

BELOW: bagpiper at Sunset Golf Course, Pebble Beach.

Map on page 184

local company operates tours out to see the gray whales on their migration between Alaska and Baja California, down Mexico way.

The 17-Mile Drive

Just north of the foot of Ocean Avenue is the Carmel Gate entrance to the **17-Mile Drive**, which meanders in a three-hour tour around the Monterey Peninsula, via the **Del Monte Forest**, to Pacific Grove. Close to the **Ghost Tree Cypress**, a big stone mansion looks like something seen in a lightning flash that cleaves the midnight darkness of the Scottish moors. The **Lone Pine Cypress**, a single gnarled and windswept tree near the top of a huge wave-battered rock, is a much-photographed site.

The drive's famous attraction is the **Pebble Beach Golf Links**, site of some of the most prestigious tournaments in the US, and usually rated by *Golf Digest* in its annual poll as the Number 1 public course in America. The 17-Mile-Drive is undeniably beautiful, but the attitude of the Pebble Beach Company

toward tourists is somewhat condescending. Motorcyles are not allowed, and the landscape is littered with "no trespassing" signs punishable by a fine and imprisonment. Because all the roads in the Del Monte Forest are privately owned, anyone traveling on the road must pay a fee to the company.

Unless you are an ardent golf fan, the 17-Mile-Drive is probably a waste of money, as the many state parks in this area are just as beautiful and are free of both the attitude and the admission charge.

Charming Carmel

The southern gateway to the Monterey Peninsula is the town of **Carmel ⑩**. Its best-known attraction is the peaceful **Carmel Mission** (open Mon–Fri 9.30am–4.30pm, Sat, Sun 10.30am–4.30pm; charge).

A few chance factors made Carmel what it is today – starving writers and unemployed painters in flight from the devastation of the 1906 San Francisco earthquake, and canny property developers who, to reduce their taxes, covered the tree-

Portuguese tile of Our Lady of Carmel, Carmel Mission.

BELOW:
Carmel Mission dates from 1771; the bell towers were added around 1820.

less acres of the local landscape with a thick, lush carpet of shady Monterey pine trees. The result is one of the most charming seaside towns on the West Coast. When the evening fog rolls in from the bay, the lights inside the cozy houses, combined with the faint whiff of wood smoke from roaring fires, give Carmel the peaceful feeling of a 19th-century European village.

The face of the earth as the Creator intended it to look.
— HENRY MILLER
ON BIG SUR

Cowboy mayor

Although some 3 or 4 million people visit each year – Carmel's popularity was boosted substantially when actor Clint Eastwood became mayor for a couple of terms – it has resisted the glare of neon signs, or the clutter of cheap souvenirs. The plazas and little shopping malls attract pedestrians to wine shops and antiques stores, art galleries and boutiques. The local market stocks fresh artichokes and has racks and racks of wines. At night, on the side streets, a dozen couples might be dining quietly by candlelight behind dark restaurant windows. In the residential parts of town, streets meander casually through the forest, sometimes even splitting in two to accommodate an especially praiseworthy specimen of pine.

Having said all this, the town is not to everyone's taste. Its sweetness and pretension can cloy, and its plethora of gift shoppes just a little too removed from real village life to digest without irony. But Carmel beach, at the bottom of the hill and within easy walking distance of the town, is still sandy and stunning.

South of Carmel is **Point Lobos State Reserve**, a rocky park overlooking the sea. Nature trails crisscross the reserve, and big natural rock pools are home to lolling sea lions. Be sure to take water and a picnic: there are no food facilities.

Highway 1 south of Point Lobos begins to swoop and curve in dramatic fashion. The San Lucia Mountains rise steeply to the left; the foamy sea to the right changes shape and color constantly. Only the two-lane road separates the two, which means the curling ribbon of road has its own distinct weather pattern (read: fog).

BELOW:
horse wranglers in the Camel Valley.

Although the sun may be shining brightly on the other side of the mountains, and can often be seen through the trees, Highway 1 can be distinctly chilly, and the fog comes on quickly, obliterating the world for unexpected moments, which can be alarming on this narrow road.

Beautiful Big Sur

This is a suitably theatrical entrance to **Big Sur ⓫**, arguably California's most beautiful stretch of coastline. One of its most popular photographic subjects is **Bixby Bridge**, north of Big Sur Village, spanning the steep gorge of Bixby Canyon.

Until 1945, Big Sur was populated by ranchers, loggers and miners, but literary people soon showed up. They were drawn to the idea of living inexpensively, growing marijuana in remote canyons and communing with what long-time resident Henry Miller called "the face of the earth as the Creator intended it to look." The **Henry Miller Memorial Library** (tel: 831-667-2574), near **Nepenthe**

restaurant where many gather for sunset, has works by and about this local hero. **Big Sur Village** is really little more than a huddle of stores and a post office. Places to stay here are scarce, and if you plan a weekend visit, book very early.

There are a couple of campgrounds, a few motels and rustic inns, like the **Big Sur River Inn** (tel: 800-588-3610), and some luxurious hot-tub-and-fireplace country inns, usually described as "hedonistic hideaways." Notable among these are the **Ventana Inn** (tel: 800-628-6500) and the **Post Ranch Inn** (tel: 831-667-2200), which was designed by local architect Mickey Muenning.

South of Big Sur Village, Highway 1 winds past several state parks, all worth visiting. One of the most beautiful is **Julia Pfeiffer Burns State Park**, with twisting nature trails and a silvery waterfall. The highway passes the 1960s alternative haven, the **Esalen Institute**, then continues south on to Hollywood-by-the-sea – remarkable **Hearst Castle ⓬** *(see page 196)*.   ❏

Map on page 184

Rustic retreats with a romantic touch.

BELOW: walking the dog, California-style.

HEARST CASTLE AT SAN SIMEON

Newspaper tycoon William Randolph Hearst was larger than life, and so is his mansion

After Disneyland, California's most visited site is the baroque home that newspaper and movie tycoon William Randolph Hearst *(left)* had built by his favorite architect, Julia Morgan. Craftsmen labored for 28 years to create La Cuesta Encantada (the Enchanted Hill) with its acres of gardens, terraces, pools and walkways.

It was Hearst's father George, a multimillionaire from gold, silver and copper mines, who acquired the 275,000-acre (111,300-hectare) property. On his parents' death, Hearst hired Morgan to design the highly ornate twin-towered main house that ended up with 38 bedrooms (some high up in the elegant belltowers), a Gothic dining room, two swimming pools and three sumptuous guest houses.

Next, he stocked the grounds with animals from all over the world, and filled the buildings with carvings, furnishings and works of art from European castles and cathedrals. To conceal a water tank on the adjoining hill, Hearst had 6,000 pine trees planted.

Hearst was the subject of Orson Welles' 1941 movie *Citizen Kane*, and at his death in 1951 he owned the country's largest newspaper chain. He lived in his 130-room hill-top mansion for 20 years until in 1947 he moved to Beverly Hills because of ill health. Ten years later, the Hearst Corporation deeded the San Simeon property to the state of California, where it is an historical monument.

Hearst Castle, San Simeon, tel:1-800-444-4445; www.hearstcastle.com. Reservations required; several different tours most days of the week.

ABOVE: Perched up so high, Hearst Castle is often wreathed in fog. All supplies were shipped along the coast by steamer, then had to be hauled up the hill.

ABOVE: This lavish room is 85 ft (26 meters) long. The 400-year-old carved wooden ceiling was shipped over, like much of the castle's detail, from Italy.

LEFT: In addition to statues, paintings and tapestries, Hearst's collection included oriental rugs, Navajo blankets, furniture, silver and stained glass.

ABOVE: The indoor swimming pool took more than three years to complete. With a Roman architectural theme and resplendent with decorative tiles in Venetian glass and hammered gold, the pool room is so massive that the space on its roof is occupied by two tennis courts.

LEFT: This enormous outdoor pool was the favorite among the castle's guests. Marble colonnades and white marble statues front an impressive Greco-Roman temple facade.

HOLLYWOOD HIGHLIFE

Virtually every weekend Hearst welcomed moviedom's elite to his San Simeon estate. A special train, with a jazz band and open bar, from Glendale station brought the party guests 210 miles (338 km) from Hollywood to San Luis Obispo, where limousines transported them through the estate's grounds filled with lions, bears, ostriches, elephants, pumas and leopards. On arrival at the floodlit mansion, each was allocated a personal maid or valet and was free to wander – except for mandatory attendance at the late-night dinner. There were also special occasions: among the hundred guests who attended a covered-wagon party were the Warner Brothers, the Gary Coopers and William Powell.

"The society people always wanted to meet the movie stars so I mixed them together," wrote actress Marion Davies *(above)*, Hearst's longtime mistress. "Jean Harlow came up quite frequently. She was very nice and I liked her. She didn't have an awful lot to say... all the men used to flock around her. She was very attractive in an evening dress because she never wore anything under it." Clark Gable was another regular guest. "Women were always running after him but he'd just give them a look as if to say 'how crazy these people are' and he stayed pretty much to himself."

BELOW: Most nights the publisher would preside over dinner at the 16th-century monastery table where catsup from bottles and the absence of tablecloths preserved the illusion of "camping out." Liquor was strictly banned (so guests drank in their rooms). After dinner Hearst often showed an as-yet-unreleased movie; *Gone With the Wind*, for example, was screened six months before its December 1939 premiere.

WINE COUNTRY

Only a couple of hours' drive from the streets of San Francisco are Napa and Sonoma, and some of the most beguiling wineries in America

Before Napa comes Sonoma – both geographically and historically. *Sonoma* is a Patwin tribal word meaning "Land of Chief Nose," and may honor a chief with a distinctive snout. Founding father Mariano Vallejo romanticized **Sonoma Valley** as the "Valley of the Moon," and Jack London took up the name, as the title of a book about urbanites rejuvenated by country living.

Sonoma County is characterized by a patchwork of country roads, orchards, hills, ridges and small towns. US 101, the wine country's only freeway, traverses the length of the county north to south, entering near the town of **Petaluma ❶**. State Highway 12 runs through Sonoma Valley to Santa Rosa, passing the towns of Sonoma and Kenwood.

Valley of the Moon

Father Altimira founded beautiful **San Francisco de Solano Mission** in 1823, California's last mission, in this fertile region. General Mariano Vallejo set up the town of **Sonoma ❷** in 1835, making it the northernmost outpost of a Catholic, Spanish-speaking realm that, at its peak, extended all the way to the tip of South America. Sonoma briefly became a republic after the Bear Flag Revolt in 1846, when Americans stormed Vallejo's home, but it was

Count Agoston Haraszthy's innovations at Buena Vista Winery about a decade later that caused residents to recognize the area's vinicultural potential. The town is pleasant, relaxed and well-heeled, and dominated by **Sonoma Plaza**. Restored adobe buildings line the plaza and nearby streets, including the mission, Vallejo's old house, **Lachryma Montis**, and the **Sonoma Barracks**, known collectively as the **Sonoma State Historic Park ❸**. Two blocks away is **Sebastiani Vineyards ❹**

Map on page 200

LEFT:
pre-wine production.
BELOW:
Sonoma Town Hall.

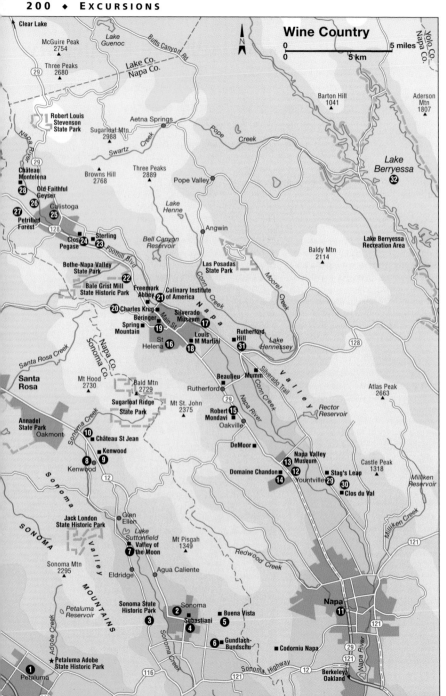

(tel: 707-933-3230), on land that previously belonged to the mission. This very large winery remains in the hands of the Sebastiani family.

East of Sonoma, **Buena Vista Winery ⑤** (tel: 800-926-1266) still retains its old-style connections with Count Haraszthy. The Gundlach and Bundschu families were involved with wine for more than 125 years, and **Gundlach-Bundschu ⑥** (tel: 707-938-5277) produces wines that are exported around the globe. Nearby is the pricey but lovely **Sonoma Mission Inn and Spa** (tel: 707-938-9000).

North on State 121, the **Valley of the Moon Winery ⑦** (tel: 707-996-6941) occupies part of George Hearst's 19th-century vineyards (George was the father of tycoon William R. Hearst). North on State 1 is the town of **Kenwood ⑧**. The **Kenwood Winery ⑨** (tel: 707-833-5891) features Zinfandel, Cabernet Sauvignon and Chenin Blanc, while Chardonnay lovers head for **Château St Jean ⑩** (tel: 707-833-4134), with medieval-style tower and excellent Johannisberg Riesling.

Napa County

Wineries, delicatessens, restaurants and country inns lie close together in **Napa Valley** and the little town of **Napa ⑪**. Although rural, the valley's mix of socialites, titled Europeans and semi-retired Hollywood directors and producers gives **Napa County** a genteel, wealthy if slightly slick, aura.

A 30-mile (48-km) thrust of flatland between the Mayacamas Mountains and the buff-colored Howell Mountains, Napa Valley is pinched off in the north by **Mount St Helena**. The valley's expanses of vineyards are broken up by farmhouses, stone wineries and a series of towns stretched along **State Highway 29**, "The Great Wine Way."

With the exception of COPIA *(see next page)*, the town of Napa is mainly an administrative center, so wine country itself begins in earnest at **Yountville ⑫**, where the vineyards abut the village's historic buildings. Yountville's city park is across from George Yount's grave at the pioneer cemetery. One of General Vallejo's beneficiaries, Yount received his huge land grant for roofing Vallejo's

Map on page 200

Sebastiani Vineyards is on land previously cultivated by the San Francisco de Solano Mission. The winery is still run by the Sebastiani family.

BELOW: the Booze Brothers.

A Wine Primer

Winemaking begins at the crusher, where the juice is freed from the grapes. Red wines are created when the grape skin and pulp are put into the fermenting tank, then yeast is added to convert sugar into alcohol. Grape skins are pressed to extract more juice, then the reds are aged in stainless steel or wooden vats. The wine is clarified, and then aged further before bottling. White wines are made from the fermentation of the juice alone, drawn off from the grapes after crushing. Yeast is added, and fermentation occurs in stainless steel vats. Leaving in the yeast creates very dry wines; controlling the yeast makes sweeter wines. Sparkling wines like Cava, Prosecco and Champagne begin the same way, and then undergo a second fermentation inside the bottle. Carbon dioxide is trapped inside creating the heady bubbles.

Most wineries are open 10am–4pm daily; some by appointment only. For more information and a list of local wineries, contact Napa Valley Tourist Information at 1310 Napa Town Center, tel: 707-226-7459, www.napavalley.org or the Sonoma Valley Tourist Information, 453 1st Street E., tel: 707-996-1090, www.sonomavalley.com.

TIP

Wine Country treats: COPIA, in the town of Napa, is a museum and cultural center that investigates and celebrates wine, food and the arts. The Culinary Institute of America near St Helena is a premier cooking school with a restaurant catered by talented students. Go to: www.ciachef.edu

BELOW: there are beautiful wineries everywhere in Napa and Sonoma counties.

Petaluma adobe – certainly one of history's more lucrative contracting deals. The town offers a chance to learn about wine in the **Napa Valley Museum** ⓭ (55 President's Circle; tel: 707-944-0500; open Wed–Mon 10am–5pm; charge). **Domaine Chandon Winery** ⓮ (tel: 707-944-2280) just west of town is French throughout. The winery, owned by Chandon of Moët & Chandon fame, makes sparkling wine in the *méthode champenoise*; fermented in the bottle from which it is poured, but not called "champagne," as this name is used only for wines made in the Champagne region of France. North of **Oakville** is the **Robert Mondavi Winery** ⓯ (tel: 888-RMONDAVI), a sleek operation, as befits the famous local name. Guided tours only.

St Helena

St Helena ⓰ has historic stone buildings, picnic parks, chic stores, upscale restaurants, country inns and about 40 wineries. The **Silverado Museum** ⓱ (open Tues–Sun noon–4pm; donations welcome) is stocked with Robert Louis Stevenson memorabilia like first editions of his work and souvenirs of the author's global jaunts. South of town, the **Louis M. Martini Winery** ⓲ (tel: 707-963-2736) is run by one of the valley's oldest wine-making clans, and offers reasonably-priced wines in an unpretentious setting. Two historic wineries lie just north of St Helena. Jacob and Frederick started the **Beringer Vineyards** ⓳ (tel: 707-963-7115) in 1876, modeling the Rhine House (1883) after their ancestral estate in Mainz, Germany. Today's winery, owned by Nestlé (yes, the chocolate people), features Fumé Blanc and Cabernet Sauvignon in the mansion tasting room. Outside, spacious lawns and a regal row of elms fronts the winery. The building of the **Charles Krug Winery** ⓴ (tel: 800-682-KRUG), dates from 1874.

The lavish **Greystone Mansion** nearby was the world's largest stone winery when it was erected in 1889 by mining magnate William Bourn; today, the building is maintained by the California headquarters of the **Culinary Institute of America** ㉑, (tel: 1-800-333-9242). The CIA's Greystone Restaurant is open to the public, with meticulous service and up-and-coming chefs guaranteed. To clear your head with a break from wine tasting, the **Bale Grist Mill State Historic Park** ㉒ is 3 miles (5 km) north of St Helena.

Between Bale Grist and the town of Calistoga are two excellent places to stop: **Sterling Vineyards** ㉓ (tel: 707-942-3345) reigns over the upper valley on top of a knoll. A tram whisks visitors 300 ft (91 meters) up on to the hill for a self-guiding tour. The tram fee is applicable toward the purchase of Sauvignon Blanc and other wines. **Clos Pegase** ㉔ (tel: 707-942-4981) is close by. Designed in 1986 by architect Michael Graves in a sleek, modern style, Clos Pegase is known for its art collection almost as much as for its wines.

The one-street town of **Calistoga** ㉕ is a gem; wooden hangings shading shopfronts give it a Wild West feel. In fact, Calistoga is a spa town, rich in mineral springs and hot, therapeutic mud. Low-key treatment centers are scattered around town, busy making beautiful Californians even more beautiful. Two miles (3 km) north, **Old Faithful Geyser** ㉖ (tel: 707-942-6463) spouts jets of boiling water into the sky. Although tickets are expensive for what takes place, there are tables inside the little waiting area, so you can have a pleasant picnic while waiting for the water to take off. West of the geyser is the disappointing **Petrified Forest** ㉗, where fallen redwoods were turned to stone millions of years ago.

Calistoga is surrounded by wineries, far too many to mention. Of note for its historic (1882) lakeside setting, however, is **Chateau Montelena** ㉘ (tel: 707-942-5105), which produces Chardonnay and Cabernet Sauvignon. A limited number of reservations are accepted for the picnic sites on Jade Lake in view of the pagoda; booking in advance is worthwhile.

The Silverado Trail

Running alongside State 29 between Napa and Calistoga, the **Silverado Trail** joins with the highway as the route into Lake County's resort and wine region. Built as the road from St Helena's cinnabar mines to Napa's river docks, the trail is a two-lane road above the valley floor offering panoramic views, uncrowded wineries and hidden valleys deep in the Howell Mountains.

Stag's Leap ㉙, a rocky promontory near Yountville where a Roosevelt elk once plunged to its death, overlooks the award-winning **Stag's Leap Wine Cellars** (tel: 707-261-6441) and also **Clos du Val** ㉚ (tel: 707-259-2225). Toward St Helena, a popular stop is the **Rutherford Hill Winery** ㉛ (tel: 707-963-1871), an ark-like structure with picnic grounds. St Helena is also the turn-off to a warm-water paradise. The Berryessa family lost sons and soil in the Mexican War; today, their land is better known as **Lake Berryessa** ㉜. Take State 128 from St Helena or State 121 from Napa to enjoy the lake's beautiful shoreline. ❏

Map on page 200

Fill high the cup with Samian wine!

– LORD BYRON

BELOW: the blessing of the grapes at Sonoma Mission.

LAKE TAHOE

Gambling makes the headlines,
but in the winter months there's top skiing
and in the summer months great hiking.
All of this is only a few hours from San Francisco

A fine place this to forget weariness and wrongs and bad business.

— JOHN MUIR

BELOW: outdoor
enthusiasts beat a
path to Lake Tahoe.

Mark Twain succumbed to the charms of **Lake Tahoe ⑬**, which straddles the borders of California and Nevada. In *Roughing It*, he wrote "The lake burst upon us," going on to describe the moment when he reached the summit overlooking Tahoe, which was a "noble sheet of blue water lifted 6,300 feet (1,920 meters) above the level of the sea, and walled in by a rim of snow-clad mountain peaks… I thought it must surely be the fairest picture the whole earth affords."

Lake Tahoe has everything an outdoors enthusiast could possibly covet – wilderness, hiking trails, hidden lakeshore caves, snow-covered backroads and quiet beaches. Recreation is the area's lifeblood, and in winter that means downhill and cross-country skiing, and lots of snowboarding. On Friday nights, the weekend exodus from the Bay Area begins, as hundreds of cars, skis strapped on their roofs like sections of picket fences, stream up Interstate 80 or US 50.

Winter paradise

The largest ski areas are **Squaw Valley** (tel: 800-403-6985) at the northwest side, and **Heavenly Valley** (tel: 775-586-7000) on the south side. Squaw Valley has a greater number of ski lifts and marked trails, but Heavenly has longer runs and more vertical drops.

Heavenly Valley is also the preferred ski area for those who like to duck into the casinos. It is located at **South Lake Tahoe**, the busiest part of the lake, near the Nevada border. The casinos can come in handy after a hard day's skiing – most offer inexpensive all-you-can-eat buffets. Gambling is, of course, the area's biggest and most lucrative business. A little down-market from the glitz of Las Vegas, the tables here compete by offering slightly better players' odds.

Many skiers, however, prefer the northern half of the lakeshore on the California side, particularly the area around **Tahoe City**. It's quieter, cleaner and the selection of ski areas is better here. In addition to Squaw Valley, skiers can choose **Alpine Meadows**, **Sugar Bowl**, **Boreal Ridge** and **Northstar**. The latter is particularly good for families, with its fine, gentle slopes. Boreal, perched on the edge of Interstate 80, is the easiest to reach. Sugar Bowl is the oldest. Alpine Meadows is preferred by experienced skiers, as runs rated "expert" make up around 40 percent of the terrain.

Summertime activities

It is often hard to choose among all the outdoor sporting options when the summer sun comes out. Rent in-line skates or a bicycle to explore the local roads, or a mountainbike to blaze down the bare ski runs at Squaw Valley. Several parks and reserves have well-marked hiking trails. The lake offers great fishing, in addition to jet-skiing, waterskiing and kayaking, and there is usually good river rafting on the **Truckee River**. The local tourist office has information on operators and rental stores. A great way to see Lake Tahoe is to take a ride on one of the vessels that cruise around the lake throughout the year. All offer lunch, dinner and dancing cruises, in addition to sightseeing trips along the shoreline and through spectacular **Emerald Bay**, an isolated, tree-lined wilderness tucked into the southwest corner.

Hikers and backpackers usually head for **Desolation Wilderness**, a lake-studded area west of the bay. A wilderness permit must be obtained . The 165-mile (265-km) **Tahoe Rim Trail** offers magnificent views and can be accessed from several points. The **Granite Peak** area is also good for backpacking, and the extremely pretty **Emerald Bay State Park**, as well as **DL Bliss** and **Sugar Pine Point** state parks, are excellent.

On any summer weekend, joggers and bicyclists take to the roads ringing the lake. The 75-mile (121-km) circle makes a strenuous one-day cycle, or a leisurely two- to three-day trip.   ❑

Map on page 184

Lake Tahoe has 18 ski and snowboarding resorts, and nearly 400 inches of annual snowfall.

BELOW: boating on Emerald Bay.

YOSEMITE NATIONAL PARK

The Ahwahneechee natives called it a holy place.
In the soft twilight evening, camped under the stars,
with the silhouette of Half Dome on the velvet horizon,
you might feel the same about Yosemite

Yosemite Valley, to
me, is always
a sunrise, a glitter
of green and gold
wonder in a vast
edifice of stone
and space.

— ANSEL ADAMS

BELOW:
Bridalveil Falls.

Because of its isolation, the Ahwahneechee tribe managed to keep Yosemite (*yo-SEH-mih-tee*) Valley secret from white settlers until 1851, a full year after California attained statehood. When news of this mountain paradise did leak out, the US Cavalry arrived and herded the natives across the Sierras to a barren reservation near Mono Lake. Subjugation of the Native Americans paved the way for settlement. During the decade following its "discovery," Yosemite Valley was fenced, farmed and logged by homesteaders. In 1864, pressure was mounted to preserve the land as a wilderness area, and the result is the spectacular **Yosemite National Park** ⓪. The park was an immediate success, so much so that by the 1980s, 3½ million people came every year. Although **Yosemite Valley** comprises only 8 sq. miles (21 sq. km) of Yosemite National Park's 1,189-sq.-mile (3,080-sq.-km) area, it plays host to more than 90 percent of all its overnight visitors.

Yosemite Village

In **Yosemite Village** Ⓐ, you can get a map, find out about campgrounds, arrange to take a guided horseback trip, and buy requisites for a longer stay. With thousands of hotel rooms and campsites, supermarkets, gift shops, a liquor store and even a jail, the valley was in danger of becoming a textbook example of overdeveloped parkland. There were traffic jams and hour-long waits in cafeteria lines, mostly centered around the village, the first large developed area on the Yosemite loop road.

Fortunately, sensible measures have been taken to manage the crowds more effectively, by reducing the amount of accommodations and parking spaces around the village, and making better use of shut-

tle buses to some of the valley's most popular sites.

There are good reasons for the crowds to come to Yosemite in such numbers. Nowhere else in the United States are there so many large waterfalls in such a small area, including 2,425-ft (739-meter) **Yosemite Falls **, the highest in North America. When Ice-Age glaciers scoured out 8-mile (13-km) long, 1-mile (1.6-km) wide Yosemite Valley, the glaciers left behind several smaller hanging valleys on either side of the main feature, high but not dry conduits for leaping torrents whose romantic names evoke their variety: **Bridalveil**, **Silver Strand**, **Staircase**, **Sentinel**, **Ribbon, Lehamite, Vernal**, **Nevada** and **Illilouette**.

In early June, one of the rarest of Yosemite sights – the "moonbow" at the foot of lower Yosemite Falls – can be seen. It shows up only in the late spring, when the falls are running full, and only in the days around the full moon, when the moonlight shines on the spray and produces a ghostly rainbow. Visitors considering the trip to Yosemite

Falls should be aware that, out of this season, the falls are often dry.

"Great is granite," wrote New England clergyman Thomas Starr King in 1878, "and Yosemite is its prophet." As the prehistoric ice floes melted and retreated, they exposed the colossal building blocks of the Sierra Nevada, shaped and polished into scenery on a grand scale – **El Capitan**, **Cathedral Rock**, **Three Brothers**, **Royal Arches** and **Clouds Rest**. In the daredevil world of technical rock climbing, Yosemite is a true mecca.

Avoiding the crowds

Travel in the east end of the valley near **Mirror Lake** has been restricted to shuttle buses, bicycles and pedestrians, and good bikeway trails make two-wheeled travel the most efficient way to get around. Rental booths can be found in Yosemite Village and at **Yosemite Lodge** (tel: 559-253-5635). Yosemite Lodge offers mid-priced accommodations, somewhere between the inexpensive cabins at the village and the lovely rustic rooms at the **Ahwahnee Hotel**.

Maps:
Area 184
Park 208

Please respect Smokey the Bear and put out all campfires.

BELOW:
sunrise over Half Dome, Yosemite National Park.

In 1864, pressure on the legislature resulted in the Yosemite Grant, the first attempt in the nation's history to preserve an area of scenic beauty from exploitation.

The time to enjoy Yosemite's most famous site, Half Dome, is during the off-season, September to May. The fall brings a rich gold to the leaves of the oak trees, and the sun's lowering angle etches the granite domes and spires into sharper relief. Nights are cool, while mornings are apple-crisp. Autumn also brings herds of bounding wild deer, migrating to winter foraging in the Sierra foothills.

Yosemite Valley is emptiest uring the winter months, when the action shifts to the ski resort of **Badger Pass ⓓ**, 21 miles (34 km) away and 3,000 ft (900 meters) higher. Badger's gentle, pine-fringed slopes offer few challenges for accomplished skiers, but are ideal for families and novice-to-intermediate skiers who don't mind the 45-minute commute from the valley. But spring is the favorite season of many. Wildflowers carpet the meadows, and the roar of wild water booms throughout the valley.

Glacier Point

To the south, State Highway 41 climbs 9 miles (15 km) to **Chinquapin** junction, where a 15-mile (25-km) paved road departs for **Glacier Point ⓔ**. From this viewpoint, 3,200 ft (975 meters) above the floor of Yosemite Valley, the entire park comes into unforgettable, stomach-clutching focus. No less compelling is the 80-mile (129-km) vista to the east and south, a panorama of lakes, canyons, waterfalls and the rugged peaks of Yosemite's High Sierra. Close at hand are the granite steps of the **Giant's Staircase ⓕ**, where Vernal and Nevada falls drop to the raging waters of the **Merced River** 320 and 594 ft (98 and 181 meters) respectively.

From Glacier Point, **Half Dome ⓖ** is the most prominent landmark, a great solitary stone thumb thrusting skyward. What became of Half Dome's other half? In fact, the dome never had another half of solid rock,

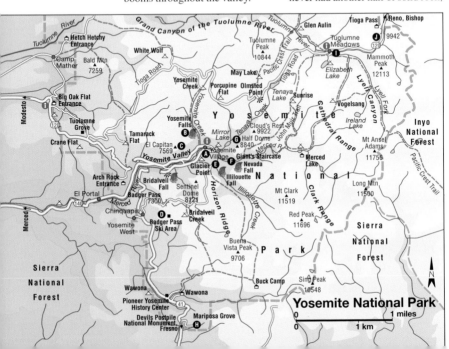

only slabs of granite on the sheer north face that were peeled away like onion skin by advancing Ice-Age glaciers.

At the height of glaciation, 250,000 years ago, Glacier Point itself lay under 700 ft (213 meters) of ice, and instructive markers explain how the 2,000-ft (610-meter) thick Merced and Tenaya glaciers ground down from the high country to merge near Half Dome and hollow out vast Yosemite Valley. The mighty glacier filled the valley to its brim, and extended all the way down the Merced canyon to **El Portal**, 15 miles (24 km) to the west.

Giant sequoias

Five miles (8 km) south of **Wawona**, a short side road leads to the lovely **Mariposa Grove** of towering sequoias, a preserve containing more than 500 mammoth redwood trees. It was here that John Muir slept under the stars alongside President Theodore Roosevelt, and persuaded the chief executive that the forest should be added to the infant Yosemite National Park.

The grove's largest tree, the **Grizzly Giant**, is at least 3,800 years old, 200 ft (60 meters) high and has a girth of 94 ft (29 meters). The best way to experience the trees is on foot, preferably alone, wandering among living things that were giants almost half their present age when Christ walked the Holy Land.

If Wawona and the Mariposa Grove are Yosemite's Black Forest, **Tuolumne Meadows** ❶ is the park's Switzerland. Reached by an hour's drive north from Yosemite Valley on the scenic **Tioga Pass** ❷, and 9,942 ft (3,030 meters) above sea level, Tuolumne is the gateway to an alpine wilderness. The only way to see the more remote areas is to hike, with a backpack that may tip the scales at 50 lbs (23 kg) or more.

A less arduous alternative, on the smoother trails, is to arrange a horse-packing trip. Details can be found locally or by calling Yosemite Park information services, tel: 209-372-8344. Tuolumne is also the site of **Tuolumne Meadows Lodge**, central star in the summer constellation of high Sierra camps. ❏

Map on page 208

TIP

Cabins, lodges and campgrounds in the park itself are extremely popular. If you plan to visit during the summer months, be sure to book six months to a year in advance.

BELOW:
Cathedral Rock is a favorite with hikers.

TRANSPORTATION

GETTING THERE AND GETTING AROUND

GETTING THERE

By Air

San Francisco International Airport (SFO), tel: 650-876-2377, www.san-francisco-sfo.com, just 14 miles (23 km) south of the city, near the town of San Mateo, is the major gateway for foreign travel. Most of the international airline companies that serve northern California land at SFO. There is no airport tax here, although this may change.

AIRLINES

US airlines that fly regularly into San Francisco include:
Alaska Airlines
www.alaskaair.com
America West
www.americawest.com
American Airlines
www.american airlines.com
Continental Air
www.continental.com
Delta Airlines
www.delta.com
Northwest
www.nwa.com
Southwest
www.southwest.com
United Airlines
www.ual.com

Oakland International Airport, tel: 510-577-4000, www.oaklandairport.com is much smaller and less crowded than SFO. A shuttle takes passengers to the Bay Area Rapid Transit (BART) station for a 30-minute ride through the underwater Transbay Tube to downtown San Francisco. Airport coaches, taxis, shuttles and AC Transit provide transportation as well.

One hour south of the city is **San José International Airport**, tel: 408-277-4759, www.sjc.org, served by the carriers Alaska, America West, American, Continental, Delta, Jet Blue, United and United Express.

The airports are served by **Airport Commuter Limo & Sedan Service**, tel: 650-876-1777, **Bay Shuttle**, tel: 415-564-3400, and Super Shuttle, tel: 415-558-8500.

By Train

Amtrak: all trains come into a depot across the Bay Bridge in Oakland, where free bus service is provided into San Francisco. Passes for unlimited travel on Amtrak are available only from a travel agent in a foreign country. Information about Amtrak's train services is available by calling toll-free: 800-USA-RAIL or online at: www.amtrak.com.

By Sea

Cruising into San Francisco Bay is a luxurious way to arrive. "Vagabond" cruises, which feature a limited number of passengers on cargo steamships, are less common than they once were, but check with the **San Francisco Port Authority** (tel: 415-274-0400) or your travel agent to determine which line has a current scheduled stop. Cruise ships representing five major lines dock regularly at Pier 35 in San Francisco. These are **Cunard**, **Holland America**, **Princess Cruises**, **Royal Viking**, and **Crystal**.

By Bus

Greyhound-Trailways provides bus services to San Francisco. Buses arrive and depart at the **Transbay Terminal**, First and Mission streets, tel: 800-231-2222. Bus systems using this terminal include **AC Transit** (East Bay), **SamTrans** (San Mateo County and the peninsula) and city tour-bus lines, including **Gray Line**.

Remember that the bus terminals are located in downtown areas and require caution for personal safety. Bus travelers should avoid walking alone at night, and use taxis or city buses to get to and from the terminals.

By Car

Major land routes into San Francisco are: US Highway 101, over the Golden Gate Bridge, from the north; Interstate 80 over the Oakland Bay Bridge from the east; and US Highways 1, 101, and 280 up the peninsula, when traveling from the south.

North–south travelers who are in a hurry use Interstate 5 to connect with I-80. Travelers from Los Angeles can cut three hours off their trip to San Francisco by taking I-5. The slower coastal routes are more scenic and pass through small towns.

The official speed limit is 55 mph (88 kpm), and 65 mph (105 kpm) on marked sections of I-5. Most federal and state highways are well maintained and policed by cops. Roadside rest and refreshment areas and service stations are well marked and placed at regular intervals. Bridge tolls are charged.

GETTING AROUND

From the Airport

Signs in the airport mark the way to the internal AirTrain **Red Line** that stops at all terminals and the BART (Bay Area Rapid Transit) which provides a metro rail service within the Bay Area station. The longer **Blue Line** links a Rental Car Center with stops for terminals, garages and the BART rail system. Service runs 24 hours per day.

There are also a variety of door-to-door shuttles – **Quake City Shuttle**, tel: 415-255-4899 and **Super Shuttle**, tel: 415-558-8500 are the most prominent and compete for passengers on the upper level of the SFO terminal at specially marked curbs. Super Shuttle operates 20 hours a day, with vans circling the upper terminal area every 20 minutes, or less often at peak periods. Call from

the terminal or simply walk out to the marked curb on the roadway island and wait. The price is marked on the window of each van and should be about $15 one-way. Tipping of around 15–20 percent is encouraged.

The shuttles are harder to come by late at night, particularly after 1am, and it's safer to call a cab after midnight. A line of cabs awaits outside the luggage terminal marked by a yellow column. Be sure to ignore hotels suggested by the drivers and have the fare quoted up front first. Limousine service is available by using the toll-free white courtesy phones in the terminal.

The **Marin County Airporter Coach** (tel: 415-461-4222) services are more expensive than the shuttles. **SamTrans**, San Mateo County's bus system, makes stops between the airport area and downtown San Francisco and is very cheap. No luggage may be taken on the "F" Express, but it may be put aboard the "7B" Local.

Airport Buses

Buses connect SFO with the Hyatt Regency Hotel at Market Street and the Embarcadero. Board on the lower level every 20 minutes from 6am to 11pm. SamTrans buses also run south – 7F (no luggage) to Palo Alto and 7B (with luggage) to Redwood City. 7F runs from about 7am to 12.30am, and 7B runs from about 6am to 1am.

Airport Parking

The airport parking garage, valet parking, long-term parking (more than six hours in lower-priced lots away from the airport) and shuttle service from distant parking lots to the airport are available for anyone who drives.

Orientation

San Francisco is 450 miles (724 km) north of Los Angeles, and flanked on three sides by water. Although often referred to as the

City of Seven Hills, there are actually over 40 hills within the San Francisco limits. The city proper is only 7 sq miles (11 sq km) and can easily be explored on foot and by bicycle, bus, trolley and cable car.

Public Transportation

You should have little problem getting around San Francisco. Many locals use their cars for trips outside the city only. There are two good reasons for this: the city streets are narrow and congested, and the public transportation network is excellent.

A map some swear by and others never figure out is published by MUNI (San Francisco Municipal Railway) and is available at drug and book store counters all over the city. For further information, refer to www.sfmuni.com.

By MUNI & Bus

For getting around in the city, San Francisco MUNI is your best bet. MUNI is responsible for all buses, streetcars, trolley cars and cable cars in San Francisco. Vintage trolleys collected from all over the world often trundle up and down Market Street; these are a delight and a regular form of transportation, unlike the tourist-laden cable cars. You must have the exact change to board.

MUNI passports (one-, three- or seven-day) are good for unlimited rides on public transportaton, or you can buy a City-Pass, which gives you seven consecutive days on MUNI, plus reduced admissions to various attractions in the city. Discounts for MUNI tickets are available for children, the disabled, and people over 65.

If you don't have a pass, you should ask for a transfer when you board; this is valid for any MUNI vehicle (except cable cars) for at least 90 minutes, but no more than two hours, from the time of issue.

Bus stops are marked by the words "Coach Stop" on the street; by a long rectangle of wide, white lines, or by a bright yellow marking on a telephone or light pole, and/or by an orange and brown route sign mounted on a bus stop pole. Service is frequent and some MUNI lines run 24 hours.

For information, tel: 415-673-6864. Be ready with your starting point, your destination and the time of day of travel, and the MUNI operator will plan your route for you. Some buses are specially equipped for wheelchairs. Some of the buses are electric, and are quiet and clean. On all buses, especially electric-powered ones, hang on to the handholds and bars as you move to your seat or stand; the jerky starts can almost throw you to the floor.

AC Transit

To travel east from San Francisco, AC Transit (Alameda-Contra Costa Transit) provides daily services from the Transbay Terminal to most cities in the East Bay area. Fares vary according to distance traveled and the exact fare is required when you board. Many buses are wheelchair-accessible. For more information, tel: 510-817-1717.

Golden Gate Transit

To travel north of the city, Golden Gate Transit buses and ferries connect San Francisco with Marin and Sonoma counties. Buses stop where green, blue and white signs are posted on the bus line poles. The exact fare is required and fares vary according to distance traveled. Golden Gate Transit buses are wheelchair- accessible. For more information, tel: 415-921-5858.

Samtrans

To travel south of San Francisco, SamTrans buses run seven days a week, connecting with AC Transit and Golden Gate

ABOVE: Embarcadero streetcar.

Transit at the Transbay Terminal. SamTrans also connects with BART at the Daly City and Hayward stations. Stops include the San Francisco International Airport, Southern Pacific Caltrain station, and the Greyhound Depot. Fares vary according to distance traveled and you need to have the exact fare when boarding. Most buses are wheelchair accessible. For information, tel: 800-660-4287.

By Train

Bay Area Rapid Transit (bart)

BART is one of the most modern, efficient, and automated regional transportation systems in the country. The sleek, clean, air-conditioned cars carry hundreds of thousands of commuters each day at speeds approaching 80 miles (129 km) an hour. BART serves 43 stations in three counties, from San Francisco to Milbrae and throughout Alameda and Contra Costa (the East Bay), Monday–Saturday, 6am–midnight, Sundays 9am–midnight. Some of the BART tracks are underground, while others are surfaced or elevated. Among the underground tracks are those inside the Transbay Tube between San Francisco and Oakland. At 3.5 miles (6 km), this tube is one of the world's longest underwater tunnels.

The trains have drivers, but are essentially controlled by track-side relays and a $40-million computer center at the Lake

Merritt BART station in Oakland. There are no cashiers (only vending machines), no ticket-takers (only automated entrance/exit gates) and no conductors (incoming trains are announced on computerized bulletin boards).

Tourists can ride BART for a special reduced fare that entitles you to stay on board for up to three hours. You must enter and exit BART from the same station. Commuters crowd the cars from 7am to 9am and 4pm to 6pm on weekdays. so plan your fun ride during off hours or you may never find a seat.

BART stations are marked with blue and white signs. Along Market Street, look for the escalators going down to the underground boarding points. For current information, tel: 415-989-2278. Outside San Francisco, local information numbers are listed in the area telephone directory under "Bay Area Rapid Transit."

Amtrak, which runs state and national passenger trains, makes daily stops not far from San Francisco in Martinez, Richmond and San Jose. Service may be ended at Oakland's 16th Street Station where a free bus service is provided to the Transbay Bus Terminal in San Francisco. For information, tel: 800-872-7245.

State-owned **CalTrain** runs passenger trains between San Francisco and San José with several stops along the peninsula. Used by many commuters, the service is most frequent northbound in the morning and southbound in the afternoons. CalTrain operates from a terminal at Fourth and Townsend streets. To receive information, tel: 800-660-4287. Since the terminal is served by many MUNI bus lines, it is easy and fun to take the train for a sightseeing excursion down the peninsula.

By Ferry

For commuters and sightseers alike, ferry boats are a convenient and scenic way to cross the bay. **Golden Gate Ferry** services are offered from the original Ferry Building at the foot of Market Street to Sausalito and Larkspur. Two lines run from the Fisherman's Wharf area: the Red & White Fleet has tours around the bay as well as ferry services to Sausalito, Tiburon, Angel Island and Alcatraz Island. The Blue & Gold Fleet also operates narrated bay cruises from the Wharf.

Information can be obtained at the telephone numbers or websites below, and it's always an idea to check the fleet and pier before arriving for a crossing. These are weather dependent and can be subject to change:

Red & White Fleet, www.redand white.com, Pier 43, 1/2 Fisherman's Wharf, tel: 415-673-2900. Round-the-Rock and Golden Gate bridge tours.

Blue & Gold Fleet, Piers 39 and 41, Fisherman's Wharf, tel: 415-773-1188. Angel Island, Sausalito, Tiburon, Oakland, Alameda.

Golden Gate Ferry, www.golden gate.org, leaves from the Ferry Building to Sausalito and Larkspur, tel: 415-921-5858.

Private Transportation

Taxis

San Francisco is so compact that taxis are a convenient alternative to walking or public transportation when you're in a hurry and going just a few miles. In busy downtown areas, taxis can be hailed from the sidewalk. but this can be difficult in other areas. Use the telephone directory and the numbers below if you need to call in advance. San Francisco cab drivers are known for their helpfulness, and the city is so small, it's difficult to get lost.

Arrow, tel: 415-648-3181.
DeSoto, tel: 415-970-1300.
Luxor, tel: 415-282-4141.
Pacific Cab, tel: 415-986-7220.
United, tel: 415-552-8562.
Veteran's, tel: 415-648-1313.
Yellow Cab, tel: 415-626-2345.

Driving

Car Rentals

There are dozens of automobile rental agencies at the airports and in San Francisco. Rates vary; insurance is extra and varies in price and coverage. Check your own auto policy before you leave home to make sure you really need the extra coverage. Read the rental agreement before you sign it. Most companies offer unlimited mileage and special weekend rates. Many will pick you up at your hotel. Shop around for the best rates and service. Often, smaller local rental companies offer better deals than national firms. If you fancy driving a dented heirloom, try Rent-A-Wreck; www.rentawreck.com. Reservations are advised.

Most rental agencies require you to be at least 21 years old (sometimes 25) and to hold a valid driver's or international driver's license and a major credit card. Drivers are required at all times to abide by local and state traffic regulations.

If you are an auto club member in another country, National Automobile Club will extend emergency cover, information and other services to you. The California State Automobile Association may extend services – you must check first. Contact www.csaa.com for details.

HOW TO PARK

Much of San Francisco's parking space is on steep hills. It is the law that wheels must be "curbed" on these inclines to help prevent unexpected runaways. Turn your front wheels into the curb on a downhill slope and away from the curb if facing uphill. Be sure to set the emergency brake. Not only are fines issued for cars that are not "curbed," but there's also the possibility of finding your car at the bottom of a hill.

Car Rental Companies

Alamo, tel: 800-882-9440, www.alamo.com
Avis, tel: 800-230-4898, www.avis.com
Budget, tel: 800-527-0700, www.budget.com
Dollar, tel: 800-800-4000, www.dollar.com.
Enterprise, tel: 800-325-8007, www.enterprise.com
Hertz, tel: 800-654-3131, www.hertz.com
National, tel: 800-227-7368, www.nationalcar.com
Thrifty, tel: 800-367-2277, www.thrifty.com

Motorcycles & Scooters

Dubbelju Motorcycle Rentals, 271 Clara Street, tel: 415-495-2774, www.dubbelju.com
Eaglerider Motorcycle Rental, 1060 Bryant Street, tel: 888-390-6500. www.eaglerider.com
Harley Motorcycle Rentals, 757 Lincoln Avenue, San Rafael, tel: 415-456-9910. www.harleymc.com
Scootcar San Francisco, 431 Beach, tel: 415-567-7994, www.scootcar.net

Bicycle Rentals

It is possible to tour San Francisco and never struggle up a hill. Both Golden Gate Park and Golden Gate Bridge have designated routes for bicycles on weekends (tel: 415-831-2700). Rental shops line Stanyan Street, at the park's entrance, and in the Marina area and Fisherman's Wharf. Many shops have route maps, too. Rental places include:
Adventure Bicycle Company, 734 Lombard St, tel: 415-771-0392.
New Holiday Adventure Sales & Rentals, 1937 Lombard St, tel: 415-567-1192.
Stanyan Street Cyclery, 672 Stanyan Street, tel: 415-668-1117.
Wheel Fun Rentals, Golden Gate Park, tel: 415-668-6699.

ACCOMMODATIONS

SOME THINGS TO CONSIDER BEFORE YOU BOOK THE ROOM

Choosing a Hotel

San Francisco offers a variety of accommodations in an ever-expanding variety of locations. The compact nature of the city allows visitors to consider many neighborhoods outside the central business and shopping areas, although many tourists find they are happy to stay in the more popular Union Square and Fisherman's Wharf areas. Information and reservation services are available to assist you in your choice. A 14 percent room tax is added to all rates.

The large hotels of San Francisco are particularly well suited to international travelers. These hotels are mostly situated in established areas, with easy access to tourist sites and public transportation.

A concierge will arrange theater tickets, tours, seats at sporting events, limousines with bilingual drivers, and airline reservations. They can also recommend restaurants, speak foreign languages, and help exchange currency.

The large hotels in San Francisco each have at least 200 rooms with air conditioning, color TV, room phones and nearby parking, restaurants, coffee shops and bars. There are

seasonal rate changes and special off-season packages. Telephone, fax, check the website or write to verify current rates and make reservations.

Smaller hotels are often renovated hotels in newly popular or changing areas, or in neighborhoods around Alamo Square, Golden Gate Park and Russian Hill. They provide services with a personal touch at rates lower than the well-known, centrally located large hotels.

Since rooms are limited in number and word spreads quickly about the good ones, be sure to arrange reservations in advance. Rates vary widely in relation to services offered, location or exclusivity, and are not necessarily less expensive than the bigger hotels downtown.

Note: Due to California's strict policy, most hotel and motel rooms are non-smoking. Be sure to check this before you book, and be prepared to shop around to find accommodation where smoking is allowed.

Reservations

Hotel reservations may be made through **San Francisco Reservations**, tel: 800-677-1570, www.hotelres.com, which deals with over 300 hotels, often at prefer-

ential rates, and there's no booking fee. The **San Francisco Convention and Visitors Bureau** (tel: 415-391-2000) can advise you regarding any special needs or give out general information about their member hotels, motels and inns. Hotel chains like **Hilton**, **Hyatt** and **Marriott** offer toll-free telephone numbers for reservations; go to: www.onlysf.visitor.org.

FISHERMAN'S WHARF, NORTH BEACH & CHINATOWN

HOTELS

Deluxe

Argonaut Hotel
495 Jefferson Street
Tel: 415-563-0800
www.argonauthotel.com
252 rooms directly opposite the Wharf's Hyde Street Pier, with a maritime theme and suites with sea views, tri-pod telescopes and hot tubs. **$$$**

Moderate

San Francisco Marriott Fisherman's Wharf
1250 Columbus Avenue
Tel: 415-775-7555
www.marriott.com
Two blocks from the attractions of Fisherman's Wharf. Great for both business travelers and families. Sauna and exercise room. **$$**

Washington Square Inn
1660 Stockton Street
Tel: 415-981-4220 or

800-388-0220
www.wsisf.com
A European-style bed and breakfast in North Beach and within walking distance of Fisherman's Wharf, Chinatown and the Financial District. **$$**

Inexpensive

Best Western Tuscan Inn
425 North Point Street
Tel: 415-561-1100 or
800-648-4626
www.tuscaninn.com
Just two blocks west of Pier 39, many of the rooms offer a spectacular view of the bay. **$–$$**

Grant Plaza Hotel
465 Grant Avenue
Tel: 415-434-3883 or
800-472-6899
www.grantplaza.com
A good bet in Chinatown: 72 immaculately clean, small rooms equipped with the basics. **$**

Hotel Boheme
444 Columbus Avenue

Tel: 415-433-9111
www.hotelboheme.com
Styled to evoke the Beatnik era, the Boheme offers an abundance of Bohemian charm. The 1950s photographs are wonderful. All rooms have free wi-fi. **$–$$**

Royal Pacific Motor Inn
661 Broadway
Tel: 415-781-6661 or
800-545-5574
www.royalpacific.citysearch.com
A budget motel located on the threshold of North Beach and Chinatown. Facilities include a Finnish sauna. **$**

San Remo Hotel
2337 Mason Street
Tel: 415-776-8688 or
800-352-7366
www.sanremohotel.com
Built in 1906, this North Beach hotel served as a boarding-house for sailors, poets and pensioners, and was a speakeasy during Prohibition. Today it's a bargain, with immaculate, well-situated

rooms without telephones or TV. Some rooms share showers. The rooftop penthouse is a real treat. **$**

The Wharf Inn
2601 Mason Street
Tel: 415-673-7411
www.wharfinn.com
In the thick of the Wharf, a 51-room gem with friendly service and rooms with balconies overlooking Pier 39. **$–$$**

PRICE CATEGORIES

The price is for a standard double room for one night:
$$$$ $350+
$$$ $225–350
$$ $150–225
$ under $150

ACCOMMODATIONS

ACTIVITIES

UNION SQUARE & THE FINANCIAL DISTRICT

HOTELS

Deluxe

Campton Place Hotel
340 Stockton Street
Tel: 415-781-5555 or
800-647-4077
www.camptonplace.com
A tranquil, intimate atmosphere, perfect for

the sophisticated and discreet traveler. Small dogs welcome. **$$$$**

Four Seasons Hotel & Residences
757 Market Street
Tel: 415-633-3000
www.fourseasons.com
With an in-house tech center, high-end stores, two-story health club with indoor pool and Jacuzzi, plus 277 rooms

in an ultra-convenient location Downtown, this recent addition to Market Street knows how to cater to its sophisticated and fairly exclusive clientele. **$$$$**

Mandarin Oriental
222 Sansome Street
Tel: 800-622-0404
www.mandarinoriental.com
Extraordinary views and decadent service.

Binoculars are provided in each accommodation, and some rooms have glass bathtubs near the windows. **$$$$**

A – Z

Expensive

Grand Hyatt
345 Stockton Street
Tel: 800-233-1234
www.hyatt.com
With a lovely fountain in the garden, this hotel towers 36 stories above Union Square. **$$$**

Hotel Nikko
222 Mason Street
Tel: 415-394-1111 or 800-645-5687
www.hotelnikkosf.com
An elegant and sophisticated Japanese hotel with 510 rooms, 22 suites and one of the city's best spa facilities. **$$$**

Sir Francis Drake
450 Powell Street
Tel: 415-392-7755 or 800-392-7129
www.sirfrancisdrake.com
Doormen are decked in Beefeater costumes, and rooms are styled as if from an English country home. **$$–$$$**

Westin St Francis
335 Powell at Union Square
Tel: 800-917-7458
www.westinstfrancis.com
A San Francisco institution since 1903, this hotel is rich in history and elegance. Meeting beneath the hand-carved grandfather clock in the lobby has long been a favorite rendezvous for locals. **$$$**

Moderate

Hilton Hotel & Tower San Francisco
333 O'Farrell Street
Tel: 415-771-1400 or 800-445-8667
With 1,685 rooms on the edge of Union Square. this is one of the largest hotels in the city. Pool, exercise room, five restaurants. **$$**

The Maxwell House
386 Geary Street
Tel: 415-986-2000 or 888-734-6299
www.maxwellhotel.com
Well-located and within most people's budgets, the owners have given this pleasant hotel an Art Deco look. **$$**

Renaissance Parc 55
55 Cyril Magnin
Tel: 415-392-8000 or 800-595-0507
www.parc55hotel.com
Part of the Park Lane hotel chain; incorporates a health club. **$$**

The Serrano
405 Taylor Street
Tel: 415-885-2500
www.serranohotel.com
A 17-story Spanish Revival building with a Moorish-style lobby, 236 rooms and 19 suites in the heart of the Theater District. Pet and kid friendly with a good restaurant, called Ponzu, downstairs. **$$**

Inexpensive

Hotel Cosmo
761 Post Street
Tel: 415-673-6040 or 800-794-6011
www.hotel-cosmo.com
Big with the arty crowd due to art openings and a lobby filled with local works. Of the 144 rooms, the corner suites with stunning views are one of the best bargains in town. **$**

Hotel Diva
440 Geary Street
Tel: 415-885-0200 or 800-553-1900
www.hoteldiva.com
This maritime themed 114-room hotel is modern and a bit sterile, but the location, in the heart of the Theater District, sells it. **$**

Hotel Rex
562 Sutter Street
Tel: 415-433-4434 or 800-433-4434
Fax: 415-433-3695
The decor of the Rex is inspired by the literary salons of the 1920s, while the lobby is a showcase of period furnishings and antiquarian books. **$**

Hotel Metropolis
25 Mason Street
Tel: 415-775-4600 or 800-553-1900
www.hotelmetropolis.com
Eco-friendly hotel with a "four-elements" theme and where each floor is painted a different color. Good, centrally located bargain for families. **$**

TENDERLOIN, CIVIC CENTER & SoMa

HOTELS

Deluxe

Clift Hotel
495 Geary Street
Tel: 415-775-4700
www.clifthotel.com
Historic hotel recently redesigned by Philippe Starke, the Clift is a fusion of old-world elegance and contemporary hipness. Home of über-cool Asia de Cuba restaurant and the Redwood Room. **$$$$**

Palace Hotel
2 New Montgomery Street
Tel: 415-512-1111 or 800-325-3535
www.sfpalace.com
An historical landmark in SoMa, and home of the magnificent Garden Court Restaurant. **$$$$**

W Hotel
181 3rd Street
Tel: 415-777-5300 or 800-946-8357
www.whotels.com
Sparse elegance and minimalist design lures the hip and the wannabees to SoMa. The delectable XYZ restaurant downstairs is top-notch. 423 rooms, each with CD players, 27-inch TVs, wi-fi and goose-down duvets. **$$$$**

Expensive

Adagio Hotel
550 Geary Street
Tel: 415-775-5000
www.thehoteladagio.com
Comfortable and chic, the Adagio Hotel has Aveda bath products, internet services, and superb customer service. **$$$**

Hotel Monaco
501 Geary Street
Tel: 415-292-0100 or 866-622-5284
www.monacosf.com
A renovated Beaux Arts building with hand-painted ceiling domes and grand Art Nouveau murals in the common areas. Rates include

morning coffee and afternoon tea, wine and cheese receptions with neck massages, and tarot readings. **$$$**

Inn at the Opera
333 Fulton Street
Tel: 415-863-8400 or
800-325-2708
www.innattheopera.com
A favorite spot for the performing artists who appear nightly in San Francisco's nearby arts centers. **$$$**

Moderate

Cathedral Hill Hotel
1101 Van Ness Avenue
Tel: 415-776-8200 or
800-622-0855
www.cathedralhillhotel.com
Rooftop pool, garden patio and 24-hour fitness center. Rooms have balconies with city views. **$–$$**

The Commodore Hotel
825 Sutter Street
Tel: 415-923-6800 or
800-338-6848
www.thecommodorehotel.com
Assets include the

swanky Red Room lounge with a neo-Deco sensibility, affordable accommodations, and the "panoramic suite" with sweeping city views.

The Mosser
54 4th Street
Tel: 415-986-4400
An ornate stained-glass window in the lobby, antique phone booths and an incredibly slow elevator are quirky reminders of this hotel's past, but the good linens, latest gadgets, prime SoMa location and good rates make it an affordable choice for young sophisticates. **$–$$**

York Hotel
940 Sutter Street
Tel: 415-885-6800 or
800-808-york
The setting for the Hitchcock movie *Vertigo* is both sophisticated and comfortable. The Plush Room Theater, once a Prohibition-era speakeasy, and now

known for its cabaret, is located here. Reasonably priced, includes breakfast, newspaper and wine. **$$**

Inexpensive

Abigail House
246 McAllister Street
Tel: 415-861-9728
www.abigailhouse.com
Boutique hotel built in 1927. Uniquely decorated rooms. **$**

Bay Bridge Inn
966 Harrison Street
Tel: 415-397-0657
www.baybridgeinn.com
Nothing but the basics here, but one attraction is that the 22 clean, motel-style rooms are convenient to the 11th Street nightclub scene in SoMa. **$**

Hotel Bijou
111 Mason Street
Tel: 415-771-1200 or
800-771-1022
www.hotelbijou.com
A 65-room hotel dedicated to cinephiles. A "film hotline" gives

patrons the latest about local movie shoots and the walls are covered in black and white images of old cinema marquees. Nightly viewings in the mini-theater with vintage cinema seating is a quirky bonus. **$**

Monticello Inn
127 Ellis Street
Tel: 415-392-8800 or
866-778-6169
www.monitcelloinn.com
Colonial-style flair right in the heart of downtown, with a bar and grill located adjacent. **$**

Phoenix Hotel
601 Eddy Street
Tel: 415-776-1380 or
800-248-9466
www.thephoenixhotel.com
Popular with touring bands and edgy celebrities, the Phoenix has 44 funky rooms with bamboo furniture and a tropical oasis touch. The adjoining Bambuddah restaurant and bar serves Asian-themed delights while you're poolside. **$**

NOB HILL

HOTELS

Deluxe

Huntington Hotel
1075 California Street
Tel: 415-474-5400 or
800-227-4683
www.huntingtonhotel.com
Plush, elegant and still family owned, this hotel is one of the city's small luxury gems. Each room and suite is uniquely decorated, the service is flawless and the style excels. **$$$$**

The Ritz Carlton
600 Stockton Street
Tel: 415-296-7465 or
800-241-3333
www.ritzcarlton.com/hotels/san_fr
ancisco
A luxury landmark hotel with 336 rooms, indoor spa with gym, swimming pool, whirlpool and sauna and an award-winning French restaurant on the premises.

Expensive

Fairmont Hotel & Tower
950 Mason Street
Tel: 415-772-5013 or
800-527-4727

www.fairmont.com
A favorite set location for filmmakers and an elegant experience, the Fairmont was about to open when the 1906 earthquake struck. Undaunted, the hotel opened a year later. **$$$**

Mark Hopkins Inter-Continental
No. 1 Nob Hill
Tel: 415-392-3434 or
800-662-4455
www. san-francisco.intercontinen
tal.com
The "Top of the Mark" restaurant and bar remains a "must,"

while the rooms never fail to satisfy. **$$$**

PRICE CATEGORIES

The price is for a standard double room for one night:

$$$$	$350+
$$$	$225–350
$$	$150–225
$	under $150

The Renaissance Stanford Court
905 California Street
Tel: 415-989-3500 or
800-227-4736
www.marriott.com
An elegant renovation credited with setting the standard for San Francisco grand-hotel revivals. **$$$**

Moderate

Nob Hill Lambourne
725 Pine Street
Tel: 415-433-2287 or
800-274-8466
www.jdvhospitality.com
Dedicated to creating a holistic environment that promotes healthy living and environmentally sound business practices, the Lambourne has Asian-inspired massages, organic mini bars and healthy Continental breakfasts. Chemical-free cleaning products are used by the housekeeping staff. **$-$$**

White Swan Inn
845 Bush Street
Tel: 415-775-1755
www.jdvhospitality.com
English-style bed and breakfast inn, the White Swan has gas fireplaces in all 26 rooms – useful in chilly and fogbound San Francisco. **$-$$**

Inexpensive

Petite Auberge
863 Bush Street
Tel: 415-928-6000 or
866-302-0896
www.jdvhospitality.com
A small, cozy French-style inn with 26 rooms. There's a pretty parlor and afternoon wine; the room rate includes a gourmet breakfast. **$**

King George Hotel
334 Mason Street
Tel: 415-781-5050
www.kinggeorge.com
Traditional rooms and afternoon tea; a favorite with Europeans. **$**

BELOW: Nob Hill elegance at the Fairmont.

CENTRAL NEIGHBORHOODS

HOTELS

Expensive

Alamo Square Inn
719 Scott Street
Tel: 415-315-0123 or
866-515-0123
www.alamoinn.com
Thirteen-room bed and breakfast with Jacuzzi, fireplaces and complimentary wine, near one of San Francisco's most photographed spots. Free parking. **$$**

The Archbishop's Mansion
1000 Fulton Street
Tel: 415-563-7872 or
800-543-5820
www.jdvhospitality.com
This exquisite French chateau mansion in Alamo Square was built in 1904 for the archbishop of San Francisco and is an historical landmark. Complimentary breakfast and wine are served. Absolutely elegant, the Archbishop is one of the city's best. **$$-$$$**

Hotel Drisco
2901 Pacific Avenue
Tel: 415-346-2880 or
800-634-7277
www.hoteldrisco.com
A 100 year-old hotel tucked away in a beautiful, historical residential area of Pacific Heights. **$$**

Moderate

The Chateau Tivoli
1057 Steiner Street
Tel: 415-776-5462 or
800-228-1647
www.chateautivoli.com
On Alamo Square, this plush Victorian bed and breakfast inn brimming with antiques and curios has 22 charming rooms, some with fireplaces and Jacuzzis. **$-$$**

Hotel Del Sol
3100 Webster Street
Tel: 415-921-5520 or
877-433-5765
www.thehoteldelsol.com
Renovated 1950s motor lodge, cheerful and bright with a fabulous swimming pool. The best on the busy Lombard strip. **$-$$**

Hotel Majestic
1500 Sutter Street
Tel: 415-441-1100 or
800-869-8966
www.thehotelmajestic.com
Constructed in 1902, the Majestic claims to be the oldest still-operating hotel in the city. Old-world atmosphere; good special rates. **$-$$**

Radisson Miyako
1625 Post Street
Tel: 415-922-3200 or
800-533-4567
211 rooms in Japantown, understated and a favorite with business travelers. **$$**

Inexpensive

The Marina Inn
3110 Octavia Street
Tel: 415-928-1000 or
800-274-1420
www.marinainn.com
The Marina, in the Lombard Street area, is a hotel that has more the feel of a countrified bed and breakfast inn than a city establishment. **$**

Queen Anne Hotel
1590 Sutter Street
Tel: 415-441-2828 or
800-227-3970
www.queenanne.com
Individually appointed rooms in a restored Victorian building near Japantown. **$**

HAIGHT-ASHBURY, GOLDEN GATE PARK & THE CASTRO

HOTELS

Moderate

Noe's Nest
3973 23rd Street
Tel: 415-821-0751
Tiny, five-room bed and breakfast inn in pretty, residential Noe Valley neighborhood beyond the Castro. Noe's nest has decks, fireplaces, a Jacuzzi and themed rooms. **$–$$**

Inexpensive

24 Henry Guesthouse & Village House
24 Henry Street
Tel: 415-864-5686 or 800-900-5686
www.24henry.com
Two refurbished late-1800s Victorian houses have been turned into hotels. Each has a parlour and five bedrooms, right in the heart of the Castro. **$**

Beck's Motor Lodge
2222 Market Street
Tel: 415-621-8212
Quintessential American motel replete with tacky carpets, garish furnishings and glasses sealed in plastic. You either think Beck's is kitsch, or you run away screaming. Prime location in the Castro. **$**

The Parker Guesthouse
520 Church Street
Tel: 415-621-3222 or 888-520-7275
www.parkerguesthouse.com
A relaxed and welcoming guest house in the Castro with 21 rooms (only two with shared baths) and terrycloth robes for every guest.

A garden and steam room complete the pleasant package. **$**

Red Victorian
1665 Haight Street
Tel: 415-864-1978
The Red Victorian is perfect for the whimsical, budget traveler. Located in the heart of the Haight-Ashbury district, this small hotel is friendly and casual with each room reflecting a different theme, like the "Flower Child Room" or the "Playground." Book in and have fun. **$**

Stanyan Park Hotel
750 Stanyan Street
Tel: 415-751-1000
www.stanyanpark.com
With 36 guest rooms and suites, some overlooking Golden Gate Park, this elegant, affordable hotel offers afternoon tea and an "expanded" Continental breakfast. **$**

MOTELS

If you are traveling by car and need only basic accommodations for sleeping, motels offer lower rates and a parking space near your room. Many motels are situated along busy streets and the degree of service and quality of amenities vary.

Major motel chains provide toll-free telephone numbers for making and confirming reservations. They also offer standard quality. The major chains include **Best Western**, **Holiday Inn**, **Ramada** and **Travelodge**.

ALTERNATIVES

San Francisco is home to one of the largest hostels in the country. The dormitory-style **Hostelling International San Francisco** includes about 200 beds and community kitchens in its Downtown location, tel: 415-788-5604, or 170 rooms located above the bay in a century-old Army dispensary at Fort Mason, between the Marina and Fisherman's Wharf, tel: 415-771-7277. The maximum stay is five nights; international hostel rules are observed. Your International Hostel Pass is honored for credit, or you can pay the night rate that includes a guest pass. Reservations are accepted and limited free parking is provided.

Another inexpensive alternative for travelers who wish to stay for a maximum of five days is provided by **European Guest House** at 761 Minna. Accommodation is dormitory style. For more information, tel: 415-861-6634. Two colleges also provide **university dormitory accommodations** during the summer months. Twin-bedded rooms with a shared bath are available for students. For information, contact **San Francisco State University**, Housing Office, 800 Font Boulevard, San Francisco, 94132, tel:

415-338-1067; or the **University of California San Francisco**, Housing Office, 500 Parnassus Avenue, San Francisco, 94122, tel: 415-476-2231. The USF facilities are located in the Haight-Ashbury neighborhood near Golden Gate Park.

For **extended visits** or for business travel, spacious accommodations are available for rent in apartments and condominiums, most of them fully equipped with kitchens. Many have maid service and require a one-week minimum stay. Locations vary throughout city neighborhoods. Specialty reservation and information services include: **American Property Exchange**, 2800 Van Ness Street, San Francisco, 94109, tel: 415-447-2061. Or go online and contact www.biz-stay.com for detailed information on extended-stay listings, including hotels.

PRICE CATEGORIES

The price is for a standard double room for one night:

$$$$	$350+
$$$	$225–350
$$	$150–225
$	under $150

TRANSPORTATION   ACCOMMODATIONS   ACTIVITIES   A – Z

ACTIVITIES

THE ARTS, NIGHTLIFE, FESTIVALS, SHOPPING AND SPECTATOR SPORTS

THE ARTS

Theater, Ballet, Opera & Concerts

The San Francisco Bay Area is a major cultural center, home to the San Francisco Ballet, Symphony, Opera and many quality museums like the Museum of Modern Art. Each is a first-rate institution. In addition, galleries, theaters, dance companies, concert halls, museums and bookstores offer choices for every taste – from classical to contemporary arts.

Many writers and artists live in the Bay Area and new works and shows are often tested here. Revivals of shows are also popular, on the stage or sometimes in ornate movie theaters.

Theater

You can choose from New York hits, local experimental works, classic revivals and more in San Francisco but tickets can be expensive for the big shows. An alternative to paying full price is to attend a preview showing, a matinee performance or to purchase same-day tickets at half price at TIX on Union Square.

The Theater District is bordered by Taylor, Sutter, Market and Post streets, not far from Union Square. Although safe when filled with theater goers, the edge of this district borders the Tenderloin *(see page 233),* so you should not walk around alone after a show.

Close to Union Square are the **American Conservatory Theater** (ACT) 415 Geary, tel: 415-749-2228 *(see next column)*; the **Curran**, 445 Geary, tel: 415-551-2000, and the **Orpheum Theater**, 1192 Market, tel: 415-512-7770, both of which present Broadway musicals that have made their way to the West Coast from New York. The **Actors' Theater**, 533 Sutter Street, tel: 415-296-9179, often does classics by such luminaries as Tennessee Williams or other innovators, Thursday–Sunday at 8pm. The **Lorraine Hansberry Theater**, 620 Sutter, tel: 415-474-8800, is home to the best known African-American theater group in the Bay Area.

Other theaters include the **Exit Theater** 156 Eddy, tel: 415-673-3847; **Golden Gate Theater**, 1 Taylor St, tel: 415-551-2000; **Cowell Theater**, at Fort Mason Center, tel: 415-441-3687; **Intersection for the Arts**, 446 Valencia, tel: 415-626-2787 (the city's oldest arts center); **Yerba Buena Center for the Arts**, 701 Mission, tel: 415-978-2787; **Theater Rhinoceros**, 2926 16th Street, tel: 415-861-5079 which offers gay and lesbian works and the **Geary Theater**, 415 Geary, tel: 415-749-2228.

The Asian American Theatre Company, at 690 5th Street, Suite 211, tel: 415-543-5738, is known for innovative Asian themes and casts who perform Thursdays through Sundays, often with matinees.

Repertory companies use smaller theaters that seat an audience of 50 to 500. Although the highly regarded **American Conservatory Theater** usually performs known works, many of the smaller groups present new material. All offerings are listed in the newspaper calendars, but you may wish to call a specific theater for more information. You can also consult www.bestofbroadway-sf.com for additional theater information.

Ballet

Known nationally for its entrepreneurial savvy and artistic innovation, **ODC Dance**, 3153 17th Street, tel: 415-863-6606, www.odcdance.org, performs a variety of modern and independent dance recitals. The Joffrey Ballet, American Ballet Theater and the Stuttgart Ballet visit the San Francisco Opera House regularly. For information, tel: 415-864-

3330. The **San Francisco Ballet**, tel: 415-865-2000, www.sfballet.org also hosts various productions throughout the year.

Opera

In addition to the **San Francisco Symphony** (tel: 415-864-6000) which performs regularly in the Davies Symphony Hall, at Civic Center, and which plays a summer pops series, a Beethoven Festival and the Mostly Mozart Festival each year, there are chamber music groups, ethnic music groups, visiting groups, and the second largest opera in the United States, the **San Francisco Opera**. The San Francisco Opera, Grove and Van Ness avenues in the Civic Center area, tel: 415-864-3330, www.sfopera.com, features internationally renowned stars of the opera world. Having entered its seventh decade of annual seasons, 10 operas are presented each year in repertory. Standing-room tickets can be purchased two hours before the performance. **Pocket Opera**, www.pocketopera.com, is also worth a look. This is a professional group that presents operatic works in English in intimate settings, with an emphasis on accessibility. The company usually performs at the Florence Gould Theater in the Palace of the Legion of Honor.

Concerts

The Bay Area is filled with wonderful concert performances. Some of the best are: **Audium**, 1616 Bush Street in the Civic Center area, tel: 415-771-1616. Audium presents contemporary and precedent-setting music, and is the first theater of sound exploration, experimenting with 136 speakers that move music around visitors in a kind of sculpture. The **Bay Area Women's Philharmonic**, tel: 415-437-0123, performs the works of women composers.
Golden Gate Park Band, Music Concourse, Golden Gate Park, tel: 415-666-7035, plays

BUYING TICKETS

TIX Bay Area is located on Powell Street between Geary and Post streets in Union Square. Half price, day-of-performance tickets are available in addition to full-price advance tickets for select events. Half-price tickets for Sun and Mon are sold Sat and Sun. Open: Tues–Thurs 11am–6pm, Fri 11am–7pm; Sat 10am–7pm; Sun 10am–3pm.
Mr Ticket, 2065 Van Ness Avenue, tel: 415-292-7328 or toll-free (800) 424-7328. Tickets for concerts and sporting events.
www.performances.org, tel: 415-392-2545, has tickets online for classical performances and lectures.

each Sunday, April to October, 1pm. Pack a picnic and enjoy a traditional brass band, free.
San Francisco Conservatory of Music, 1201 Ortega, tel: 415-564-8086 or 415-759-3477 (a 24-hour tape recording lists music activities) has professional chamber music as well as student recitals. With graduates like Isaac Stern to its credit, the San Francisco Conservatory is regarded as the best music school on the West Coast.

Museums & Galleries

Museums

Museums are scattered all over the city, with the majority in the SoMa and Civic Center areas, as well as a few in far-flung neighborhoods; check websites for upcoming shows and ticket information. The biggest or most frequented museums are:
The **Yerba Buena Center for the Arts and Gardens Complex,** 701 Mission Street, tel: 415-978-ARTS, www.ybca.org.
San Francisco Museum of Modern Art, 151 3rd Street, tel:

415-357-4000, www.sfmoma.org
Cartoon Art Museum, 655 Mission Street, tel: 415-227-8666, www.cartoonart.org
Asian Art Museum, 200 Larkin Street, tel: 415-581-3500, www.asianart.org
California Palace of the Legion of Honor, Lincoln Park at 34th Avenue, tel: 415-863-3330, www.thinker.org
MH de Young Museum, Golden Gate Park, tel: 415-863-3330, set to open in late 2005.

Art Galleries

San Francisco has an active visual arts community. Pick up a copy of the *Art Now Gallery Guide – West Coast*, available in galleries all over town, for information on special events and shows. Galleries are located Downtown, in the Civic Center, South of Market and on Fisherman's Wharf. The art is for sale and the shows change. At Fisherman's Wharf, art ranges from commercial to quality prints. Galleries are located on Pier 39, at Ghirardelli Square, along the side streets, and in the Cannery.

The established art dealers are on Maiden Lane, Sutter, Grant, Post and other Civic Center area streets. Some notable galleries are:
111 Minna Street Gallery, 111 Minna Street, tel: 415-974-1719, www.111minnagallery.com
Catherine Clark Gallery, 49 Geary Street, tel: 415-399-1439, www.cclarkgallery.com
Dolby Chadwick, 210 Post Street, Suite 205, tel: 415-956-3560, www.dolbychadwickgallery.com
Folk Art International Gallery, 140 Maiden Lane, tel: 415-392-9999, is housed in a stunning Frank Lloyd Wright building with a swooping circular interior.
Hackett-Freedman Gallery, 250 Sutter Street, Suite 400, tel: 415-362-7152, www.realart.com
Simmons Gallery, 565 Sutter St, tel: 415-986-2244.
Stephen Wirtz Gallery, 49 Geary Street, tel: 415-433-6879, www.wirtzgallery.com

NIGHTLIFE

Cocktails, dancing, entertainment, musical revues and more await the visitor's pleasure. San Francisco is noted for its talented comedians who go on to national fame and fortune after getting experience in local comedy clubs. The city is also known as the birthplace of the first American pizza restaurant and, later, the first topless club in America. Choose from these listings and from the listings in the various entertainment sections of local publications. All clubs have cover charges, which vary according to the quality of entertainment.

Music Venues

Bimbo's 365
1025 Columbus Avenue
Tel: 415-474-0365
Swank throwback nightclub with swing, jazz, rock and big bands.

Bottom of the Hill
1233 17th Street
Tel: 415-621-4455
Small, rockin' venue for punk, alternative, and rockabilly among several others.

Café Du Nord
2170 Market Street
Tel: 415-861-5016
Swing, jazz, spoken word, and eclectic music at this funky, intimate venue.

Elbo Room
647 Valencia Street
Tel: 415-552-7788
Jazz, hip-hop, acid jazz, and spoken word at this always-hip club.

The Fillmore Auditorium
1805 Geary Boulevard
Tel: 415-346-6000
Historic venue from the 1960s featuring major headlining acts.

Great American Music Hall
859 O'Farrell Street
Tel: 415-885-0750
Rock, punk, country, and more at this former bordello.

Last Day Saloon
406 Clement Street
Tel: 415-387-6343
College rock, tribute bands and fun R&B bands play this thumping club.

Thee Parkside
1600 17th Street
Tel: 415-503-0393
Potrero neighborhood joint for rock, roots, country and rockabilly.

Jazz and Blues Clubs

Biscuits & Blues
401 Mason Street
Tel: 415-292-2583
Subterranean music venue in the Theater District near Union Square featuring blues and blues-based rock.

Boom Boom Room
1601 Fillmore Street
Tel: 415-673-8000
Blues, funk, jazz, boogie woogie and much more at this good, late-night club.

Enrico's
504 Broadway
Tel: 415-982-6223
Dinner jazz and great people watching in North Beach.

Jazz at Pearl's
256 Columbus Avenue
Tel: 415-931-4242
North Beach jazz joint with traditional bands and combos.

Rasselas
1534 Fillmore Street
Tel: 415-567-5011
Both traditional and experimental jazz music are performed here.

BELOW: sax and the city.

INFORMATION IN PRINT

SF Weekly, a free arts and entertainment weekly newspaper, is widely available on racks and in cafés.
Bay Guardian, another free arts, entertainment and news weekly, is also widely available in stores and cafés.
Datebook, also referred to as the "Pink Pages," is an insert in the Sunday edition of the *San Francisco Chronicle* newspaper and contains comprehensive events listings.

Dance Clubs

Bambuddha Lounge
601 Eddy Street
Tel: 415-885-5088
DJ music, beautiful people and poolside cocktails all happen on a heated patio.

The End Up
401 6th Street
Tel: 415-357-0827
Tweakers dance until dawn and beyond.

Harry Denton's Starlight Room
450 Powell Street
Tel: 415-392-7755
Big band orchestras, Motown, and jazz performed high above Union Square.

Ruby Skye
420 Mason Street
Tel: 415-693-0777
Former theater turned hip nightclub featuring local and international DJs.

Bars & Pubs

Edinburgh Castle
905 Geary Street
Tel: 415-885-4074
Scottish pub in the heart of the Tenderloin hosts readings and other literary events.

El Rio
3158 Mission Street
Tel: 415-282-3325
Fun and funky mainstay of the Mission District has a patio for outdoor drinking.

The Irish Bank
10 Mark Lane
Tel: 415-788-7152

After-work watering hole and European sports bar. Can get rowdy after 5pm.

Liverpool Lil's
2942 Lyon Street
Tel: 415-921-6664
Comfy pub with tasty food.

O'Reilly's Bar & Restaurant
622 Green Street
Tel: 415-989-6222
Locals, tourists and Irish expats mingle with Guinness and (sometimes) Van Morrison.

Tonga Room
950 Mason Street
Tel: 415-772-5278
Tiki bar extraordinaire with indoor rainstorms, great cocktails and *pupu* platters.

Tosca Café
242 Columbus Avenue
Tel: 415-986-9651
Politicos, entertainers and other swells listen to opera records over Irish coffee.

Zeitgeist
199 Valencia Street
Tel: 415-255-7505
Hipsters, bike messengers and other locals drink and eat barbecue in the backyard.

Cabaret

Beach Blanket Babylon
Club Fugazi, 678 Green Street
Tel: 415-421-4222
Steve Silver's wacky and whimsical musical revue has earned the status of a San Francisco institution – the longest running musical in the city. The show goes on eight times a week, including a Sunday matinee.

Comedy Venues

San Francisco is a city with a rich tradition in stand-up comedy, beginning in North Beach with the days of Lenny Bruce and Mort Sahl taking on the establishment at the Hungry i, and the Smothers Brothers, Jonathan Winters and Phyllis Diller at the subterranean Purple Onion.

The city's clown prince, Robin Williams, exploded out of a scene that was the flashpoint for a national comedy boom, and a reputation for cutting edge,

original material is ongoing well-deserved. Watch for p wit Will Durst, absurdist Arj Barker, or jokeslinger Jim Si

San Francisco has four fi time comedy clubs, and a wi variety of comedy in theater a alternative spaces. Subject m ter and language are of the "a thing goes" variety, so the eas offended beware.

Cobb's Comedy Club
915 Columbus Avenue
Tel: 415-928-4620
The biggest names in television play this, the city's biggest comedy room.

The Punch Line
444 Battery Street
Tel: 415-397-4337
The best national stand-up comics regularly headline this small club – Dave Chappelle, Dave Attell, Greg Proops and David Cross among them.

QComedy LGBT Center
1800 Market Street
Tel: 415-541-5610
www.QComedy.com
Outspoken, outrageous and out-of-the-closet comics in a showcase of the queer comedy scene.

Mock Café
1074 Valencia Street
Tel: 415-826-5750
Local showcases one night a week at this fun and funky spot next to the Marsh Theater.

The Purple Onion
140 Columbus Avenue
Tel: 415-217-8400
www.purpleonioncomedy.com
This historic, intimate nightclub has comedy and music, with superb food from its Italian restaurant upstairs, Caffe Macaroni Sciue Sciue.

Gay & Lesbian Venues

For the thriving gay and lesbian communities in San Francisco, the Castro and South of Market districts are the locus of activities and nightlife, as well as Polk Street in between Sutter and California. For information covering gay and lesbian entertainment listings to counseling and health resources, two free weekly publi-

ABOVE: nighttime in SoMa.

cations, *Bay Times* and the *Bay Area Reporter*, offer the most comprehensive coverage and good classified ads.

In addition to the **Halloween** bash that takes place in the heart of the Castro each year – it has become San Francisco's own version of Mardi Gras, and draws thousands who party on the streets into the wee hours – San Francisco also hosts the annual **Lesbian/Gay Pride Celebration** on the last Sunday of June, culminating in a Market Street parade which regularly draws up to 250,000 people.

The **Castro Street Fair** is held usually in September or October. A candlelight march each November in the Castro area honors former city supervisor Harvey Milk, the gay community leader who was brutally gunned down along with Mayor George Moscone at City Hall in 1979.

Along with the city's plethora of gay bars, cafés and nightclubs (in SoMa go to: The End Up, Lone Star Saloon and Rawhide II; in the Castro check out : Badlands, Bar on Castro, Detour and many others), there is a growing number of theaters drawing gay audiences to alternative performance shows, including those at the fun and funky **Theater Rhinoceros** (2926 16th Street).

ACCOMMODATIONS

ACTIVITIES

A – N

...rld. Macintosh Comput-
...annual tradeshow and new
products exhibition. www.mac-
world.com

**Dr Martin Luther King Jr's Birth-
day Celebration**

February

Chinese New Year Parade. One
of the world's top 10 parades
and one of the largest events of
its kind outside Asia. www.chinese
parade.com

Pacific Orchid Exposition.
www.orchidsanfrancisco.com

March

San Francisco Garden Show.
Acres of extraordinary gardens,
seminars and shopping.
www.gardenshow.com/sf

St Patrick's Day Parade. A full
day of celebration at Civic Center
and one of the longest running
parades in the United States.
www.teamproevent.com

April

Cherry Blossom Festival (Japantown street fair). Two weekends
of Taiko drumming, tea cere-
monies, calligraphy, marital arts,
Ikebana flower arrangement,
Japanese food and bonsai.

**San Francisco International Film
Festival**. www.sfiff.org

Whole Life Expo. Workshops, lectures and exhibits on alternative
health practices and products.

May

Bay to Breakers. A 7½-mile (11-
km) footrace in which participants don outrageous costumes.
www.baytobreakers.com

Carnaval. The Hispanic Mission
district explodes with colorful
floats, costumed dancers and
Latino music and flavors at this
cultural celebration.
www.carnavalsf.com

Kaboom. Local radio station KFOG
sponsors a synchronized concert
and firework display.
www.kfog.com

June

Haight Street Fair. Always one of
the city's wildest street fairs.
www.haightstreetfair.org

North Beach Festival. San
Francisco's oldest street fair.
www.sfnorthbeach.org/festival

**San Francisco Pride Celebration
and Parade**. A weekend of events
including live music, shows, parties and a huge Sunday parade to
celebrate San Francisco's gay,
lesbian, bisexual and transgen-
dered populations. www.sfpride.org

**Stern Grove Midsummer Music
Festival**. Classical, jazz, ethnic
music and picnics in the Grove
(June–August).
www.sterngrove.org

July

**Cable Car Bell Ringing Competi-
tion**. www.cablecarmuseum.org

**Fourth of July Waterfront
Festival**. An annual Independence Day celebration featuring
live music and fireworks over the
bay. www.pier39.com

Jewish Film Festival. www.sfjff.org

August

Nihonmachi Street Fair. A celebration of the many diverse Asian
and Pacific American communities in the Bay Area.
www.nihonmachistreetfair.org

September

Folsom Street Fair. Gay leather
event. www.folsomstreetfair.com

Opera in the Park. Opera's
"greatest hits" performed by the
San Francisco Opera in Golden
Gate Park. Free.
www.sfgate.com/chronicle/events/opera

San Francisco Blues Festival.
One of America's largest blues
festivals is a prestigious music
festival drawing big name talent.
www.sfblues.com

San Francisco Fringe Festival.
Independent theater, performance art and comedy held in
various venues. www.sffringe.org

**San Francisco Shakespeare
Festival**. Free Shakespeare in
the Park, Shakespeare camps
and urban youth programs.
www.sfshakes.org

October

Comedy Day. A day of free,
stand-up comedy in Golden Gate
Park.
www.comedyday.com

Fleet Week. Fisherman's Wharf
welcomes the US Navy. Highlights include the Blue Angels air-
show. www.fleetweek.com/sf

Halloween SF. A huge costumed
block party in the Castro is an
annual tradition on October 31.

November

**Christmas Tree Lighting Cere-
monies**. The city lights up in
Union Square on the Saturday
after Thanksgiving.

Dia de los Muertos. The Mexican
Day of the Dead is celebrated
with drummers, decorative altars
and dancing skeletons.
www.dayofthedeadsf.org

December

Festival of Lights. The lighting of
a massive Hanukkah menorah in
Union Square.

Grace Cathedral Concerts.
www.gracecathedral.org

**SFNYE (San Francisco New
Year's Eve)**. Citywide celebration
with live music and fireworks.

SHOPPING

What to Buy

It's always a joy to shop in San Francisco. While bargains are a rarity, especially for tourists, browsing is fun and shopping is a serious event. There is no shortage of distinct shopping areas, each offering a different type of retail experience. From large malls and shopping centers to neighborhood streets crowded with small stores and boutiques, the consumer can find designer fashions, local arts and crafts, food and gifts and vintage clothes stores. The tourist areas in Union Square have all the big names in shopping, including high-end fashion houses like Chanel.

Small boutiques specializing in everything from local fashion designers to specialty foods, crafts and gifts are found in local shopping areas like Hayes Street between Gough and Webster, Polk Street between Sutter and Green, Union Street between Gough and Fillmore and Chestnut Street between Fillmore and Divisadero.

Thrift shopping is another favorite pastime in San Francisco. Some spots, especially those in the Haight-Ashbury district, are picked over and hardly worth looking at, while those in less popular areas are a gold mine of vintage or used fashion.

Most museums have excellent gift stores, especially the San Francisco Museum of Modern Art, the California Palace of the Legion of Honor and the Exploratorium.

Where to Buy: By Area

San Francisco Shopping Center
Market Street at the base of Powell Street.
The opulent San Francisco Shopping Center mall and its surrounding Downtown environs (Union Square is just a few blocks away) epitomize the shopping experience. It is home to some of the world's largest American chains, including a five-story Nordstrom's, a two-level Abercrombie & Fitch, numerous outlets such as Victoria's Secret and Bebe, and high-end retailers like Kenneth Cole and Club Monaco.

Union Square
Post, Stockton and Geary between Grant and Powell streets.
A mecca for shopaholics ringed by Macy's, Saks, Neiman Marcus and Levi's stores along with colorful flower stands and street performers. Surrounding streets feature stores like Virgin Megastore, Gump's and Britex Fabrics along with boutiques for Coach, Bulgari, Cartier, Thomas Pink, Louis Vuitton, MaxMara, Emporio Armani, Diesel, Prada, Celine, Escada, Gucci, Guess, Hermès, Agnès b, Betsey Johnson and Wilkes Bashford. DSW is a large discount shoe warehouse across from stores like Urban Outfitter's, Bath and Body, French Connection and Sephora (a huge make-up warehouse).

Chestnut Street
Chestnut Street between Scott and Fillmore streets.
Chestnut Street is lined with a

BELOW: the fabulous Neiman Marcus store in Union Square.

mix of sophisticated stores, beauty outlets and restaurants alongside brand name retailers. While unique and offbeat in nature, Chestnut Street retains a distinctive neighborhood feel. Shoe boutiques like Rabat feature trendy but functional footwear and specialty stores like Blue Bird, a gift shop, carry kitschy gifts like porcelain dolls and oversized potato heads. Well-known retailers like Gap Body mix with the small, unique Chadwick's of London for cotton and lace lingerie, lending mass appeal. Williams-Sonoma, a neighborhood fixture, has the best in cookware, utensils and cookbooks. For beauty care, go to Bare Essentials or the Body Shop. On any day, Chestnut Street is bustling with shoppers, professionals meeting for coffee at The Grove or neighborhood moms with strollers shopping at Books, Inc. The highlight of this cozy neighborhood is a sophisticated and energetic ambience and streamlined stores conducive to walking.

Chinatown
Grant and Stockton streets between Bush St and Broadway.
Enter the Dragon Gates for candles, vivid silks, delicate lace embroidery, colorful robes and window fronts filled to the brim with made-in-China delights like noisy toys, carved Buddhas, paper parasols and regal mahogany furniture, perfect for exotic gifts or indulgent tourist souvenirs. Apothecaries abound, selling delicate green teas, rose-scented black teas and a variety of other ailment-banishing brews by the ounce. The fragrant Fortune Cookie Factory, tucked away on Ross Alley, is a postcard worthy find.

Embarcadero Center 1–4
Sacramento Street between Clay, Sansome and Front streets.
Embarcadero is an under-utilized shopping expanse that caters to the professionals who work in the nearby towers. It is retail heavy with brand names like Gap,

ABOVE: picture pretty in chic *chapeaux*.

Banana Republic, Ann Taylor, Liz Claiborne, and Victoria's Secret as well as smaller boutique-like chains. The mall's spacious outdoor and indoor design lends itself to a comfortable and easy shopping experience. The Embarcadero is contoured for the busy shopper with wide walkways and well-placed stairwells. The shopping mall is also home to the Embarcadero Theater, a movie house that shows alternative and independent films by local and top directors.

Fillmore Street
Fillmore Street between Washington and Geary streets.
On Fillmore, it's easy to feel pampered with several well-known beauty retailers and ritzy interior design boutiques straight out of New York. Rachel Ashwell's Shabby Chic furniture and bedding store is near Betsy Johnson's runway store and the MAC boutique. Perfumeries, jewelry stores, paper designers and specialty beauty outlets like Aveda fill the spaces in between in this deluxe area. For shopping fuel, stop at Peet's coffee or the locals-frequented Grove café.

Haight Street
Haight Street in between Ashbury and Stanyan streets.
This stretch of stores, referred to by locals as the "Upper Haight," was the center of 1960s psychedelia. Despite gentrification and the proliferation of stores like Ben & Jerry's and The Gap – as well as some small cutting-edge

designer stores of its own – the neighborhood still retains its hippie counterculture credentials, and is dotted with Victorian houses, anarchist bookstores, piercing salons, funky clothing stores and head shops. Shoppers can find just about anything, from hardware to punk gear, and fishnets to upscale vintage. For music-philes, the bowling alley turned record store, Amoeba Records, is one of the Haight's biggest draws.

Hayes Valley
Hayes Street between Gough and Octavia.
The Hayes Valley is a beautiful blend of art and commerce in a small neighborhood brimming with art galleries, contemporary boutiques, interior design studios, outdoor cafés and wine bars. This stretch of shopping street, in view of the San Francisco Symphony and Opera House, is a great place to find out-of-the-ordinary items like crafted ultra-modern club chairs, Italian shoes and hand-blown glass ornaments.

North Beach
Grant Street and Columbus Avenue.
The unmistakable Italian district of San Francisco has an Italian style and energy that permeates every boutique and restaurant. North Beach is the perfect shopping destination because visitors can stop at Italian cafés after discovering the European-inspired boutiques along Grant Avenue.

Aria is the ultimate curiosity shop with everything from vintage European family photos to Victorian mirrors. AB Fits will help you find the perfect jeans for your body type and MAC (Modern Appealing Clothing) has Anna Sui and Yoshi Kondo – all for women.

Mission Street
Valencia Street between 16th and 24th streets.
The Mission is the perfect place to cater to unconventional whims. This colorful stretch with offbeat boutiques and funky ethnic clothing and furniture stores includes wonderful *taquerias* where a California-style burrito will set you back $5. Standout boutiques include Therapy, a funky gift shop and furniture store with clothing and jewelry, Dema, a local dressmaker and 826 Valencia, San Francisco's very own pirate store.

Polk Street
Polk Street in between Union and California streets.
One of the most divergent shopping neighborhoods, offering a blend of high-end consignment stores, affordable retail outfits, antique dealers and low-end clothing stores. Shopping here accommodates different tastes and budgets; the outdoor enthusiast will love Lombardi Sports; Americana buffs will love all the quirky antique and gifts stores like Molte Cose; and the fashion-conscious in search of an affordable Chanel jacket can look in CRIS, an upscale-only consignment store. Polk is best for out-of-town shoppers who like the gritty mixed in with some high style, the upscale with the zany.

Sacramento Street
Sacramento Street between Presidio and Laurel streets.
This shopping area, on the cusp between Pacific Heights and Presidio Heights in a quiet residential neighborhood, features deluxe shopping with fantastic finds squeezed into a compact little block. Main attractions are the interior decor stores, children's clothing, shoes and

furniture shops and high-end clothing boutiques, including some great consignment stores. There are household items from small to large — from cashmere sofa throws and scented Florentine soaps to oversized Persian rugs and 19th-century French tables. Shoppers should also look for Brown Eyed Girl (closer to Fillmore Street), a store designed to look like the interior of a hip apartment, and view Jimmy Choo sandals and Prada heels at Fetish shoes on Presidio.

Where to Buy: By Item
Antiques & Furniture
Antique stores are scattered into various shopping districts and offer some wonderful European and Asian furnishings and Americana artifacts. The highest of the high-end retailers are found on Maiden Lane in Union Square and Jackson Square off the old Barbary Coast Trail. Market Street between Van Ness and Valencia has an array of stores that sell primarily Art Deco pieces. Valencia Street between 14th and 24th has a few stores with furniture, art and household wares. SoMa has a number of good furniture stores, especially on the 9th Street corridor between Bryant and Folsom. Most of these tend toward the modern aesthetic. Union Square, as well as Union Street and Polk Street, has quite a few stores that carry Asian objects, housewares, maps and memorabilia. Generally, there are re-sale shops all around.
Art & Reproductions
The major museums and art galleries sell excellent reproductions of their paintings, and numerous small commercial galleries sell original oil paintings, watercolors, sculpture, drawings and installations. Union Square and the Jackson Square Historical District (call 296-8150 for the Jackson Square Art & Antique Dealers Association) are the primary locations of most galleries.

Books
The city has an exceptionally large selection of new and used bookstores and specialty bookshops, many of which host readings and other literary events. For second-hand books of general interest, Green Apple Books, 506 Clement, has the largest selection. City Lights, 261 Columbus Ave, in North Beach is the famed publishing company and bookshop founded by Lawrence Ferlinghetti and made famous by the Beat legacy. Be sure to visit the Poetry Annex upstairs. A Different Light, 489 Castro Street, has an extensive stock of books for and about the queer community. The San Francisco Mystery Bookshop, 4175 24th Street, and Kayo Books, 814 Post Street, have excellent collections of hard-boiled, pulp and other vintage and new mysteries. William Stout Architecture Books, 804 Montgomery Street, is known for books on urban planning, design and rare editions relating to the field of architecture. Limelight Film and Theater Bookstore, 1803 Market Street, is dedicated to books on the thespian arts.
Clothes & Shoes
San Francisco has several huge department stores in the heart of Union Square; coming soon are Bloomingdale's and H&M. Loehmann's, 222 Sutter Street, sells cut-rate designer clothes and shoes. But it's the creative

juice of the Bay Area that fuels many of the charming boutique stores in smaller neighborhoods. Grant Street in North Beach between Columbus and Green has some lovely high-end boutiques with lingerie, custom overcoats, knits and denim. Hayes Street is for the ultra-hip, with vintage couture, shoes and other luxuries. Sacramento Street in Presidio Heights has some wonderful high-end consignment stores and Fillmore, Union and Chestnut streets are filled with boutiques outfitting women and men from head to toe.
Jewelry
Jewelry stores all over town have eye-catching displays of modern and traditional pieces, some original and designed on the spot. There are a host of stores on Powell Street and Sutter Street in Union Square that sell diamonds and estate pieces, but it's a good idea to have a firm grasp of the market before stepping into these shops. De Vera, 29 Maiden Lane and Gallery of Jewels, 2115 Fillmore Street, feature local creations you'll want to take home.
International Finds
San Francisco is a mixture of many different cultures, each with their own neighborhoods filled with specialty import stores. Chinatown is awash with Chinese trinkets and Asian-inspired porcelain and art. Japantown has traditional Japanese

THRIFT SHOPPING
San Francisco has a staggering array of thrift stores where you can rummage for almost anything to outfit your home, your children or yourself at a quarter of the price of regular stores. The Mission and Haight-Ashbury districts have the largest concentration. In the Mission, the place to be is Valencia and Mission streets between 16th and 24th. Clothes Contact, 473 Valencia St, charges by the pound; Thrift Town, 2101 Mis-

sion Street, has a good selection of vintage shoes and musty books; and the Goodwill Superstore at 1580 Mission Street (at Van Ness) has the largest selection of clothes. If you're on Haight Street, try Wasteland or Held Over for fashions that take you back in time. Peek-a-Boutique at 130 Castro Street in Noe Valley is a wonderful place for previously worn children's clothing, as the neighborhood is so popular with young families.

CLOTHES CHART

The chart listed below gives a comparison of United States, European and United Kingdom clothing sizes. It is always a good idea, however, to try on any article before buying it, as sizes between manufacturers can vary enormously.

● **Women's Dresses/Suits**

US	Continental	UK
6	38/34N	8/30
8	40/36N	10/32
10	42/38N	12/34
12	44/40N	14/36
14	46/42N	16/38
16	48/44N	18/40

● **Women's Shoes**

US	Continental	UK
4½	36	3
5½	37	4
6½	38	5
7½	39	6
8½	40	7
9½	41	8
10½	42	9

● **Men's Suits**

US	Continental	UK
34	44	34
—	46	36
38	48	38
—	50	40
42	52	42
—	54	44
46	56	46

● **Men's Shirts**

US	Continental	UK
14	36	14
14½	37	14½
15	38	15
15½	39	15½
16	40	16
16½	41	16½
17	42	17

● **Men's Shoes**

US	Continental	UK
6½	—	6
7½	40	7
8½	41	8
9½	42	9
10½	43	10
11½	44	11

hardware stores and a mall that sells teapots, housewares, books, paper goods and lanterns. And Mission Street between 16th and 24th streets gives off a distinctive Mexican feeling – most of the trinkets are cheaply made and inexpensive, while the people watching is superb.

Gifts

For cheap souvenirs like snowglobes, magnets and other San Francisco ephemera, Chinatown and Fisherman's Wharf offer the best deals. Wine, cheese and specialty artisan foods can be found at the newly remodeled Ferry Building at the foot of Market Street. And to bring back a piece of history, Haight Street has a huge selection of tie-dyed shirts, Grateful Dead posters, pot paraphernalia and other 1960s era goodies. Ghirardelli Square is also a good spot for tourist gift shopping.

Tax

Be advised, there is an 8.5 percent sales tax that applies to most non-food purchases.

SPORTS

Spectator Sports

Baseball

The **San Francisco Giants**, www.sfgiants.com, play at stunning SBC Park in the South Beach neighborhood at 4th and King streets, one of the newest and one of the best ballparks in Major League baseball. Public transportation is abundant and absolutely necessary. Fans with boats have been known to hang around outside the field, sailing by in McCovey Cove.

The **Oakland As,** www.coliseum.com, play at the Network Associates Coliseum in Oakland, a short and comfortable ride from the city on BART. Tickets can be bought at the gate or booked in advance. Check the websites for each team for game schedules and ticket availability.

Basketball

The **Golden State Warriors** play at the Oakland Arena, www.coliseum.com, tel: 888-479-4667. The team has been marred by years of conflict between coaches and players; see them in action and catch up with all the sports gossip.

Football

The **'49ers** (www.sf49ers.com, tel: 415-656-4900) are the Bay Area's most successful professional team, winning several Super Bowls. Every game is sold out to season-ticket holders, so visiting fans must go to a ticket agency or a scalper on the day of the game to get tickets. The construction of a new stadium to replace Monster Park (formerly Candlestick) was approved, but its future remains in doubt.

The **Oakland Raiders**, www.coliseum.com, play at the Network Associates Coliseum in Oakland, though for how long is anyone's guess. Owner Al Davis moved the team to LA in the 1980s, then back to Oakland in 1996. Despite threats to move them again, fans remain loyal.

Horse Racing

Though not within the city limits, two reasonably close tracks provide excitement for thoroughbred and quarter-horse race fans. There is a general admission price and clubhouse seating. Bets can be placed for small sums of money, so even novices have fun. **Bay Meadows** is on the peninsula, south of San Francisco just off Highway 101 at the Hillsdale exit.

Bay Meadows is the oldest, busiest and one of the most beautiful ovals in California. There is seating for general admission, plus a clubhouse and a Turf Club (where a dress code is enforced). Valet parking is available. Tel: 650-574-7223 for information. **Golden Gate Fields** is in the East Bay, near the water, just off Highway 580 in Albany, tel: 510-559-7300.

ACTIVITIES ♦ 229

TRANSPORTATION

ABOVE: sailing through the fog.

Participant Sports

The vistas and the weather draw people outside on a regular basis. Climbing hills keeps most people fit and generally there are as many active sports participants as there are spectators. The **Recreation and Park Department** oversees 52 public areas with a variety of facilities in addition to the extensive and beautiful Golden Gate Park complex.

For information about archery, basketball, baseball, bicycling, boating, fishing, football, golf, horseback riding, photography, target shooting, swimming and tennis, tel: 415-831-2700.

Along with the vast selection of free public facilities, there are private clubs which issue guest memberships, equipment rental and lessons. *City Sports*, a free monthly publication, is an excellent up-to-date reference for sports events, clubs and classes. Look for the oversized magazine stacked in cafés and sidewalk news boxes or try www.citysportsmag.com

The **Golden Gate National Recreation Area** encompasses 35,000 acres (14,000 hectares) and 69 sq miles (178 sq kms) of waterfront. The facilities for bicycling, birding, bocce ball, exer-

cise, fishing, hang gliding, hiking, running, jogging, swimming, and walking in San Francisco include **Fort Mason**, **Aquatic Park**, the **Golden Gate promenade** and **Marina Green, Crissy Field, Baker Beach, China Beach, Land's End, Ocean Beach** and **Fort Funston**.

Women who are interested in getting involved with sports should check out *Women's Sports Connection* or try one of the many classes and clinics offered by **Adventurous Woman Sports**, tel: toll-free 800-80WOMAN, or www.adventurous.com. Among the classes for women, taught by women, are rock climbing, inline skating, sea kayaking, hiking, mountain biking and windsurfing in the beautiful bay.

Boating

San Francisco Bay is challenging even for the most experienced sailor, and some of the best **sailing** in the country can be enjoyed without ever going beyond the Golden Gate Bridge.

If you're experienced, you can try the **windsurfing** or **kitesurfing** off Crissy Field, between the Marina Green (Marina District) and the Golden Gate. Beginners should call Kite Wind Surf (tel: 510-522 WIND or toll-free, tel: 877- 521-WIND) in Alameda for information about lessons and equipment.

Sea kayaking is popular with sports men and women of all ages. Lessons for all abilities, equipment, sail and power boat rentals are listed in the *Yellow Pages* of the phone book.

You also can choose to float in smaller vessels and calmer waters like **Stow Lake** in Golden Gate Park, tel: 415-752-0347. **Bay Adventures**, Schoonmaker Point Marina, Sausalito, tel: 415-331-0444, has various vessels in which you can enjoy the bay.

Bowling

Bocce ball and lawn bowling are popular local sports. For information, tel: 415-831-2700. For

indoor bowling, **Presidio Bowling Center**, Bldg 93, Montgomery Street at Moraga in the Presidio, tel: 415-561-2695 has 12 lanes and a cocktail lounge.

Fishing

Deep sea fishing boats leave Fisherman's Wharf on regular schedules. Catches include salmon, seabass, halibut, rock fish, bonito, shark and albacore. You can rent equipment but you'll need a fishing license. If you want to impress the folks back home, your catch can be smoked, packed and shipped to most places in the United States (check about shipping internationally, as some countries have strict regulations about food imports). For the fishing trip, plan for wind and some rough seas. Bring along motion sickness preventatives and warm clothing. Check the *Yellow Pages* for sport fishing trips.

Fresh water fishing is available at the **Lake Merced Boating and Fishing Company**, just south of the city at 1 Harding Road, where Skyline Boulevard and the Great Highway come together. Large trout are stocked in the 360-acre (146-hectare) lake that is open year-round. Boats, licenses, bait and tackle are available. For information, tel: 415-753-1101.

Before you go to Lake Merced, you might want to practice at the **Fly Casting Pools** near the Anglers' Lodge in Golden Gate Park, off Kennedy Drive, close to the Buffalo paddock, tel: 415-831-2700. Sportsfishing expeditions set out to the high seas from **Miss Farallones**, Fisherman's Wharf, tel: 415-346-2399.

Golf

San Francisco has a few very beautiful municipal golf courses. Although it's often possible to find a partner while there, call ahead for reservations, as the courses are very popular. Rental equipment is usually available. **Harding Park Golf Club**, south of the city at Skyline Boulevard and

ACCOMMODATIONS

ACTIVITIES

A – Z

ABOVE: kite flying on Marina Green is a time-honored tradition.

Harding Park Road near the Pacific Ocean, tel: 415-661-1865, www.harding-park.com, has two courses: the **Fleming Course** is nine holes, 2,316 yards (2,105 meters), par 32, while the **Harding Course** is 18 holes, 6,637 yards (6,040 meters), par 72. A 2002 renovation has brought the club, established in 1925, up to top-notch scratch. **Lincoln Park Course**, 34th Avenue and Clement Street, tel: 415-221-9911, www.playlincoln.com, is situated on a cliff with spectacular views. It has 18 holes, 5,081 yards (4,620 meters), par 68.

Hang gliding

There's more hang gliding in California than in any other state because the good coastal winds are consistent. One of the best spots to watch or participate is the 200-ft (60-meter) cliff at **Fort Funston**, just south of San Francisco, at the end of the Great Highway near Lake Merced.

Computerized up-to-the-minute wind condition information is available, tel: 415-333-0100. See the *Yellow Pages* of the phone directory for lessons and equipment rentals. The **San Francisco Hang Gliding Center**, 977 Regal Road in Berkeley, tel: 510-528-2300, specializes in scary tandem flights.

Horseback riding

You'll have to venture out of the city limits to ride; there are stables in Half Moon Bay (to the south) and (to the north) in Marin County, but you can ride on the beach in Bodega Bay, just off Highway 1, at **Chanslor Ranch**, tel: 707-875-3333. **Sonoma Cattle Company** and **Napa Valley Trail Rides** operate out of Glen Ellen in the bucolic Sonoma wine country, tel: 707-255-2900.

Jogging

Although there are jogging paths designated in Golden Gate Park and along the Marina Green and Crissy Field, the entire city seems to be one big joggers' paradise. You can stick to the waterfront and avoid the hills, or challenge yourself with an intense vertical workout. (You could even try jogging along Lombard Street, for jogging at its dizziest.)

The annual **Bay to Breakers** run in May is one of many running events that take place in San Francisco but is by far the most outrageous. Participants dress up in wild costumes and don't dress at all for the run/walk that spans the entire city from east to west. Check the information sources listed above for all kinds of jogging, striding and walking events, including the **San Francisco Marathon** and **Escape from Alcatraz Triathlon**.

Kite flying

In the meadows of Golden Gate Park, on the beaches, and especially in the Marina Green area of the Marina District, kite flying is very serious stuff, and the windy weather makes it a perfect sport. It's also colorful and fun. Specialty stores around town sell all types of kites, including one on Pier 39 that features demonstrations out front on the Fisherman's Wharf promenade.

Skating

Inline skating is a popular sport that has found a niche in skate-friendly San Francisco. Parts of Golden Gate Park are closed to traffic on Sundays, making it an ideal place to skate.

Along the Marina and the Embarcadero are smooth, flat expanses that are often filled with skaters. Friday Night Skate is a social group open to skaters of all levels, male and female, who meet weekly at 8pm at the corner of Bryant Street and the Embarcadero.

Rentals are available in all sizes from **Golden Gate Skate & Bike**, 3038 Fulton Street, tel: 415-668-1117 and 1818 Haight Street, tel: 415-752-8376.

Tennis

Tennis is a popular year-round sport. San Francisco has 142 public courts in 42 locations, including some floodlit courts for night play. All are free except for the 21 courts located in the **Golden Gate Park Tennis Complex**. Here, reservations are required on weekdays, but it's first-come, first-served during busy weekends. Generally, people are polite about observing the time limit rules (this is San Francisco, after all) that are posted at each court.

It is not impolite to inquire about the status of the time or game limits when you approach a court that is in use. There is an excellent women's tennis program. For Golden Gate Park information, tel: 415-753-7001. There are also private tennis clubs in the Downtown and South of Market areas. See the telephone book's *Yellow Pages* for information.

SIGHTSEEING TOURS

Walking Tours

There are many independent walking tours in the city; the internet is a good source for locating the right one. The **Victorian Home Walk**, tel: 415-252 9485, www.victorianwalk.com, will take you where buses can't. Learn about

San Francisco architecture and history from longtime residents. **Wok Wiz Walking Tours**, tel: 650-355 9657, www.wokwiz.com, offers Chinatown history, culture and folklore lectures during a guided insider's view of one of the largest Chinatowns outside China. **FOOT!** tours, tel: 415-793-5378, www.foottours.com, are fun, informative, and led by professional comedians. Also, check www.sfcityguides.com for details about 20 free architecture and history tours.

On-the-Road Tours

Several companies offer narrated tours in buses, vans or limousines. The typical tour choice is a half-day city tour combined with a visit across the Golden Gate Bridge to Muir Woods and/or Sausalito, or in combination with a bay cruise. Check the *Yellow Pages* or the internet for the tour best suited to your interests.

Sky Tours

Tours by air are also available. They are expensive but memorable. Your tour can be customized and cover the coast from Monterey to Mendicino, or from the Golden Gate to the Sierras. Most require a minimum of two people, and be sure to take a sweater, no matter how hot it

may seem at the time; the weather can be different up there in the sky. Telephone for current rates and information. **Otis Spunkmeyer Air**, tel: 800-938-1900, offers champagne flights over the Bay Area in historic DC3s, and **SF Helicopter Tours & Charter**, tel: 800-400-2404, is another reputable carrier.

Cruises

With all cruises, be sure to check the departure pier, as these are subject to change.

Alcatraz

Most tour companies offer day or evening tours and combination Alcatraz/San Francisco tours. Shop around or check eBay for deals. Advance reservations are advised. Most tours include an excellent audio guide; park rangers also conduct people around. Ferries leave every half hour from Pier 41. Dress warmly as it can be chilly or cold out on the bay.

Reputable companies include: **Blue & Gold Fleet**, tel: 415-705-8200 (admin offices) or 415-705-5555 (tickets); www.blueandgoldfleet.com; **Brighter Images Alcatraz Tours & Tickets**, tel: 800-700-3151, www.alcatraztrips.com; **All San Francisco Tours**, tel: 800-566-5868, www.allsanfranciscotours.com

Ange
For ti
ules
can
44
pa
in
station for ....
balmy weather even when ...
the bay, along with hiking, bicycling and panoramic views. Ferries run back and forth from Piers 41 and 43, going direct to the island or connecting with the Tiburon-Angel Island Ferry. The park has a comprehensive website with details on docent-led tours, kayak tours and nature walks: www.angelisland.org

Bay Cruises

These include sunset or dinner cruises as well as daytime trips. **Blue & Gold Fleet**, Pier 39, tel: 415-773-1188 or toll-free 800-426-8687, www.blueandgoldfleet.com **Hornblower Yachts**, Pier 33, tel: 415-394-8900; www.hornblower.com **Red & White Fleet**, Pier 41, tel: 415-447-0597; www.redandwhite.com

Whale-watching Tours

Blue & Gold Fleet *(see above)* December–April to Point Reyes. **Oceanic Society Expedition**, Marina, tel: 415-441-1104, www.oceanic-society.org, organizes a few gray-whale spotting tours during winter and spring.

SPECIALTY TOURS

A Day in Nature, tel: 415-673-0548. Personalized tours of the Marin Headlands with an experienced naturalist as a guide.
Bay City Bike, tel: 415-346-BIKE (2453) or www.baycitybike.com Bike rentals and tours; rides include Golden Gate Park, Golden Gate Bridge, Mount Tamalpais and Sausalito.
Backroads, 801 Cedar Street, Berkeley, tel: 800-GO ACTIVE or www.backroads.com. Cycling and hiking tours.
California Parlor Car Tours, 1101 Van Ness Avenue, tel:

415-474-7500 or 800-227-4250 or www.calpartours.com. Tours are conducted in large motorcoaches.
Golden West Sports Tours, 3185 Mission Street, tel: 415-566-8466. Hunting, shooting and fishing outings.
Green Tortoise Adventure Travel, 494 Broadway, tel: 415-956-7500 or 800-867-8647. The Green Tortoise has been hitting the hippie trails for more than a quarter of a century.
Incredible Adventures, tel: 415-759-7071 or 800-777-8464 or www.incadventures.com. Tours of

Yosemite, Muir Woods, Wine Country and Tahoe. River rafting tours and surf lessions.
Key Holidays, 1141 Bont Lane, Walnut Creek, tel: 800- 783-0783 or www.keyholidays.com. Amtrak train tours to Hearst Castle, Yosemite, Reno, Monterey and Napa.
Viviani INC, Destination Management, tel: 800- 658-9997 or www.viviani.com. Private, customized tours of California's Wine Country, where patrons get to sample the vintages, indulge in gourmet lunches and meet the winemakers.

A – Z

DIRECTORY

A dmission Charges

Most of San Francisco's large museums have reasonably moderate entrance fees – typically $7 to $15 for the first visit. Smaller art galleries tend to be free. Student travelers can often get special discounts by showing a student card, and many places offer discounts for people 65 years and older. Call or check the website of a specific attraction for any days on which admission is free, or for special circumstances where charges might be lowered.

B udgeting for Your Trip

If you're looking for a hotel room with an acceptable minimum level of comfort, cleanliness and facilities, a reasonable starting point for the price of a double room is $85 in budget-class hotels; upping your budget from there to around $150 will make a significant difference in quality. For between $150 and $300 a whole range of hotels opens up, from bland business traveler places to hip little boutique hotels in the heart of Union Square. Beyond this, and cer-

tainly beyond $350, you're moving into deluxe territory; though you don't really arrive at "discreet hideaway for celebrities" status until $500 and above.

Food costs range from $5–10 for a perfectly acceptable sandwich, burrito or Asian delicacy, to $40 for a two or three-course meal at a cute California-cuisine type restaurant. Expect to pay $50–100+ at a fine restaurant.

Getting around by public transportation (bus, BART and cable car), within city limits, can cost as little as $3–5 a day. Taxi fares for journeys in the city center can

CLIMATE CHART

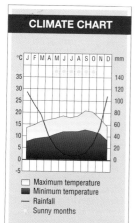

- ☐ Maximum temperature
- ■ Minimum temperature
- — Rainfall
- · Sunny months

range from as little as $5 to as much as $15, depending on the length of your journey. A taxi to the airport should cost $30–45, while a shuttle to the airport will cost $15–20, excluding tip.

Business Hours

Normal shopping hours differ from neighborhood to neighborhood. In Union Square and Fisherman's Wharf, business hours are 9am–6pm, seven days a week, with extended hours at night for the larger chains. Smaller boutique shops in surrounding areas are open as late as noon and close as late as 9pm. Banking hours vary, and some branches offer a limited Saturday service.

C limate

Summers in San Francisco can be foggy and chilly; in wintertime, expect rain. September and October are the warmest months, when temperatures occasionally reach 80°F (32°C). **Daily weather forecast**: tel: 415-936-1212.

Crime & Safety

In general, it is safe to walk the streets during the day in most

parts of the city, but use special caution in the following areas, especially at night: the Western Addition (bordered by Gough, Divisadero, Geary and Golden Gate streets – between Golden Gate Park and Civic Center); Hunter's Point (the peninsula just north of Monster Park); the small streets of the Mission District (unlit passages between Dolores, Potrero, 10th and Cesar Chavez streets); the Tenderloin (bordered by Bush, Powell Market and Polk streets, which is near the Theater District frequented by tourists).

Whenever possible, travel with another person while sightseeing or shopping, particularly at night. Do not walk in deserted or run-down areas alone. If driving, keep your door locked even when moving and never leave luggage, cameras or other valuables in view. Put them in the glove compartment or trunk to avoid any break-in. Park your car below a streetlight.

With regard to your personal belongings, you should never leave your luggage unattended. While waiting for a room reservation, for example, keep your property in view. Rather than carrying your bags around with you, ask the hotel captain, the restaurant waitress or the department store security guard if you can check your luggage. Never leave money or jewelry in your hotel room, even for a short time. Report any loss to the nearest police station or tel: **911**.

Try to carry only the cash you need. Use credit cards and traveler's checks whenever possible and avoid displaying large amounts of cash. Automated teller machines (ATMs) provide a convenient way to withdraw cash around the clock, but travelers should be careful when using ATMs alone or after dark. Most outlets are equipped with security cameras but are otherwise unattended. If you're concerned, a safe bet is to use an ATM located inside a convenience store and pay any surcharge.

Customs Regulations

If you are 21 or over, you are allowed to bring in 200 cigarettes, 50 cigars or 3 lb (1.3 kg) of tobacco, 1 US quart (1 liter) of alcohol and gifts up to a value of $800. You are not allowed to bring in food items, seeds, plants or narcotics. Customs officials are strict.

There is no limit to the amount of money you can bring in, but if the amount exceeds $10,000, you must fill out a report at the airport or on the plane. Anything you have for your own personal use may be brought in duty-and tax-free. **Duty-free shopping** is available to those who are leaving San Francisco for a destination in another country. You must show your flight number and date of departure, then you can purchase retail goods duty-free at the San Francisco airport.

D isabled Travelers

The US Welcomes Handicapped Visitors is a 48-page booklet available from the **Advancement of Travel for the Handicapped**, 1012 14th Street, No. 803, Washington DC 20005. Or you can write to the **Consumer Information Center**, Pueblo, CO 81109, Colorado for travel tips.

There is a **Recreation Center for the Handicapped** at 207 Skyline Boulevard, tel: 415-665-4100. The facility includes an adapted gymnasium, sports/physical fitness area, therapeutic warm water swimming pool, three outdoor parcourses, weekend overnight respite facilities, dining facility, arts and crafts.

E lectricity

The standard electric current is 115–120 volts, requiring a voltage converter and adapter plug for European appliances. Many hotel bathrooms have plugs for electric shavers that work on either current.

Embassies & Consulates

Australia: 625 Market Street,
Tel: 415-536-1970
Canada: 555 Montgomery,
Tel: 415-834-3180
Great Britain: 1 Sansome Street,
Tel: 415-617-1300
Ireland: 100 Pine Street,
Tel: 415-392-4214
New Zealand: no SF address.
Tel: 415-399-1255
South Africa: 6300 Wilshire Blvd,
Suite 600, Los Angeles,
Tel: 323-651-0902

Emergency Telephone Numbers

Police, Fire and Ambulance,
Tel: 911
Violent Crime Victims' Hot Line,
Tel: 800-842-8467
Red Cross Hotline,
Tel: 415-427-8000
MUNI Lost and Found,
Tel: 415-923-6168.
Travelers' Aid
Tel: 415-255-2522.
24-Hour Suicide & Crisis Hotline
Tel: 415-781-0500.
Poison Control Center
Tel: 800-222-1222

Entry Requirements (Visas & Passports)

Canadians may enter the US
without a visa. Most Dutch,
French, Italian, Japanese, Spanish, Swedish, Swiss, UK and German citizens do not need a visa
for travel of 90 days or less if
they enter on an airline or cruise
line which participates in no-visa
travel and have a return or
onward ticket. Citizens of other
countries require a visa and a
health record if they are from (or
have passed through) an infected
area. For clarification, contact the
nearest American embassy or
consulate.

Since September 11, 2001,
entry requirements to the US
have undergone extensive
review. It's an idea to check with
your local representative before

setting out. Upon arrival at a US
airport immigration desk, expect
to be questioned, perhaps
searched, and to have your eyes
scanned as part of an identity
profile assessment.

Extending your Stay

A foreign visitor who comes to
the US for business or pleasure
is admitted initially for a period of
not more than six months. Exten-
sions of stay are likewise limited
to six months. Visitors may not
accept employment during their
stay. Check with your consulate
for more details.

G ay & Lesbian Travelers

San Francisco is known as one of
the world's most welcoming
places for gay men and lesbians.
No one really agrees on what
made it into the current thriving,
politically influential gay community it is today, but it doesn't matter. Queers are everywhere and
everybody's used to it. The best
source for up-to-date information
on new clubs, shows, films,
events and gay news are the free
newspapers, notably the *Bay
Times* and the *Bay Area Reporter
(BAR)* found in cafés or street-
corner boxes. **The Center**, at
1800 Market Street,
www.sfcenter.org, has become a vital

nexus for the LGBT (lesbian, gay,
bisexual and transgender) community and has numerous fliers
and listings for events. **The
Women's Building**, www.womens
building.org, houses various non-
profit organizations and you'll
find newspapers, bulletin board
postings and information here
too. Two free weekly newspapers, the *Bay Guardian* and
SF Weekly, have useful listings
and information as well.

H ealth & Medical Care

There is nothing cheap about
being sick in the United States. It
is essential to be armed with
adequate travel medical insurance and to carry identification
and/or policy numbers at all
times. Consult the local telephone *Yellow Pages* for a nearby
pharmacist or physician. If
expense is a concern, turn first to
county hospitals that offer good
service and do not necessarily
charge a fee. If you need immediate attention, go directly to a hospital emergency room. If you have
to be treated, make sure your
insurance company is informed
within 24 hours.

Medical Services

To contact the **San Francisco
Medical Society Referral
Service**, tel: 415-561-0850; the
Dental Society Referral Service,
tel: 415-928-7337. An additional
free **Physician Referral Service**
is available by telephoning 885-
7777. General assistance and
referrals can be obtained from:
Dept Social Services, tel: 415-
557-5000.

Hospitals

Some of the larger hospitals with
24-hour emergency services are:
the **California Pacific Medical
Center,** with buildings at 3700
California Street, 3898 California
Street, 2333 Buchanon Street,
and the **Davies Medical Center**
(at Castro and Deboce streets).
Main telephone number and
information, tel: 415-387-8700.

24-hour medical services are also provided at the **San Francisco General Hospital**, 1001 Potrero Ave, tel: 415-206-8000. Other hospitals include:

Children's Hospital Oakland
tel: 510-428-3000; 24-hour emergency, tel: 510-428-3240

Kaiser-Permanente Medical Center
2425 Geary Boulevard
Tel: 415-833-2000

St Francis Memorial Hospital
900 Hyde Street
Tel: 415-353-6000

St Luke's Hospital
3555 Cesar Chavez Street, at Valencia Street
Tel: 415-647-8600

St Mary's Medical Center
450 Stanyan Street, at Hayes St
Tel: 415-668-1000

San Francisco General Hospital
1001 Potrero Avenue, at 22nd St
Tel: 415-668-1000

UCSF Parnassus Campus
505 Parnassus Avenue
Tel: 415-476-1000

UCSF Mount Zion Campus
1600 Divisadero
Tel: 415-567-6600

Outpatient Clinics

Low-cost outpatient clinics provide good care but the wait can be long. These include:

Haight-Ashbury Free Medical Clinic
558 Clayton
Tel: 415-487-5632

St Luke's Hospital Neighborhood Clinic
1580 Valencia Street
Tel: 415-647-8111

Women's Options Center
1001 Potrero Ave
Tel: 415-206-8476

Pharmacies

Certain drugs can only be prescribed by a doctor. Most drugstores stock a variety of drugs and have a pharmacist on duty. These stores are open long hours or 24 hours:

Walgreen Drugs: there are over 60 locations throughout the city; check the phone directory for its extensive listings.

USEFUL WEBSITES

www.sfgate.com: the *San Francisco Chronicle*'s website reproduces the daily newspaper online and has archives of information on everything from restaurant reviews to events listings.
www.sfweekly.com and www.sfbg.com: both of the free weeklies have corresponding websites with entertainment, arts and cultural events listings.
www.craigslist.org: a community site with a cult-like following.
www.sfstation.com: a hip, comprehensive site dedicated to food, entertainment and activities in San Francisco.
www.citysearch.com: another informative guide to the city.

Internet & Websites

It 's relatively easy to get on-line in San Francisco because there are so many ways to do it. Wireless spots are in abundant supply. For a ragtag listing of cafés and other relaxing spots with free wireless connections, check www.cheesebikini.com/wifi-cafes. Another site, www.wifihotspotlist.com/browse/us has a searchable list of spots across the US and can help you find a location in San Francisco as well as other Bay Area locations. Some cafés ask you to pay a minimal service fee for use of their wireless router. Others, like Starbucks, require that you purchase an account (daily or monthly) with their preferred service. This is all helpful, of course, if you have your own computer with you.

Internet cafés are a bit harder to find, but they are out there. Some have scanners, fax machines and other extras. Kinko's, a national chain, has many locations throughout the city that are helpful to the business traveler. Check the *Yellow Pages* for locations and numbers.

Golden Gate Perk is open six days a week, 401 Bush Street, tel: 415-362-3929. The California Welcome Center and Internet Café at Pier 39 is open seven days a week, tel: 415-397-0898. A quaint internet café in the Mission, Red Tap, 1360 Valencia Street, tel: 415-285-0585, is open Monday through Saturday and attracts a hip crowd. The Main Library, 100 Larkin Street at the Civic Center plaza, tel: 415-557-4400, has free terminals on the first floor that are available for 15 minutes on a first-come, first-served basis.

Most hotels have dataports in the rooms; the more expensive offer high-speed internet connections and a laptop, while many cheaper hotels have at least one computer for guest use.

Left Luggage

Leaving luggage has got trickier since September 11, 2001. No airports have lockers, but larger hotels may allow you to leave bags with them. Or use this agency: Airport Travel Agency, tel: 650-877-0421, in SFO's international terminal.

Lost Property

Lost property is handled by the SF police department, and found items are held at the Property Clerk's Room for 120 days. To report lost property, phone a local police station, or from Mon–Fri 6am–6pm, call the Property Clerk, tel: 415-553-1392, fax: 415-553-1555. Faxing serial numbers, descriptions, or photos of items may aid in recovering lost or stolen valuables.

Restaurants, taxicabs, nightclubs, stations etc are not responsible for your personal property, but you might have luck calling up and asking for lost and found. Be friendly and patient, and you may have a reunion. Try phoning again during business hours if you are not successful during the evening.

TRANSPORTATION

ACCOMMODATIONS

ACTIVITIES

A – Z

Maps

If you find yourself confused and mapless, look for a MUNI bus shelter, which often has a detailed map of the city, including a close-up map of Downtown. *Insight FlexiMap: San Francisco* has a laminated surface and contains text and photography about essential sites. The Rand-McNally store on Market Street at the corner of 2nd Street sells maps of the major cities of the world. Some corner shops and gas stations also sell maps.

Media

Television & Radio

The major television stations in the San Francisco area include Channels 2 (**KTVU**), 4 (**KRON**), 5 (**KPIX-CBS**), 7 (**KGO-ABC**), 9 (**KQED-Public Television**), and 11 (**NBC**). There is also a variety of foreign-language stations, mainly Spanish and Chinese. Dozens of other cable channels are available through the city's local cable company, **Comcast**. Complete television listings appear daily in the *San Francisco Chronicle* newspaper.

Newspapers & Magazines

The major daily newspaper is the *San Francisco Chronicle*. The *San Francisco Examiner* is a free daily tabloid. The Sunday *Chronicle* includes special sections, such as the "Pink Pages," which is a comprehensive guide to various current sports, entertainment, cultural and artistic events.

Free weekly papers include the *San Francisco Bay Guardian* and the *SF Weekly*, both featuring coverage and commentary on everything from arts to city politics and include film, music and arts listings. Sidewalk racks and cafés carry a variety of other free magazines, from real-estate publications to neighborhood papers and literary journals.

Besides the English-language

RADIO STATIONS

Formats are often subject to change, but the most popular local radio stations include:

AM

560:	**KSFO**: talk
610:	**KFRC**: oldies
680:	**NBR (NBC)**: sports, talk
740:	**KCBS (CBS)**: news, sports
810:	**KGO (ABC)**: news, talk and sports
960:	**KABL**: pop, soft rock
1260:	**KOIT**: lite rock
1646:	**KDIA**: Christian

FM

88.5:	**KQED**: PBS, NPR, news
89.5:	**KPOO**: soul, blues
94.9:	**KYLD**: urban, top 40
95.7:	**KZQZ**: top 40
96.5:	**KOIT**: lite rock
97.3:	**KLLC**: rock, alt., top 40
98.1:	**KISQ**: soul, R&B, urban
99.7:	**KFRC**: oldies
102.1:	**KDFC**: classical
103.7:	**KKSF**: smooth jazz
104.5:	**KFOG**: rock, alternative
105.3:	**KITS**: alternative
106:0	**KMEL**: urban, hip hop
107.7:	**KSAN**: classic rock

publications, various communities publish daily and weekly papers in foreign languages. These are available at a number of places, including: **Juicy News**, 524 Geary, tel: 415-441-3051; **Dave's Smoke Shop**, 2444 Durant Street, Berkeley, tel: 510-841-7292; and **De Lauer News Agency**, 1310 Broadway, Oakland, tel: 510-451-6157.

Money

Current dollar exchange rates are usually listed in the travel section of the *San Francisco Chronicle* Sunday edition.

Traveler's Checks: Since visitors may face problems changing for-

eign currency, it is better to use American-dollar traveler's checks. When lost or stolen, most traveler's checks can be replaced and they are accepted in most stores, restaurants and hotels. Banks readily cash large traveler's checks, although be sure to take along your passport. Smaller denomination traveler's checks (provided you have adequate identification) are usually accepted for purchases in stores and supermarkets.

Exchange: The airport is the best place to change currency, since only certain banks perform this service for customers who do not have accounts. In the city, you can exchange currency at **Bank of America**, 345 Montgomery Street, tel: 415-622-2451; **Foreign Exchange Limited**, 415 Stockton Street, tel: 415-397-4700; and **Thomas Cook Currency Services**, 100 Grant Avenue, tel: 415-362-3452.

Cash: Most banks belong to a network of ATMs (automatic teller machines) which dispense cash 24 hours a day.

Credit cards: Not all credit cards are accepted at all places, but most places accept either **Visa**, **American Express** or **MasterCard**. Major credit cards can also be used to withdraw cash from ATMs. (Look for an ATM that uses one of the banking networks indicated on the back of your credit card, such as Plus, Cirrus and Interlink.) There will be a charge for this transaction.

Photography

Many museums and galleries allow no pictures, and flash photography is seen as rude and disruptive during public performances. The use of tripods is also restricted in many public places. For photographic equipment or services in the down-town area, avoid the shops along Grant or Kearny streets. The same can be said of Market Street, with the exception of the excellent store, **Ritz Camera**, tel:

415-835-7318 at Hallidie Plaza near the Powell Street cable car turnaround. For consumer and professional supplies, including digital gear and rental equipment, **Calumet** at 2001 Bryant in the Mission District, tel: 415-643-9275, is the best stocked, with fair, non-negotiable prices and international warranty support from locations in Germany, Belgium and the UK.

Postal Services

The **United States Post Office General Mail Facility** is located far away at 1300 Evans Avenue, tel: 415-550-5247. Many of the city's 50 postal stations are open for extended hours on weekdays and also open limited hours on Saturday. For current postal rates and any other information, tel: 415-550-6500. If you wish, you can have mail addressed to you care of "General Delivery" at the post office of your choice. You will need the zip code of the station and you must pick up your mail in person.

Stamps may be purchased from the post office or from vending machines in hotels, stores, supermarkets, transportation terminals, and the lobbies of post office stations.

The Art Deco **Rincon Center Post Office**, 180 Steuart St, is the jewel of the city's postal history, with beautiful murals and a philatelic center. The building makes "doing the mail" a pleasant experience.

But **Federal Express**, or **FedEx**, is the postal service of choice these days, as the US postal system is not what it used to be. Call 1800-GO-FEDEX to schedule a pick up or delivery.

Public Holidays

Most government agencies close during the holidays listed below. Local banks and businesses may also be closed. Since schools are often closed for these holidays, you may want to consider whether to avoid the extra crowds during these periods. (*For a list of local festivals, see page 224.*)
New Year's Day: January 1.
Martin Luther King's Birthday: January 15.
Abraham Lincoln's Birthday: February 12.
Presidents' Day: third Monday in February.
Memorial Day: last Monday in May.
Independence Day: July 4.
Labor Day: first Monday in September.
Admission Day: September 9.
Columbus Day: second Monday in October.
Veterans' Day: November 11.
Thanksgiving: fourth Thursday in November.
Christmas: December 25.

Public Toilets

San Francisco has about 25 public pay toilets scattered about the city in an experimental effort to help travelers and deter the homeless from using the city streets for relief. They are green and gold and cost a quarter. Most are acceptably clean, but avoid public toilets in the Tenderloin especially, as they are notorious for illicit activity.

R eligious Services

There are places to worship in all denominations in a variety of unique and historic venues.
Catholic services
Archdiocese of San Francisco,
Tel: 415-614-5500.
St Mary's Cathedral
111 Gough Street
Tel: 415-567-4040
Saints Peter and Paul
666 Filbert Street
Tel: 415-421-0809
Mission Dolores Basilica
3371 16th Street
Tel: 415-621-8203
Jewish services
Jewish Community Federation
of San Francisco
Tel: 415-777-0411
Jewish Community Center
3200 California Street
Tel: 415-292-1200
Other services
Grace Cathedral
1100 California Street
Tel: 415-749-6300
Glide Memorial United
Methodist Church
330 Ellis Street
Tel: 415-674-6000
Buddhist Church of
San Francisco
1881 Pine Street
Tel: 415-776-3158
Kong Chow Temple
855 Stockton Street
Tel: 415-788-1339

S enior Travelers

Senior citizens (over 65 for men, over 62 for women) are entitled to many benefits, including reduced rates on public transportation and for entrance to museums. Seniors who want to be students should write to **Elderhostels**, 80 Boylston Street, Suite 400, Boston, MA 02116, Massachusetts, for information on places that provide both

accommodation and classes. The Bay Area has a number of Elderhostel locations.

Smoking

San Francisco's famed tolerance is not extended towards smokers. California state law bans smoking in bars, clubs, restaurants, within 25 feet (7.5 meters) of playgrounds or sandboxes, and within 20 feet (6 meters) of all public buildings, even though the governor of California, movie star Arnold Schwarzenegger, has his own "smoking tent" on the grounds of the Capitol, and the state's residents are notorious for their gas-guzzling vehicles.

San Francisco law also prohibits smoking in all city-owned parks, plazas and public sports facilities. Even in blues bars and the city's famed coffee houses, smoking is considered uncool, despite its beatnik heritage. You may find it difficult to reserve a hotel room where smoking is allowed; be sure to check at the time of booking.

Student Travelers

Most museums offer discounts to students who have a valid student identification card from their university or school.

The café at the San Francisco Art Institute at 800 Chestnut Street is open to the public and is known for in-expensive vegetarian meals and one of the best views of the city.

T elecommunications

Western Union, tel: 800-225-5227 will take your messages by phone. Many smaller, local message and wire transfer service companies are listed in the *Yellow Pages* of the San Francisco telephone directory.

Telephones

A shrinking number of telephones are located in hotel lobbies, bars, restaurants and other public places as more and more people turn to cellphones. California is adding to its existing telephone codes extremely fast and with little warning area codes can change; if in doubt over an area code, contact an operator.

Long-distance rates vary but discounts are available during specified calling times; check the local telephone directory or dial 0 for operator assistance for both local and international calls. Pre-paid calling cards offer a cheaper and more convenient alternative when using public phones.

Toll-free numbers for various services or businesses are indicated by an **800** or **888** prefix. The **Directory** for toll-free numbers is (800) 555-1212. To call the **Information Operator** for all other

TOURIST OFFICES

**San Francisco Visitors
& Convention Bureau**
900 Market Street
San Francisco, CA 94103
Tel: 415-391-2000
www.sfvisitor.org
**Berkeley Convention
& Visitors Bureau**
2015 Center Street
Berkeley, CA 94704
Tel: 510-549-7040
Tel: 800-847-4823
www.visitberkeley.com
Carmel Chamber of Commerce
PO Box 4444
Carmel, CA 93921
Tel: 831-624-2522
Tel: 800-550-4333
www.carmelcalifornia.org
Lake Tahoe Visitors Authority
1156 Ski Run Boulevard
South Lake Tahoe, CA 96150
Tel: 530-544-5050
(reservations)
Tel: 800-AT TAHOE
www.virtualtahoe.com
**Marin County Convention
& Visitors Bureau**

1013 Larkspur Landing Circle
Larkspur, CA 94939
Tel: 415-925-2060
www.visitmarin.org
**Monterey Peninsula Chamber
of Commerce**
380 Alvarado Street
Monterey, CA 93940
Tel: 831-648-5360
www.mpcc.com
**Napa Valley Conference
& Visitors Bureau**
1310 Napa Town Center
Napa, CA 94559
Tel: 707-226-7459
www.napavalley.org
**Oakland Convention
& Visitors Bureau**
463 11th Street
Oakland, CA 94607
Tel: 510-839-9000
www.oaklandcvb.com
**Sacramento Convention
& Visitors Bureau**
1608 I. Street
Sacramento, CA 95814
Tel: 916-264-7777
www.sacramentocvb.org

**Sausalito Chamber of
Commerce**
10 Liberty Ship Way
Bay 2, Suite 250
Sausalito, CA 94965
Tel: 415-331-7262
www.sausalito.org
**San Jose Convention
& Visitors Bureau**
408 Almaden Boulevard
Suite 1000
San Jose, CA 95110
Tel: 408-295-9600
www.sanjose.org
Sonoma Valley Visitors Bureau
453 First Street E.
Sonoma, CA 95476
Tel: 707-996-1090
Tel: 800-326-7666
www.sonomavalley.com
Yosemite National Park Service
P.O. Box 577
Yosemite, CA 95389
Tel: 209-372-0200
www.nps.gov/yose
(for park information)
www.yosemitepark.com
(for park accommodation)

TRANSPORTATION

TELEPHONE CODES

415: San Francisco, Sausalito, Larkspur, Mill Valley, Tiburon.
510: Oakland, Berkeley.
650: San Mateo, SFO airport, Palo Alto.
707: Napa, Sonoma, Mendocino.
408: San Jose.
831: Monterey, Carmel, Santa Cruz.
209: Yosemite.
530: Lake Tahoe.

numbers, dial **411**. There is a charge for this service.
    To dial another country from the United States, the prefix **011** must precede the country code and number. To dial another area code within the US, add the prefix **1**.

Cell phones

To use your GSM cellular phone in the US, you must have a tri-band phone and contact your service provider before you leave to set up international roaming. If you'd rather rent a cellular phone in San Francisco (it may be cheaper than roaming charges), try AllCell Rentals, tel: 877-724-2355, www.allcellrentals.com. They are open 24 hours a day and may charge a delivery fee.

Time Zone

California is in the Pacific Time Zone, which is two hours behind Chicago, three hours behind New York City and eight hours behind London. On the last Sunday in April, the clock is moved ahead one hour for Daylight Savings Time. On the last Sunday in October, the clock is moved back one hour. For local time, call **POPCORN** (tel: 415-767-2676).

Tipping

The accepted rate for porters at the airports is $1 or so per bag. Hotel bellboys and porters usually expect the same. A doorman should be tipped if he unloads or

parks your car. Tip your chambermaids at the end of your hotel stay, a few dollars per day should be sufficient. Depending on the quantity and quality of service rendered, 15 to 20 percent of the bill before tax is the going rate for most other help such as taxi drivers, barbers, hairdressers, waiters, waitresses and bar persons. In some restaurants, the tip or a service charge is included in the bill if it is for a large group; be sure to check first.

Tour Operators & Travel Agents

There are many tour operators in San Francisco offering a variety of options. The best place to start is at the **San Francisco Visitors & Convention Bureau**. They can be extremely helpful in choosing activities and operators. You can call or visit the centrally located offices at Hallidie Plaza, Powell and Market streets, Monday–Friday from 9am–5pm, Saturday–Sunday 9am–3pm, tel: 415-391-2000, www.sfvisitor.org
The **International Visitors' Center** (tel: 415-986-1388) provides professional appointments and tours for guests of the US Government. Their services include home hospitality, sightseeing suggestions and translation assistance. Open: Monday–Friday 9am–5pm.
The **San Francisco Chamber of Commerce** at 465 California Street, tel: 415-392-4511, primarily a business organization, can provide information and referrals to Chamber member businesses and professionals.

Useful Numbers

Police, fire, ambulance, tel: 411.
Customs, tel: 415-744-1530.
American Civil Liberties Union, tel: 415-621-2488.
Senior Citizen Information, tel: 800-510-2020.
Consumer Fraud – check the phone directory for its listings.

ACCOMMODATIONS

Weights & Measures

The US uses the Imperial system of weights and measures. Some conversions:

1 inch	=	2.54 cms
1 quart	=	1.136 liters
1 foot	=	30.48 cms
1 gallon	=	3.8 liters
1 yard	=	0.9144 meters
1 ounce	=	28.40 grams
1 mile	=	1.609 kilometers
1 pound	=	0.453 kilograms

What to Bring & Wear

San Francisco is a city best explored on foot, so remember to bring a comfortable pair of walking shoes. Also keep in mind that San Francisco's infamous fog and wind can conspire to make summer days wintery. Even if you're visiting during summer, you should bring warm clothes, a windbreaker, and a coat. The key to comfort is to dress in layers, since temperatures are known to drop considerably over the course of the day, particularly when the fog rolls in.
    San Franciscans do dress up, but in a more casual way than in New York or Europe. Some restaurants employ a dress code, so bring a jacket and tie.

ACTIVITIES

A – Z

WHAT TO READ

History

Ambrose Bierce, The Devil's Lexographer by Paul Fatout, University of Oklahoma Press (1951).

Citizen Hearst by W.A. Swanberg, Charles Scribners Sons (1961).

The Gate: The True Story of the Design and Construction of the Golden Gate Bridge by John Van der Zee, Simon & Schuster, New York (1986).

The Hearsts by Lindsay Chaney and Michel Cieply, Simon & Schuster (1981).

Jazz on the Barbary Coast by Tom Stoddard, Heydey Books (1982, 1998).

Inside the Walls of Alcatraz by Frank Heaney, Bull Publishing, Palo Alto (1987).

The Madams of San Francisco by Curt Gentry, Doubleday (1964).

San Francisco, You're History by J. Kingston Pierce, Sasquatch Books (1995).

Superspan: The Golden Gate Bridge by Tom Horton, Chronicle Books, San Francisco (1983).

Treasure Island by Richard Reinhardt, Square Books (1978).

General

The Art of the Fillmore by Gayle Lemke, Acid Test Productions (1997).

art-SITES San Francisco: the Guide to Contemporary Art-Architecture-Design by Sidra Sitch, art-SITES Press (2003).

Beneath the Diamond Sky: Haight-Ashbury 1965–1970 by Barney Hoskyns, Simon & Shuster (1997).

California Wildlife Viewing Guide by Jeanne L. Clark, Falcon Press (1996).

The Dashiell Hammett Tour by Don Herron, City Lights Books.

Dr Weirde's Weirde Tours: A Guide to Mysterious San Francisco by Dr Weirde, San Francisco (1994).

Footsteps in the Fog: Alfred Hitchcock's San Francisco by Jeff Kraft and Aaron Leventhal, Santa Monica Press (2002).

Gay by the Bay by Susan Stryker and Jim Von Buskirk, Chronicle Books (1996).

Haunted San Francisco: Ghost Stories from the City's Past edited by Rand Richards (2004).

The Literary World of San Francisco and Its Environs by Don Herron, City Lights Books, San Francisco (1990).

Mirror of the Dream by T.H. Watkins and R.R. Olmsted, Scrimshaw Press (1976).

Midnight at the Palace: My Life as a Fabulous Cockette by Pam Tent, Alyson Books (2004).

Outdoor Adventures by Tom Sienstra, Foghorn Press (1989).

San Francisco Almanac by Gladys Hansen, Chronicle Press (1995).

San Francisco Stories edited by John Miller (contributors include Tom Wolfe, Dylan Thomas, Hunter S. Thompson, H.L. Mencken, Jack London and Amy Tan), Chronicle Books (1990).

The Secrets of Success Cookbook: Signature Recipes and Insider Tips from San Francisco's Best Restaurants by Michael Bauer, Chronicle Books (2000).

Shanghaied in San Francisco by Bill Pickelhaupt, Flyblister Press (1996).

Shot on the Site by William A. Gordon, Citadel Press (1995).

Stairway Walks In San Francisco by Adah Balalinsky, Lexicos, San Francisco (1984).

Tales of the City and More Tales of the City by Armistead Maupin, Chronicle Books.

Walking San Francisco on the Barbary Coast Trail by Daniel Bacon, Quick Silver Press (1997).

The World of Herb Caen edited by Barnaby Conrad, Chronicle Books (1996).

Other Insight Guides

Nearly 100 titles and maps in the acclaimed *Insight Guides* series cover the United States, from Hawaii to New York to Florida.

Insight Guides are award-winning, highly visual titles, combining stunning photography with the best in local writing.

Insight Pocket Guides, have an itinerary-based approach, with a "local host" in each destination highlighting the best attractions.

Insight Compact Guides offer a highly portable encyclopedic travel guide packed with carefully cross-referenced text, photographs and maps.

Insight Fleximaps combine clear, detailed cartography with essential travel information. The laminated finish makes the maps durable.

SAN FRANCISCO STREET ATLAS

The key map shows the area of San Francisco covered by the
atlas section. An index of street names and places of interest
shown on the maps can be found on the following pages.
For each entry there is a page number and grid reference

Map Legend

▭▭	Freeway with Junction
‒ ‒ ‒	Freeway (under construction)
═══	Divided Highway
───	Main Road
───	Secondary Road
───	Minor road
▬ ‒ ▬	International Boundary
─ ─ ─	State Boundary
─ • ─	National Park/Reserve
─ ─ ─	Ferry Route
✈✈	Airport
†⛪	Church (ruins)
†	Monastery
🏰 🏚	Castle (ruins)
∩	Cave
★	Place of Interest
☀	Viewpoint
◤	Beach
═══	Freeway
═══	Divided Highway
═══ }	Main Roads
─── }	Minor Roads
───	Footpath
▬▪▬	Railroad
▭	Pedestrian Area
▬	Important Building
▭	Park
Ⓜ	Metro
🚌	Bus Station
ⓘ	Tourist Information
✉	Post Office
✝	Cathedral/Church
✡	Synagogue
⚑	Statue/Monument

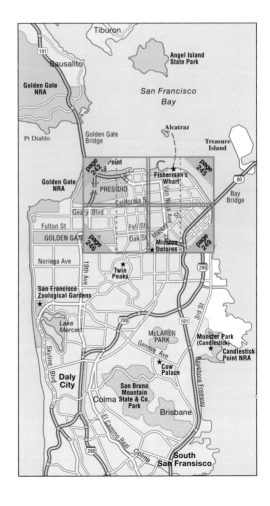

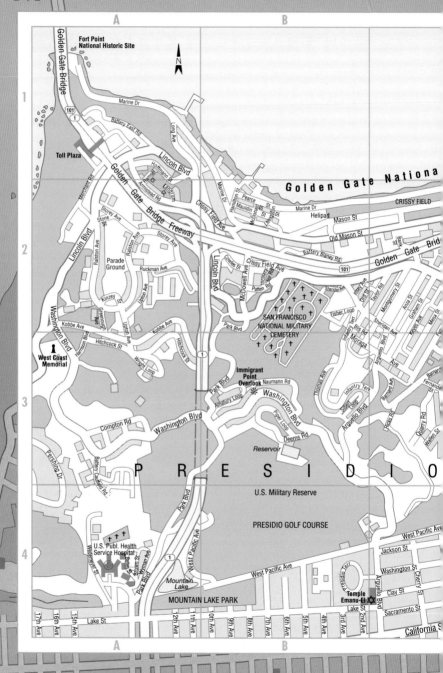

Fort Point
National Historic Site

Golden Gate Bridge

Marine Dr

101
1

Toll Plaza

Battery East Rd

Long Ave

Lincoln Blvd

Hoffman St

Merchant Rd

Golden Gate Bridge Freeway

Armistead Rd

Lincoln Ct

Golden Gate Nationa

CRISSY FIELD

Marine Dr

Pearce
Mauldin
McDonald
Johnston St
Marine Dr

Mason St

Helipad

Old Mason St

Battery Blaney Rd

Golden Gate Brid

101

Storey Ave

Stone St

Ralston Ave

Storey Ave

Crissy Field Ave

McDowell Ave

Lincoln Blvd

Cowles St

Crissy Field Ave

Treacher's Rd

Patten Rd

Lincoln Blvd

Washington Blvd

Ralston Ave

Parade
Ground

Ruckman Ave

Upton Ave

Kobbe Ave

Kinzey St

Greenough Ave

Upton Ave

Park Blvd

SAN FRANCISCO
NATIONAL MILITARY
CEMETERY

Sheridan Ave

Fisher Loop

Infantry Terr

Bliss Rd

Taylor St

Sheridan Ave

Montgomery St

Anza St

Graham St

Mesa St

Keyes Ave

Moraga

Arguello Blvd

Ave

West Coast
Memorial

Kobbe Ave

Hitchcock St

Harrison Ave

Wright Loop

Hitchcock St

Park Blvd

Immigrant
Point
Overlook

Naumann Rd

Amatury Loop

Washington Blvd

Thomas Ave

Infantry Terr

Storey Loop

Arguello Blvd

Barnard Ave

Ruckman Ave

Brooks Rd

Quarry Rd

Wallen St

Barnard

Fernande

Compton Rd

Washington Blvd

Piper Loop

Deems Rd

Reservoir

Pershing Dr

Battery Caufield Rd

P R E S I D I O

U.S. Military Reserve

PRESIDIO GOLF COURSE

West Pacific Ave

Park Blvd

West Pacific Ave

Jackson St

Washington St

Clay St

Arguello Blvd

Cherry St

U.S. Publ. Health
Service Hospital

Wedemeyer St

Brown St

Barnard St

1

Mountain
Lake

MOUNTAIN LAKE PARK

West Pacific Ave

Temple
Emanu-El

Lake St

Sacramento St

17th Ave

16th Ave

15th Ave

Lake St

12th Ave

11th Ave

10th Ave

9th Ave

8th Ave

7th Ave

6th Ave

5th Ave

4th Ave

3rd Ave

2nd Ave

California St

A

B

0   400 yards
0   400 m

Marina Small Craft Harbor

Recreation Area

Yacht Rd

West Harbor

East Harbor

Fort Mason Center

S.F. Craft & Folk Art Museum

Marina Green Dr

MARINA GREEN

Marina Blvd

Marine Dr

Jauss St

Allen St

Mason St

Marshall St

Doyle Dr

Exploratorium

Marina Blvd

Jefferson St

Beach St

North Point St

Bay St

Francisco St

Chestnut St

Baker St

Broderick St

Scott St

Prado St

Avila St

Casa Way

Rico Way

Retiro Way

Cervantes Blvd

Mallorca

Pierce St

Capra Way

MARINA

Alhambra St

Toledo Way

Way

Jefferson St

Beach St

North Point St

Bay St

Buchanan St

Laguna St

Bay St

FUNSTON PLGD

Chestnut St

Magnolia St

Lombard St

St

Greenwich St

Filbert St

Vedanta Temple

Union St

Green St

Vallejo St

Broadway

Gordes Ave

Birmingham Rd

Thornburg Rd

Edie Rd

Letterman Army Institute of Research

Lincoln Blvd

Lagoon

Palace of Fine Arts

Bay St

Letterman Digital Arts Center

Kennedy Ave

Truby St

Richardson Ave

Lyon St

Lombard St

Baker St

Broderick St

Divisadero St

Scott St

Pierce St

Steiner St

Moulton

Pixley

Fillmore St

Webster St

Lombard St

Greenwich St

COW HOLLOW PLGD

Filbert St

Union St

Green St

Vallejo St

Baker St

PACIFIC HEIGHTS

Convent of the Sacred Heart

Normandie Terr

Presidio Blvd

Letterman Dr

Dewitt Rd

Lombard St

Sherman Rd

Simonds Loop

Simonds Loop

Shafter Rd

Clark St

Lynch Ave

Sibley Rd

Morton St

Rodriguez St

Sanches St

McArthur Ave

Summer Ave

Bay Infantry

West Broadway

Raycliff Terr

Broadway

Pacific Ave

Pierce St

Pacific Ave

Jackson St

Bromley Pl

Jackson St

Webster St-Hist. Distr.

Washington St

JULIUS KAHN PAYGROUND

Pacific Ave

PRESIDIO HEIGHTS

Spruce St

Locust St

Laurel St

Walnut St

Presidio Ave

PRESIDIO HEIGHTS PLGD

Jackson St

Washington St

Clay St

Sacramento St

Baker St

Lyon St

Broderick St

Divisadero St

Scott St

Clay St

ALTA PLAZA PARK

Steiner St

Fillmore St

Sacramento St

Perine Pl

Pacific Medical Center

FILLMORE

California St

Pine St

Webster St

Orben St

Cottage Row

LAUREL HEIGHTS

Mayfair Dr

California St

Pine St

S.F. Fire Department Museum

California St

Pierce St

Bush St

Wilmot St

Sutter St

101

101

A   B

N

Alcatraz

Municipal Pier

Historic Ships
Balclutha
Eppleton Hall
C.A. Thayer

Hyde Street Pier
Alma
Eureka

Pier 45
S.S. Jeremiah
O'Brien
U.S.S.
Pampanito
Pier 43

Pier 39

S.F. Maritime
National Historic Park

Musée
Mécanique

Fisherman's Wharf

The Embarcadero

Aquarium
of the Bay

Pier 47

S.F. Maritime
NHP Visitor
Center

**Fort Mason
Center**

Mexican
Museum

Museo Italo
Americano

FORT MASON

AQUATIC
PARK

Maritime
Museum

Ghirardelli Square

Jefferson St

The
Anchorage

The Cannery

Leavenworth St

Jones St

Taylor St

Mason St

Powell St

Beach

Stockton St

North Point Stre

Beach
St

Hyde St

Polk St

North Point Street

Columbus Ave

Larkin

Vandewater
St

Francisco St

Pfeff

**Golden Gate
National Recreation Area**

Bay St

Bay St

Octavia St

Gough St

Franklin St

Chestnut St

Van Ness Ave

Francisco St

North Cuba St

Chestnut St

Lombard St

Franklin St

Greenwich St

Grant St

Greenwich St

RUSSIAN
Reservoir
HILL PARK

Lombard St

Filbert St

San Francisco
Art Institute

Powell-Hyde Line

Houston
St

Water St

Menard
Alley

Fielding St

RUSSIAN

Lurmont
Terr

MICHELANGELO
PLGD

Jansen St

Reach
Val.

paraiso St

Richard

NORTH
BEACH
PLAYGROUND

Tuscany
Alley

Powell-Mason-Line

NORTH

Sts Pe
& Pau

Washington
Square

BEACH

Alley

HILL

Allen St

Havens St

Macondray Ln

North Beach
Museum

Alley

Filbert St

Laguna
St

Harris Pl

Union St

Octagon
House

ALLYNE
PARK

Octavia St

Gough St

Union St

Vallejo St

Green St

Bonita St

Polk St

Larkin St

White St

Rockland

East

Hyde St

Leavenworth St

Jones St

Glover St

Taylor St

Florence St

Auburn

COOLBRITH
PARK

Eaton Pl

Mason St

Fallon St

Powell St

Church St

Allen St

R. Levy Tunnel
Bernard St

Waldo
Alley

Waldo
Alley

Auburn

Dorie
Alley

John St

Stone

Filbert St

Union Charl-
ton Ct

Green St

Vallejo St

Buchanan St

Broadway

Broadway

Van Ness Ave

101

HELEN
WILLS PLGD

Pacific Ave

Morrell
McCor-
mick St

Lynch St

Burgoyne
Wal Pl

Cable Car
Powerhouse

Whittier
Mansion

Haas-Lilienthal
House

Jackson St

Jackson St

Washington St

Reed St

Priest St

Jones St

Pleasant
St

Stroule
St

Miller Pl
Bayer Pl

Taylor St

Mason St

Coleman St
Wetmore St

Dewey Ct

Pacific Ave

Spreckels
Mansion

Franklin St

NOB HILL

Troy
Alley

Clay St

Larkin St

Hyde St

Kimball

Pleasant
St

HUNTINGTON
PARK

Grace
Cathedral

Fairm
Hotel

Pacific Medical
Center

**LAFAYETTE
PARK**

Laguna St

Washington St

Gough St

Clay St

Sacramento St

Polk St

Acme Alley

Leavenworth St

Mark Hopkins
I-C Hotel

Masonic
Auditorium

Renaissan
Stanfor
Court Hot

Sacramento St

California St

California Street-Line

Mulford
Alley

California St

Pine St

Austin St

Hemlock
St

Buchanan St

Gough St

Octavia St

Van Ness Ave

Pine St

Bush St

Fern St

Sutter St

Hemlock St

St Francis
Memorial
Hospital

Joan P.

Leavenworth St

Jones St

Cosmo Pl

Shannon St

YWCA

Hobart
Alley

Wes
St Fran

Austin St

Bush St

Sutter St

Post St

Fern St

Daniel
Burnham Ct

Van
Ness Ave

Cedar St

Geary St

Post St

A   B

0   400 yards
0   400 m

Pier 35
Pier 33
Pier 31
Pier 29
Pier 27
Pier 23
Foreign Trade Zone
Pier 19
Pier 17
Pier 15
Pier 9
Pier 7
Pier 3
Pier 1

y St
Kearny St
Montgomery St
Winthrop St
nut St
Lombard St
Sansome St
Battery St
The Embarcadero
TELEGRAPH
Coit Tower
Greenwich St
ike y
HILL
Filbert St
Levi's Plaza
Alta St
Calhoun Terr
Union St
Castle St
Montgomery St
Clubhouse Alley
Merchant
Commerce
Green St
N.E. Waterfront Hist. Dist.
Battery St
Vallejo St
Davis St
Front St
Sansome St
Pfeiffer Pl
Prescott Ct
Kearny St
Dunnes Alley
Broadway
Fresno St
Nottingham Pl
Adler
Pacific Ave
SIDNEY WALTON PARK
Columbus Ave
Gold St
Custom-house
Jackson St
Maritime Plaza
Grant Ave
Osgood Pl
Jackson Square
Golden Gateway
Washington St Center
Justin Herman Plaza
World Trade Center
Ferry Plaza East
Chin. Culture Center
Transamerica Pyramid
Clay St
Ferry Building
Ferry Plaza
Tien Hou Temple
Portsmouth Square
Wells Fargo Bank History Room
Embarcadero Center
Drumm St
Hyatt Regency Hotel
Ferry Building Market
Pier 2
Commercial
Montgomery St
Sansome St
Battery St
Sacramento St
Contemporary Jewish Museum
Temple
Old St Mary's Church
Halleck St
California St
Front St
Davis St
Federal Reserve Bank
Steuart St
The Embarcadero
Promenade
FINANCIAL
Embarcadero
M
Pine St
Main St
Mission St
Rincon Center
Bank of America
Market St
Beale St
Howard St
Spear St
Folsom Station
Transbay Terminal
Chinatown Gateway
Kearny St
Bush St
Fremont St
Steuart St
Pier 24
Bay Bridge
Harlan Pl
DISTRICT
Sutter St
1st St
Transbay Terminal
Folsom St
Ricon Point
Hallidie Bldg
Crocker Galleria
Lick Pl
Post St
Tillman Alley
Minna St
Natoma St
Beale St
Main St
80
Pier 26
Campton Pl
M
Montgomery St
2nd St
Zeno Pl
Fremont St
Harrison St
Lower Deck
Pier 28
Maiden Ln
Sheraton Palace Hotel
Annie St
Tehama St
1st St
Bryant St
Pier 30
Geary St
Grant Ave
Cartoon Art Museum
3rd St
Clementina St
Pier 32
O'Farrell St
Market St
Stevenson St
Museum of the African Diaspora
San Francisco Museum of Modern Art

RICHMOND

California St

19th Ave
RICHMOND PLGD
18th Ave
16th Ave
15th Ave
14th Ave
Park Presidio Blvd
Funston Ave
12th Ave
11th Ave
10th Ave
9th Ave
8th Ave
California St
7th Ave
6th Ave
5th Ave
Cornwall St
4th Ave
3rd Ave
2nd Ave
California St
Palm Ave
Jordan Ave
Arguello Blvd
Euclid Ave

1

Clement St
17th Ave
Tacoma St
Clement St
Clement St
CLEMENT STREET
Clement St

1

Geary Blvd
Geary Blvd
Geary Blvd

ARGONNE PLGD
18th Ave
19th Ave
17th Ave
16th Ave
15th Ave
14th Ave
Funston Ave
12th Ave
11th Ave
10th Ave
9th Ave
Anza St
8th Ave
ARGUELLO PARK
French Hospital
5th Ave
4th Ave
3rd Ave
Columbarium
Stanyan
Almaden
Lorraine
Anza St
6th Ave
ANGELO ROSSI PLGD
Rossi Ave
Arguello Blvd

Anza St

Edward St

Turk Blvd
Willard St N
Golden Gate
Pat

2

Balboa St
Balboa St
Balboa St

Cabrillo St
Cabrillo St
Cabrillo St

Arguello Blvd
McAllister St

Balboa St
19th Ave
18th Ave
17th Ave
16th Ave
15th Ave
14th Ave
Park Presidio Blvd
Funston Ave
12th Ave
11th Ave
10th Ave
9th Ave
8th Ave
7th Ave
6th Ave
5th Ave
4th Ave
3rd Ave
2nd Ave
Arguello Blvd

Fulton St
Fulton St
Fulton St

Park Presidio By-Pass Dr
John F. Kennedy Dr
Conservatory Dr W
Conservatory

Prayer Book Cross
John F. Kennedy Dr
Heros Grove
Redwood Memorial Grove
De Young Museum
Conservatory of Flowers

Boat House
Pioneer Log Cabin
Stow Lake Dr
Music Concourse
California Academy of Sciences
Lily Pond
Tennis Courts

3

Stow
Japanese Tea Garden
Morrison Planetarium (reopens 2008)
Middle Dr East
Bowling Green Dr

Cross Over Dr
Strawberry Hill
Lake
G O L D E N   G A T E   P A R K
Big Rec Ball Field
Bowling
Greens
CHILDREN'S PLGD
Kezar Dr
Kez Stad

Strybing Arboretum
County Fair Building
Martin Luther King Jr. Dr
Martin Luther King Jr Dr

Lincoln Way
20th Ave
19th Ave
18th Ave
17th Ave
16th Ave
15th Ave
14th Ave
Funston Ave
12th Ave
11th Ave
10th Ave
9th Ave
8th Ave
7th St
Hugo St
6th Ave
5th Ave
4th Ave
3rd Ave
2nd Ave
Arguello Blvd
Carl St
Hillway Ave

Irving St
Irving St

4

N

Judah St
Parnassus Ave
Medical Center

Judah St
Upper Service Rd

0   400 yards
0   400 m
SUNSET
Kirkham St
6th Ave
5th Ave
4th Ave
Kirkham St
University California

A   B

1

Post St

Japan Center
★ Peace
Pagoda

Webster St
Hollis St

Geary Expressway

Laguna St

Cleary Ct

Starr KingWay

Gough St

Franklin St

Olive St

St Mary's
Cathedral

Ellis St

Willow St

Willow St

Eddie St

Jefferson Square

Turk St

HAYWARD PLGD

Golden Gate Avenue

McAllister St

Ash St

**WESTERN
ADDITION**

Western Addition
Cultural Center

Fulton St

Birch St

Grove St

HAYES VALLEY

Ivy St

Ivy St

Fillmore St

Hayes St

101

Linden St

Linden St

Fell St

Fell St

Hickory St

Hickory St

Lily St

Oak St

Oak St

Laguna St

Octavia

Gough St

Franklin St

Page St

Lily St

Page St

Rose St

Rose St

Haight

**University
of California**

Webster St

Buchanan St

Haight St

Germania St

Hermann St

**U.S.
Mint**

Guerrero St

Elgin

Pink Alley

Pearl St

Market St

Gough St

Duboce Ave

Sanchez St

Belcher St

Church St

Reservoir

14th St

Church St

Clinton Pk

Brosnan St

Rosemont

Pl

Ramona Ave

Hidalgo

Terr

M Church St

Dolores St

15th St

Albion St

Caledonia St

Sanchez St

Sharon St

Church St

Landers St

Alert
Alley

Spencer St

16th St

16th St

**Mission
Dolores**

Chula Ln

Abbey

17th St

Dolores St

Ford St

Dorland St

Prosper St

Guerrero St

17th St

Dolores Terr

Dorland St

18th St

M

0   400 yards

0   400 m

Oakwood St

Linda St

Lapidge St

San Carlos St

Lexington St

19th St

MISSION

Geary St

Myrtle St

Van Ness Ave

O'Farrell St

Great
American
Music Hall

Ellis St

Eddie St

Larch St

Elm St

101

Redwood

**State
Building**

Pioneer Hall

**Civic
City
Hall
Center**

**Veterans
Bldg**

**War Memorial
Opera House**

**Davies
Symphony Hall**

Grove St

Health
Center

Larkin St

Hyde St

Dodge St

Brooks Hall
(Underground)

Brooks Hall

Polk St

Auditorium

Hayes St

Board of
Education

Fell St

Franklin St

Oak St

11th St

M Van Ness

Rose St

12th St

Market St

Goulding St

Otis St

McCoppin St

Plum St

Valencia St

Mission St

Woodward St

Julian St

Minna St

Natoma St

16th St

Capp St

Hoff St

Rondel Pl

Clarion Al

Sycamore St

Dearborn St

Bird St

Camp St

Albion St

Wiese St

Shotwell St

South Van Ness Ave

Adair
St

**16th
St
Mission**

17th St

18th St

Mission St

Capp St

TENDERLOIN

Turk St

**Federal
Building**

**State
Building**

Asian Art
Museum

**Federal
Building**

United Nations
Plaza

**Public
Library**

**Orpheum
Theater**

Civic
Center

Glide Memorial
Methodist Church

Antonio St

Cohen

YMCA

Hastings
Law Coll

McAllister St

Leavenworth St

Jones St

Eddy St

Golden Gate Avenue

Market St

7th St

Stevenson St

Jessie St

Greyhound
Bus Terminal

Stevenson St

Jessie St

Mission St

Minna St

Natoma St

Howard St

9th St

10th St

Washburn St

Dore St

Grace St

Folsom St

Tehama St

Clementina St

Lafayette St

12th St

Kissling St

Burns
Pl

Norfolk St

12th St

Central Skyway

Erie St

Harrison St

14th St

South Van Ness Ave

Shotwell St

Folsom St

15th St

16th St

Folsom St

Enterprise
St

17th St

18th St

Shotwell St

Folsom St

O'Farrell St

Steveloe
Pl

Mason St

BOEDDEKER
PARK

Taylor St

Eddie

Turk St

Golden Gate
Theater

Golden Gate Avenue

8th St

6th St

5th St

Julian St

Laskie St

Langton St

Rausch St

Sumner St

Ringold St

Sheridan St

10th St

Harrison St

Dore St

Br

Juniper St

Alameda

Florida St

Bryant St

15th St

Alabama St

Harrison St

Treat Ave

Folsom St

Bryant St

16th St

17th St

18th St

Mariposa St

Alabama St

Florida St

Bryant St

FRANKLIN
SQUAR

Harrison Ave

Harrison St

Mistral St

2

3

4

A   B

SOUTH OF MARKET

Mexican Museum (Opens 2008)
Contemporary Jewish Museum (Opens 2007)
San Francisco Museum of Modern Art
Center for the Arts
F. Visitor formation enter
Metreon
San Francisco Museum of Craft & Folk Art
Yerba Buena Square
Moscone Convention Center
Old Mint
California Academy of Sciences
Zeum

Upper Deck

The Embarcadero

Pier 32
Pier 34
Pier 36
Brannen Station
Pier 38
Pier 40

South Beach Harbor

James Lick Skyway

SOUTH PARK

2nd & King Station

SBC Park

McCovey Cove

China Basin St
Pier 48
Newsprint Terminal

Mission Rock Terminal
Pier 50
Boat Launch Ramp
Pier 52

Hall of Justice

San Francisco Caltrain Depot

SAN FRANCISCO PARK

4th & King Station

Southern Embarcadero Freeway

Mission Creek Marina

CHINA BASIN

Mission Rock St
Pier 54

El Dorado St

Pier 64

AGUA VISTA PARK

JACKSON PARK

POTRERO

Mariposa St

Southern Embarcadero Freeway

James Lick Freeway

STREET INDEX

ART & PHOTO CREDITS

GENERAL INDEX

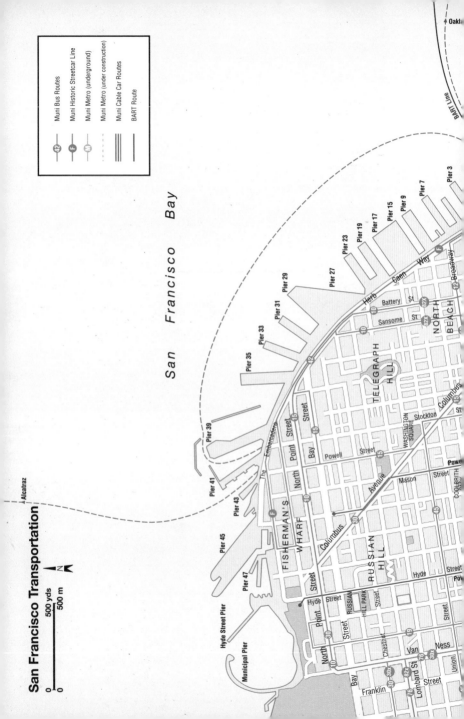

San Francisco Transportation

0 500 yds
0 500 m

N

Muni Bus Routes
F — Muni Historic Streetcar Line
M — Muni Metro (underground)
— — — Muni Metro (under construction)
‖‖‖ Muni Cable Car Routes
—— BART Route

San Francisco Bay

Alcatraz

Oakl

BART Line

Pier 3
Pier 7
Pier 9
Pier 15
Pier 17
Pier 19
Pier 23
Pier 27
Pier 29
Pier 31
Pier 33
Pier 35
Pier 39
Pier 41
Pier 43
Pier 45
Pier 47

Hyde Street Pier
Municipal Pier

Broadway
NORTH BEACH
Columbus
Stockton
St
Herb
Caen
Way
Battery St
Sansome St
TELEGRAPH HILL
WASHINGTON SQUARE
Powell Street
Powe
Mason
Avenue
COOLBRITH
Hyde
Street
Pow
Stockton
RUSSIAN HILL
RUSSIAN HILL PARK
Columbus
FISHERMAN'S WHARF
Hyde Street
Point
North
Street
The Embarcadero
Point Street
North
Bay
Street
Chestnut
Van
Ness
Lombard St
Franklin
Bay
Union
Street